BLACK POWER AND THE GARVEY MOVEMENT

BLACK POWER AND THE GARVEY MOVEMENT

by

Theodore G. Vincent

The *Ramparts* Press

To Theodore Burghardt Vincent
Frederick Lewis Vincent
and Marilyn Mavis Vincent

CONTENTS

PREFACE

In the early 1960s I wrote a weekly column for the Los Angeles *Herald Dispatch* called "The Hidden Past of Afro-Americans." The paper's editor, Pat Patterson, was a strong supporter of the late Malcolm X and the Nation of Islam, and she suggested I do some columns on the Garveyites, the forerunners of the Muslims. I had read through David Cronon's *Black Moses: The Story of Marcus Garvey and the Universal Negro Improvement Association* without developing much of an interest in Garvey, but with Pat Patterson's prodding I got hold of a ragged copy of volume 1 of the *Philosophy and Opinions of Marcus Garvey*. Reading this book was the beginning of my realization that Cronon and most other scholars dealing with Garvey had misunderstood their subject, and had written off as unimportant a man who founded a most significant movement for black freedom.

A few years later I ran across a copy of Amy Jacques Garvey's *Garvey and Garveyism* in the UCLA library. (Quite recently I found that Mrs. Garvey had taken her life savings and mailed unsolicited copies of this book to hundreds of libraries all over the world.) Through *Garvey and Garveyism* I became interested in learning more about the individual followers of Marcus Garvey, who were depicted in this book as reasonable and rational men and women, rather than as dupes of a demagogue, as Cronon's book implied. While in New York I visited the Schomburg Collection in Harlem, and discovered the Universal Negro Improvement Association weekly, the *Negro World*. Sitting there in that library, reading through its small file of the Garvey newspaper, I experienced a sense of discovery akin to the excitement of the archaeologists who first entered Tutankhamen's tomb. Here was a working example of the type of movement militants of the 1960s hoped to build. Constructive and workable approaches to problems of black identity, economic hardship, social discrimination, political disenfranchisement and the need for international alliances were all there, wrapped up in one gigantic organization. The story cried out to be told.

The errors of the Garveyites during their heyday in the 1920s were well documented and widely publicized by a host of black militants, including Dr. W. E. B. DuBois. In later years, as the relevance of the Garvey approach became more apparent, many of Garvey's one-time enemies, including Dr. DuBois, adopted a more favorable stance toward Garveyism. But nonetheless the early criticisms have retained a dominant position in the historical appraisal of Garveyism. To present a more balanced picture, I have found it necessary to present in this study a chapter analyzing some of the basic assumptions of Garvey's opponents. Obviously, one chapter cannot do justice to a myriad of social protest movements. Since the subject of this study is the Universal Negro Improvement Association, other organizations are discussed primarily in terms of how they related to issues which Garveyites felt were important.

* * *

Invaluable assistance in writing this book was provided by my wife Selma. The many evenings I spent with Mrs. Amy Jacques Garvey helped immeasurably to clarify my understanding of Garveyism. I would like to acknowledge the help of the late Professor Robert Starobin in reviewing the manuscript, and also to thank Professor Leon Litwack of the University of California at Berkeley, Professor Leonard Jefferies Jr. of the Black Studies Department at San Jose State College, and W. F. Elkins of Stanford University. My students at the Center for Participant Education at the University of California at Berkeley were most helpful in class discussions about material in this book. Much of the material in the book is based on information provided by James B. Yearwood, Harry Haywood, Ted Poston, Rudolph B. Smith, Professor St. Clair Drake, Len Nembhard, Dr. Muriel Petioni, Alfred A. Smith, Richard B. Moore, Alfred Lannon, Ruth Beckford, Reynold R. Felix, Herbert Hill, Lionel Winston Greenidge, and the relatives of Evelyn R. Donawa and Marie Duchaterlier, to all of whom I am most grateful. My thanks are also due to Bill Taylor, curator of the Cyril Briggs Papers, and Ann Reed of the University of California library.

1

AN INTRODUCTION TO GARVEYISM

THE UNIVERSAL NEGRO IMPROVEMENT ASSOCIATION may conjure up images of Marcus Garvey in a cocked hat and imperial dress reviewing his African Legionnaires marching to military music through the streets of Harlem, or of thousands of blacks crowding to see the maiden voyage of the Black Star Line, which would carry them back to Africa. By means of exclusions and distortions, historians have left us with an impression of Garveyism as an oversized sect or cult, an escapist pseudo-religion of which Garvey was God while many of his followers were only a cut above fools. But in its time the UNIA was the most powerful organization of black people in the world and was as active in political struggles as in the social sphere. Founded by Marcus Garvey in 1914, by the early 1920s it had over eight hundred chapters in forty countries on four continents; it had nearly a million members and two to three times as many participating in its activities. The leaders of the Garvey movement worked on the premise expressed by W. E. B. DuBois in 1898: "The problem of the twentieth century is the problem of the color line—the relation of the darker to the lighter races of men in Asia and Africa, in America and the islands of the sea." [1]

Garveyites subsequently conceived and popularized a host of new approaches to the struggle for black freedom. They constructed a framework for a future world government for black people. They became masters of psychological warfare and propaganda. In an age of anticolonialism, Garveyites were the first organized group in this country to wage mass-based struggles for independence from colonial rule. As ideologues, they formulated almost every version of black power to gain currency in the United States in the twentieth century. The Black Muslims were an outgrowth of the UNIA, as

13

were most black nationalist organizations formed in the thirties and forties. The Republic of New Africa's idea of a separate black republic within the United States was discussed and rejected as impractical by the Garveyites. The Black Panther Party's call for a United Nations plebiscite is reminiscent of Garvey's petitions to the old League of Nations, and recent international black power conferences resemble UNIA conventions in their attempt to bring together all proponents of black nationalism and black power.

Like the cultural nationalists of recent years, the Garveyites argued that spiritual and cultural development could best be served by separation from whites and white ideas. Garvey taught his followers to be proud that they were black, to cherish their African past, and to build for themselves their own civilization of the future. The UNIA sought to build an international alliance of all the black nationalist and black power groups that had sprung up after World War I—a coalition that would be for nationalism what the Third International was for Socialist and Communist parties.

On the one hand, in their construction of the ideological basis of modern black nationalism and black power, and in their success as organizers of a worldwide movement, the Garveyites were indeed victorious. On the other hand, when Garvey died on the eve of World War II his organization was in ruins, its extensive business ventures bankrupt, its once vibrant press silenced, and its membership dwindling and diffused among a plethora of splinter groups and offshoots. It should be noted that the prime of the UNIA came in the early 1920s and that the Garveyites ran against a tide of reaction, which was embodied in a revitalized Ku Klux Klan in America, in the nascent fascism that was making tremors throughout Europe, and in the vicious repression that characterized relations between the mother countries and their colored colonies all over the globe.

Historians who have written about Garveyism generally agree, as Roi Ottley says, that "the movement set in motion what was to become the most compelling force in Negro life—race and color consciousness, which is today that ephemeral thing that inspires 'race loyalty'; the banner to which Negroes rally; the chain that binds them together."[2] But despite this acknowledgment, only four volumes on the Garveyites have been published during the last fifty years, and the dozen or so black history texts which discuss the movement usually do so in shallow and often condescending terms.

The situation has improved somewhat recently insofar as four publishing houses are circulating reissues of the *Philosophy and Opinions of Marcus Garvey*,[3] an important two-volume work which was out of print for forty years. Amy Jacques Garvey's *Garvey and Garveyism*[4] has also been reissued. Nonetheless, only two books dealing directly with the Garvey movement have been written by "outsiders" in the last thirty years. Len Nembhard's *Trials and Triumphs of Marcus Garvey*[5] was published in 1940, and David Cronon's *Black Moses: The Story of Marcus Garvey and the Universal Negro Improvement Association* was published in 1956.[6] Nembhard is concerned mainly with Garveyite activities in the West Indies. Cronon's more general history, despite the author's negative attitude toward black nationalism, has doubtless helped to keep the public aware of Garveyism. Cronon made a conscious attempt to overcome the integrationist bias which pervaded the movement for black equality in the 1950s, but his work still reflects the misunderstanding which has led others to ignore Garveyism entirely or to deal with it only in passing.

In being ignored by scholars and social analysts, the UNIA has shared the neglect accorded many organizations restricted to black members, and as an organization of working-class people acting outside traditional black bourgeois spheres the UNIA did not enjoy the intellectual respectability of the NAACP and the Urban League. Chroniclers of black history have often chosen to report only what whites want to hear. Propaganda from the black middle class, designed to minimize the importance of the Garveyites, may also have influenced outside observers.

Cronon perpetuated a number of myths which were broadcast by Garvey's critics in the early years of the UNIA. Discussing the "inherent weaknesses of Garveyism," he states that "Garvey sought to raise high the walls of racial nationalism at a time when most thoughtful men were seeking to tear down these barriers."[7] These "thoughtful men" were the traditional American liberals, black and white, who believed that the only constructive social movement was one which eliminated differences, who believed that the American "melting pot" would solve the race problem, whose only models for racial nationalism were nazism and fascism. "One may question," Cronon commented, "whether Garvey was aware of all the connotations of either fascism or communism, but certainly his UNIA, with its fierce chauvinistic nationalism and strongly centralized leadership, had fascist characteristics."[8] Cronon could not visualize a black nationalism which was neither reactionary nor demagogic, and he finally concluded that Garvey's racial nationalism was the product of ignorance rather than intent.*

Obviously there are activists in the United States and abroad who promote a black version of the views of Dale Carnegie and Norman Vincent Peale and who call their mind-over-matter philosophy "black nationalism" or "black power." However, the Garveyites constructed a movement which, in addition to emphasizing the subjective qualities of blackness and the value of black culture, was actively involved in political struggles for power and was relevant to genuine attempts to liberate blacks from capitalist oppression and to build a new society offering individual freedom, economic security, and equality.

Through the Universal Negro Improvement Association there developed the philosophical-political system of Garveyism. The creation of international solidarity among all people of African descent was a prime objective for Garveyites. All blacks were to be considered brothers, although they differed from one another in language, religion, societal structures, and other ways. Garvey's slogan, "Africa for the Africans," had significance for black Americans in that once Africa had been freed from colonial rule, blacks in the United States could be given aid in their fight for equal rights, much as the Zionists in Garvey's time sought to make in Palestine a bulwark for international Jewry. For black Americans the future prospect of a powerful international alliance provided much of the inspiration and hope through which the UNIA became the largest black organization ever developed in this country.

---

* Cronon's work has helped promulgate the view that the Garvey movement was primarily intended to take black Americans back to Africa. Garvey and his leading lieutenants planned for relatively few—at most, a hundred thousand—blacks to "return." They were to help develop the African continent, and to strengthen ties between blacks in the Eastern and Western hemispheres. Cronon does note that mass exodus "was never Garvey's intention," but elsewhere he uses the back-to-Africa plan as an easy way of criticizing the UNIA's separatist program. In his conclusion, he declares that, through the emigration plan, "Garvey asked his followers to abdicate their hard-won, admittedly incomplete rights in the United States and . . . turn the country over to white supremacists of the Ku Klux Klan variety"—thus completely ignoring the UNIA's opposition to discrimination and its attempts to fight it.[9]

Until the coming of Garvey there had not been a movement in the mainstream of black American politics based on allegiance to a power beyond the borders of the United States. The prevailing view was that black Americans—who in many cases had a longer history in this country than whites—could gain the rights and privileges of full participation in the American system. It was believed that strong support for democratic ideals as proposed by the founding fathers of the United States would best suit the aims of achieving full citizenship. While many well-intentioned blacks of Garvey's time did not see through the facade of American democracy, Garvey did. Developments in recent years have proved Garvey right.

Garvey's reputation as a charismatic leader and powerful orator was based on his ability to argue persuasively that the development of a separate black society was more important than winning the right to participate in the American mainstream. He made this argument because his long-range goal was freedom within a separate society, rather than escape from that society into the American white world. Garvey's view is echoed today by the Reverend Albert Cleage Jr., of Detroit: "We are in the process of becoming a Black Nation, a Nation that is as real as if it had a capital, a Congress and a president. . . . We were afraid to fight because we felt that if we fought we would fight alone and we would die alone. That is the way we were. The difference now is that we are coming together. We are no longer just individuals. We are becoming a Nation. . . . We are a Black Nation in a white man's world. . . . Now we are in our own world, our own Nation, so much so that sometimes we feel uncomfortable because we have to go out into their enemy world to work and to shop."[10] Garvey recognized that for the foreseeable future many blacks would still have to work in that enemy world. His organization was officially on record as condemning discrimination and forced segregation; his weekly newspaper, *Negro World*, condemned such racist practices in issue after issue; and placards carried at UNIA parades denounced lynching, political discrimination, and other expressions of racial exclusion. But since Garvey's major emphasis was on building a separate world, his critics ignored UNIA civil rights activity.

Through the Garvey system, black Americans were provided alternative institutions to those offered by mainstream America, black or white. Garveyites began the development of businesses, churches, and social organizations as an aid to their membership recruitment efforts. In their day, Garveyites were criticized by many well-intentioned blacks for emphasizing institutional development when that energy might have been expended in direct challenges to white racism. Replying to this criticism, Garvey argued that without an independent base of operations, challenges to white racism would require alliance with one or another segment of that racist society and would be self-defeating. "Hence it is advisable for the Negro to get power of every kind. POWER in education, science, industry, politics and higher government. That kind of power that will stand out signally, so that other races and nations can see, and if they will not see, then FEEL." [11]

Working on Garvey's principle of economic independence from whites, the UNIA built an extensive system of business enterprises—a scheme which has often been equated (and therefore damned) with the program of Booker T. Washington, who was the leading advocate of black capitalism in the years just prior to the founding of the UNIA. But unlike Washington, Garvey received no support from existing black businessmen. They stood aloof as Garvey launched his Black Star Line steamship company and his Negro Factories Corporation. Ultimate control of UNIA businesses rested in the annually elected leadership of the Association. Established black businessmen could not deal with a man who made economics an integral part of political struggle. The UNIA also differed from the pro-Washington crowd in that it was not considered "safe" by the white power structure and did not receive support from white philanthropists.

Religion had an important role in the UNIA, but the Garvey movement did not attract a single prominent Negro minister. Garveyites encouraged blacks to leave existing churches and to form new ones within the UNIA that were based on a black theology and on a willingness to join the struggle for self-determination.

Although Garveyites did formally participate in American electoral politics and, like most black organizations, endorsed candidates on their merits as "race men" rather than on the basis of political party affiliation, such activity was secondary to the building of international political power. And the first big step in that direction, for Garveyites, would be the liberation of Africa. There were some American Garveyites who didn't want to be involved in electoral politics at all, but there were many others who were as active in the fight for voting rights as were spokesmen of the NAACP. The UNIA's official demands, set down in a Declaration of Rights of the Negro Peoples of the World, included the right to vote, a fair share of political patronage, representation on juries and on the judge's bench, and full freedom of press, speech, and assembly for all.[12] The UNIA sought these basic freedoms primarily to create and strengthen a separate black world, while groups like the NAACP would utilize these freedoms primarily to create an integrated world.

Socially, the UNIA was a huge club and fraternal order, but it drew little support from established Negro lodges or Greek-letter societies. The black fraternities and sororities trained their members to ape white middle-class society. For Garveyites, there was the fraternal camaraderie of all the black people of the world. UNIA parades, Saturday night parties, women's group luncheons, etc., had a significance far beyond that of providing social diversion. Their affairs were designed to build a pride and confidence in blackness. This "soul" of Garveyism is recaptured today every time one black greets another with the fraternal handslap, every time a group studies black history, eats at a soul food restaurant, listens to black music, dances to it, sings with it. The UNIA did include a "Noble Order of the Knights of the Nile," but the top positions in it were reserved for those who had made significant contributions to the black struggle.

* * *

The legacy of Garvey and his followers goes beyond the many programs they initiated. Garvey and many of his leading lieutenants were masters of psychological warfare. Garvey tried to restore to the black man the masculinity stolen from him during the centuries of slavery. With his belief that even the best programs would come to naught unless the black man overcame his "trembling fear" of white authority, Garvey could be aggressive and purposely intemperate—as in this challenge to the Ku Klux Klan: "They can pull off their hot stuff in the south, but let them come north and touch Philadelphia, New York or Chicago and there will be little left of the Ku Klux Klan. . . . Let them try and come to Harlem and they will really have some fun."[13] In his *Negro World,* Garvey wrote that the colonies of Africa were the property of the blacks, and "by God we are going to have them now or some time later, even if all the world is to waste itself in blood."* [14]

For a short time in the early 1920s, the Garveyites held together an unprecedented black coalition which included cultural nationalists, political nationalists, opponents of organized religion (atheists, separatists, or simply reformers), advocates of armed rebellion, pacifists, women's liberation fighters, participants in Democratic and Republican machine politics, a smattering of left-wingers, many who wanted no contact with whites, and a small but significant number who wanted the UNIA to cooperate with integrated civil rights organizations to end discrimination and segregation.

Obviously, with such diversity in the coalition there were strong differences of opinion expressed in the UNIA. The coalition did not last out the decade; those who wanted to make alliances with whites were among the first to go. Their departure was hastened by the development of bitter animosity between established civil rights organizations and the UNIA. Garvey, coming from Jamaica, was not really in tune with some of the subtle nuances of the black American situation, and by expressing a pro-black bias in chauvinistic rhetoric he alienated many Americans who had experienced enough racial bias from the other side to make them suspicious of any prejudice—positive or negative. However, Garvey considered himself an advocate of "the bigger brotherhood," in which all ethnic groups took pride in their own identity, while maintaining respect for the shared humanity of others. The following statement typifies Garvey's tone and style.

What We Believe

The Universal Negro Improvement Association advocates the uniting and blending of all Negroes into one strong, healthy race. It is against miscegenation and race suicide.

It believes that the Negro race is as good as any other.

It is against rich blacks marrying poor whites.

It is against rich or poor whites taking advantage of Negro women.

---

* He was in this instance referring to the African territories formerly under German control.

20

It believes in the spiritual Fatherhood of God and the Brotherhood of Man.

It believes in the social and political physical separation of all peoples to the extent that they promote their own ideals and civilization, with the privilege of trading and doing business with each other. It believes in the promotion of a strong and powerful Negro nation in Africa.

It believes in the rights of all men.[15]

The militants of today might quarrel with Garvey's emphatic opposition to miscegenation and with other specifics, but it is generally agreed that separate and viable bases of black power are essential to black liberation, whether or not there is association with whites, political or social.

Today's black militants often ask whether the Garveyites were truly radical or revolutionary. The most common statement made by Garveyites interviewed by this writer was that their leader had been misunderstood in his day because he was ahead of his time—when the leader of a protest movement holds views which are too advanced for that period in history, then he is usually considered a radical. Whether or not Garvey was a revolutionary is another question, though he did employ the inflammatory rhetoric of a revolutionary, particularly in his periodic warnings of an impending world war of the races. In one of many such projections he told a reporter for the Pittsburgh *Courier,* "Within the next twenty years . . . there will be a great world upheaval. The white and darker races will clash and there will be a fight to the finish. . . . We of the UNIA are aware of these world indications and we intend to be ready when the changes come." [16] "Be Ready to Strike If New War Breaks" ran a banner headline over a Garvey *Negro World* editorial.[17] "England's doom is at hand," declared Garvey at a rally in Philadelphia, "and as the Czar lost his throne some years ago, so I fear George of England may have to run for his life, and that will be the chance for the Negro. . . . Let us pray for the 'downfall of England.' Why do I want the downfall of England? Because I want the freedom of Africa." [18]

Like black power advocates of today, Garvey could conceive of only two versions of the future—either the black man would receive his freedom or war would be inevitable. But in his forebodings of the future struggle Garvey avoided directly stating that his organization would instigate a revolutionary uprising. He sought to motivate black people, to prepare them for action by arming them with a belief in the essential moral integrity and reasonableness of black nationalist and black power demands. Garvey's approach involved petitions, delegations, and declarations to public bodies asking for a dialogue and understanding. "If we are to have world peace," wrote Garvey in 1922, "it will only come when a greater inter-racial conference is called. When Jew will meet Gentile; when Anglo-Saxon will meet Teuton; when the great Caucasian family will meet the Mongolian, and when all will meet the Negro, and then and there straighten out the differences that have kept us apart for hundreds of years, and will continue to keep us apart until Doom's Day, if something is not done to create better racial understanding." [19]

Garvey's calls for peace and understanding on the one hand, and his demands for self-determination on the other, reflect the ambiguity which so often confronts black leaders working in the United States. Describing "national liberation in the black colony" Eldridge Cleaver said, "We start with the basic definition: that black people in America are a colonized people in every sense of the term and that white America is an organized imperialist force holding black people in colonial bondage." [20] However, the struggle to liberate the colony in America is complicated by factors not present in the Third World. Where black and white are as interrelated as they are in this country, a geographically separate nation, as proposed by groups like the Republic of New Africa, is at best a remote possibility. Garvey's objective was to give to blacks a consciousness of the nationhood which already existed, and to conduct this effort without being jailed, assassinated, or exiled, as so many recent radicals have been. The late Malcolm X, whose father was a Garveyite, had a vision of the black nation similar to that of Marcus Garvey. The Oakland cultural nationalist Donald Warden recalled an evening with Malcolm X: "I asked Malcolm where the new nation would be and he said, 'It is right here, in the community, and in every black community in America'."

Many of the ideas and programs of the old UNIA are now being seriously considered. The idea of emigration to Africa is not today as strange a prospect as it once appeared. In the past decade, several thousand Afro-Americans have either visited or permanently emigrated to Africa, including many who were engaged in short-term work projects, such as those arranged by black church groups. There is also a growing contingent of black American businessmen working in Africa or through Africa with offices in New York. Political turmoil in Africa has discouraged many prospective permanent residents, but interest in emigration to the homeland appears to be growing rather than diminishing. Political repression in the United States has caused some exodus to Africa, and militant black Americans in Africa have been asking individual states to grant automatic citizenship to Afro-Americans wishing to emigrate.

Garvey's idea of emigration did not end with one-way tickets to Africa. He also wanted to increase the migration of black people to and from the United States and the West Indies. The UNIA's Declaration of Rights of the Negro People states, "We declare it unjust for any country, state or nation to enact laws tending to hinder and obstruct the free immigration of Negroes on account of their race and color."[21] For Garvey, migrations were a means of solidifying ties between blacks of different countries and continents; and what Garvey tried to do in an institutionalized manner, blacks today are doing piecemeal—visiting Africa, smuggling themselves into Cuba, and vacationing in Jamaica.

The UNIA call for "all . . . churches, lodges, fraternal organizations, civil and uplift bodies"[22] to join in annual conventions has been echoed by the broadly representative Black Power Conferences, which were first held in Newark in 1967 and now are annual affairs. The promoters of these conferences have gone to great lengths to maintain a comprehensive representation of black groups of various persuasions, and with greater success than Garvey enjoyed—perhaps because they do not face such vociferous and well organized opposition to black power from within black society. This concern with racial unity is predicated on the realization that blacks cannot act strongly without solidarity which cuts across class and ideological differences. Black power conferences, black student unions in colleges, and black caucuses in the labor movement bring together the widest possible collection of black people, held by general agreement on the need for black unity.

The unity of today's radical black groups is dangerously threatened by differences over economic theory. Cultural nationalists denounce socialism, and black socialists, particularly the Black Panther Party, refuse to cooperate with people labeled cultural nationalists. In the 1920s, conflicts over economics were central to the fights between Garveyites and their black opponents. Marcus Garvey became an ardent foe of organized socialist and communist movements, especially as found in the United States. With the heritage of the Garvey era in mind, many of today's black nationalists feel compelled to denounce socialists, this opposition being part of their emphasis on independence from whites and white ideas.

Garvey's position, however, has been greatly misunderstood. His opposition to organized socialist groups was based primarily on a dislike for their integrationist views and the socialist concept of black and white political alliance. Garvey was certainly not an exponent of black capitalism as proposed today by Richard Nixon. Conscientious militants who are trying to follow today's eleventh commandment of maintaining black unity should find comfort in Garvey's overall approach to economics. Keeping in mind that economic theory was quite secondary in Garvey's philosophy, one can see that Garvey was adamantly opposed to the economic imperialism of whites in the Third World and to the exploitation of blacks by American black capitalists. Garvey did endorse capitalism, under certain conditions and restrictions, but he was certainly not the economic reactionary he was made out to be by his left-wing critics. This is an important point for understanding Garveyism. It should also be a consideration in the attempts of various militants to overcome ideological differences and to work together. In order to overcome the divisions which now go under the labels of "cultural nationalists" vs. "socialists," there will have to be compromise. That a man of Marcus Garvey's solid cultural nationalist reputation also fought against economic colonialists and exploitative black capitalists offers hope that compromise is possible—at least on the part of nationalists. (Later in this study, attention will be given to the African Blood Brotherhood, a Marxist organization which attempted to compromise with cultural nationalism.)

Garvey's eclectic approach to economic questions angered the dogmatists on all sides. In an age of extremism on the question of socialism versus capitalism, Garvey separated the national liberation struggle from a narrow economic context. Stokely Carmichael has argued, in a similar fashion, that socialism is designed for the economically depressed classes and cannot by itself free the black American who suffers most directly from colonialism and the suppression of his nation. National liberation for the black American requires a united front of the black bourgeoisie and the working class. To turn black liberation into a purely working-class struggle will leave the bourgeoisie free to sabotage the movement, and there will be plenty of white money provided to aid the black middle class in its treacherous cause.[23] Unlike Fidel Castro's Cuba, where the disgruntled bourgeoisie can be put on airplanes bound for Miami, black America must keep together all segments of its population.

Garvey's first concern was the building of a nation, and anyone who stood in the way of this struggle was to be opposed, whatever economic theory he espoused. For the most part, Garvey refrained from endorsing either major economic system, much as latter-day African leaders have steered a course between the ideologies of East and West. But if any economic label fits Garvey, it would be "welfare-state liberal"; his People's Political Party platform for Jamaica, drawn up in 1929, states that the government of a black nation should guarantee the workers social security, steady employment, and compensation in case of injury, and that it should have the right to appropriate private lands for public use. The UNIA Negro Factories Corporation and the Black Star Line were more cooperatives than corporations, and the proposed colony in Liberia was to consist of family-unit farms along with five thousand–acre cooperative farms run by the Association. "Capitalism is necessary to the progress of the world," wrote Garvey in his *Philosophy and Opinions,* "but there should be a limit to the individual or corporate use or control of it. No individual should be allowed the possession, use or privilege to invest on his own account more than a million, and no corporation should be allowed to control more than five million. Beyond this, all control, use and investment of money should be the prerogative of the State with the concurrent authority of the people." [24]

Although the young Garvey was an ardent follower of Booker T. Washington (because Washington sought to build independent black economic power), Garvey later said in his *Philosophy and Opinions,* "If Washington had lived he would have had to change his program. No leader can successfully lead this race of ours without giving an interpretation of the awakened spirit of the New Negro, who does not seek industrial opportunity alone, but a political voice." [25] And in 1921, Garvey said, "We have been misrepresented by our leadership. We have been taught to beg rather than to make demands.

Booker T. Washington was not a leader of the Negro race. We do not look to Tuskegee. The world has recognized him as a leader, but we do not. We are going to make demands." [26] Again, at the 1924 UNIA convention Garvey denounced "the capitalist class of Negroes whose only concern is to rob and exploit the unfortunate of their own race. . . . The Negro people are suffering under exploitation by a privileged class of Negroes, businessmen and professional men who have no more consideration for their own unfortunate people than the white exploiter. Their selfishness is their only motive, their contempt for the masses of their people is great, and their only mission is to rob and exploit the unfortunate brothers of their own race. The Negro real-estate man in New York is the greatest devil we have to combat." [27]

Garvey was far more concerned with the evils of imperialism than with domestic economic policies. He termed dollar diplomacy a "disgrace to our civilization" and decried the practice whereby underdeveloped nations granted "concessions" to foreigners for the exploitation of natural resources. "Men like Morgan, Rockefeller, Firestone, Doheny, Sinclair and Gary should not be allowed to entangle the nation in foreign disputes, . . . for the sake of satisfying their personal, individual or corporate selfishness and greed for more wealth. . . ." In Garvey's opinion, "Modern wars are generally the outgrowth of dissatisfied capitalistic interests. . . . Until a universal adjustment takes place the State or nation should have the power to conscript and use, without any obligation to repay, the wealth of such individuals or corporations through whose investments or interests, in foreign countries or among foreign or strange peoples, wars are fomented and made." [28] In a lengthy polemical poem titled "The Tragedy of White Injustice," Garvey wrote:

> The bankers employ men to shoot and kill
> When we interfere with their august will.
> They take the savings of deaf, dumb and poor,
> Gamble with it here and on foreign shore;
> In oil, gold, rum, rubber they speculate,
> Then bring their foreign troubles upon the State.
> Friends in government they control at will,
> War they make for others, our sons to kill. [29]

When Garvey suggested that the government should appropriate surplus corporate profits to forestall investment abroad, he was proposing state regulation of the economy, but he did not envision this as an endorsement of socialism. Garvey declared that both capitalists and socialists were capable of imperialist exploitation; his black nationalism held that white industrial powers could fleece colonial nations regardless of their particular economic system. Describing the western socialist movement in his *Black Man* monthly, he wrote: "The people who make up the rank and file are of the lower and upper working classes. They organize, they agitate and they fight because they desire primarily to improve their economic status." In Garvey's view, this was already an elevated status "enjoyed at the expense of the oppressed and suppressed darker and Black races who are ruthlessly exploited by the capitalist class in their respective colonies. . . . If the Communist or Socialist in America or England receives $4 or 16*s* a day as his average wage, that $4 or 16*s* is the result of the supply of the cheap raw materials of the native countries by the native populations of Africa, India and China. So to maintain the present wage scale in America and in England the native must be paid 2*s* a day and the coolies in India 3*d* a day. It means therefore, that a higher wage standard of the American or English white worker must result in a lower standard for the exploited natives in their country." Hence when white workers "inveigle darker peoples into Communism, they are only endeavoring to use them to gain a greater advantage in the economic scale. . ."[30]

The use of surplus capital from colonies to bribe the proletariat of developed nations was first noted by Karl Marx himself. In recent years, Marxists have accused "revisionists" in Europe and America of complicity in their government's neo-colonialism, accusations which bring bitter denials today. Garvey's attempt at such criticism went unanswered by his left-wing opponents, who found it most difficult to make analytical rebuttals to his ideological position. His consistently "color-first" viewpoint seemed to the theorists of class struggle to be an intellectual morass of contradiction and hypocrisy; since the white socialists of Garvey's day could not understand the meaning of or the need for black power, they could not fathom Garvey's economic views. Garvey, in turn, saw nothing of benefit to the black nation in the programs of American and European leftists. "Fundamentally, what racial difference is there between a white Communist, Republican or Democrat?" he asked.[31] For posing such questions, Garvey was called a narrow-minded racist, just as black power spokesmen today are labeled reverse racists for similar remarks.

According to his critics, Garvey won followers by presenting emotion-laden arguments that were void of any realistic appraisal of the black situation. Garvey and leading Garveyites realized that the "race first" perspective had emotional appeal, and to balance this they attempted to set forth the practical rationale for their position. An example of this appears in an evaluation of "white liberalism" by Ernest E. Mair, a Garveyite *Negro World* columnist. Mair concluded that Christian liberals were "hypocrites" who would not open their churches to the brotherhood of man and that League of Nations liberals were a "society of thieves" because they would not free Africa. Socialists, in Mair's view, "tell you that they see no reason why they should single the Negro out for favor when there are so many of their own race in need, in which I concur, and by the same sign I will have none of them or their works." He found organized labor "the most conservative of all the supposed liberal movements," pointing out that unions were asking black men not to scab, but refusing to let them join. Mair added that he was not opposed "to the principle of unionizing. If one is to be honest he must admit that practically everything gained by the people that work with their hands has been due to the efforts of organized labor. Considered . . . as a movement for the general betterment of workingmen the labor movement is highly desirable. But we are not so considering it here. We are considering its usefulness as a liberal element of white society, able, if it will, to make life a whole lot more tolerable for the black man. And from that standpoint it is a miserable failure." As to communists, "those ultra-radicals . . . hated by all good capitalists. Well, I don't hate them [and no matter how bad communism is] it can't be worse than the system now in practice. Let us be truthful. We know that however well we thought of the system it would be economic suicide for us to embrace it, for the powers that be give us starvation wages now; if we developed Communistic leanings they would see to it that we had no jobs at all." [32]

The Garveyite refusal to work with white leftists was in most instances a reaction to the situation in the United States, where socialist movements were directed by whites. In the Third World, where there were instances of indigenous black-led socialist struggles, Garveyites worked with socialists. Today there are shining examples of independent socialist nations in Africa; no longer is it necessary for blacks in the Third World or in America to think of socialism as purely the white man's prerogative.

In the past few years Marcus Garvey's son, Mwalimu Marcus Garvey, who has emerged as an important leader in the Jamaican black power movement, has been developing an ideology called African National Socialism which attempts to bring ideas of the old UNIA up to date. African National Socialism, which Mwalimu calls "black power in its highest form," will unite Garvey's "African Nationalism . . . with the African socialism of Kwame Nkrumah." The new ideology is based on three concepts:

> First, the belief in the one God, the God of Africa and the Black Race. . . . Just as the white man whitewashes all the external paraphernalia of his religion, so must we do likewise. . . . Marcus Garvey has taught us that we must see our God through the spectacles of Ethiopia, and it was for this reason that he together with Archbishop [sic] McGuire* raised the Black Christ and the Black Madonna of the African Orthodox Church. So let it be. The African must have a theology rooted in his own ancestry and heritage and illustrated in conformity with his own physical appearance.
>
> Second, the black man must take power of every kind— power that is exclusive. The black man must be in a position to determine his own destiny. He can do this only when he has power firmly in his own black hands. . . . The power which our race needs at this time can only be realised by action from within our own closed institutions. The alien must not be allowed to penetrate authentic African institutions. There must be a wall past which they cannot see; there must be a door to which they have no key.
>
> Third, the African society must be organized on the basis of African Socialism. The basic concept is that the wealth of the black community must be in the hands of the black people, and there must be an equitable distribution and sharing of this wealth. In order to obtain these

* George Alexander McGuire was bishop of the Garveyite African Orthodox Church and was chaplain general of the UNIA.

desirable results, the state must plan and direct the economy. . . . African Socialism however, is not doctrinaire but flexible. Private ownership is not something to be exorcised or swept away, rather it is something to be controlled. The socialist concept of the greatest good for the greatest number is in accordance with African thinking. African National Socialism postulates the following types of ownership which have their proper places in the complete system: (a) state ownership, (b) cooperative ownership, (c) individual ownership, (d) state and individual ownership. In all cases the aim should be to allow the workers to participate in the ownership of the enterprises of which they are a part.[33]

As for the relevance of Garveyite objectives to today's black struggle, suffice it to say that they are increasingly embraced throughout the black world and that no nation can call itself free if it does not allow its citizens to work for these ends.

2

THE
NEW NEGRO:
GARVEYITES
AND OTHERS

WORLD WAR I BROUGHT new hope to black people in many parts of the world. Liberation came to few, but a great number of black people became convinced that, with a concentrated effort, the long era of white domination over blacks could be brought to a close. The new confidence was worldwide, affecting blacks in Africa and Latin America as well as in the United States, and it was part of a larger change that had begun in some places as early as 1910. But for the most part the change came with the war. The Garvey movement was nurtured by, and blossomed in, the climate of hope and the dramatic changes of life-style among black people that followed World War I.

For traditional Western European civilization, World War I was an unmitigated disaster. Militarists, capitalists, despots, benevolent monarchs and liberal democrats joined to direct a grotesque scenario which brought about an unprecedented waste of human lives—and all for that shallowest of motives, the rights of Empire. Blacks and others of the Third World, so long propagandized into thinking of themselves as the "white man's burden," began to question the ability of white colonial rulers who were unable to maintain peaceful relations. This new understanding could not eradicate all vestiges of ingrained inferiority, but it started many in the direction of psychological freedom. Further, blacks fought on battlefields in Africa, the Near East and Europe, and proved themselves the equals of whites as soldiers; close to one million blacks from Africa, the Caribbean and North America served in World War I (including three hundred seventy thousand from the United States). Even those who did not fight could not fail to notice that the supposedly omni-potent white rulers had been forced to plead for black support in their military efforts.

A heightened political consciousness had been building among black people during the years of World War I in the course of a debate within black society over black involvement in the war. For many it seemed ridiculous for blacks to involve themselves in a war to save democracy in Europe when blacks didn't have democracy at home. One issue of the Richmond *Planet,* a black weekly, was barred from the mails because it contained an article urging blacks not to volunteer for military service. Uzziah Miner of Howard University Law School published—at his own expense—a small book criticizing the hypocrisy of the war and the use of black troops. [1] Meanwhile, a future leading Garveyite, J. C. St. Clair Drake, was telling his friends that he couldn't feel much sympathy for the suffering Belgians after what Belgians had done to blacks in the Congo. [2] Some, however, chose to keep their anti-war sentiments to themselves, since a widespread pro-war chauvinistic hysteria made outspoken opposition dangerous. As in so many wars, the strongest opposition came from the young, and the main support from the old; these stands on the war foreshadowed the coming division in black society between "New Negroes" and "Old Negroes."

The new awareness reached a dramatic height in the United States at the end of World War I as black troops returned from Europe. Writing in the NAACP magazine *Crisis* in 1919, W. E. B. DuBois exemplified the militant mood of the day: "We return. We return from fighting. Make way for Democracy! We saved it in France, and by the Great Jehovah, we will save it in the United States of America, or know the reason why." [3] Men who had seen a compara-tively non-racist France wanted to bring some non-racist culture home, and returning blacks refused to accept segregated facilities and protested discriminatory practices. When white America tried to terrorize the Negro back into his "place" by bringing lynch mobs into black communities, the black man fought back. The newly returned black troops took a leading role in defense against the mobs, as the community expected them to. Black soldiers had learned how to fight and, as some three dozen post-war race riots showed, black people pressed together in the compact ghetto could now snipe at invading whites and then escape in the maze of tenements. Participation in community defense was for many a first step toward involvement in a broad political struggle.

The worst of these post-war battles (there were more than twenty in 1919 alone) were fought in Chicago, Omaha, Knoxville, Washington, D.C., Tulsa and Charleston, and in smaller centers such as Elaine, Arkansas; Longview, Texas; and Waukegan, Illinois.[4] Isolated incidents involving blacks and white citizens or white police broke out sporadically in larger cities such as New York and Philadelphia during 1917 and 1918.[5] But the days of the lynching bee were past; white mobs invading black communities now faced well-placed gunfire. In Chicago the death count after two weeks of warfare totaled thirty-five blacks and thirteen whites, and almost every black victim had been killed *outside* the ghetto, usually going to or from work in a white neighborhood. "The colored troops fought nobly. We have something to fight for now," a black defender in Chicago wrote a friend in riot-torn Washington, D.C.[6] In Tulsa, the final toll was one hundred fifty blacks and fifty whites killed, but both sides suffered almost equally for the first two days, with whites unable to cross defensive positions at the railroad tracks which segregated the black community. One Negro weekly headlined its report on Tulsa "Colored Rioters Poorly Armed, But Casualty List Favorable."[7] These strong defenses effectively ended large-scale invasions of black neighborhoods by white mobs. From then on, whites would call upon their trained military, police or National Guard to do the job.

The new militancy was mirrored in Africa and the Caribbean. In the year following the Armistice, strikes and large demonstrations against colonial rule were reported in Sierra Leone, the Gold Coast, South Africa, Trinidad and British Honduras, and blacks in Panama and Costa Rica conducted a series of strikes for better working conditions and an end to racial discrimination.[8] This violent response had been presaged by a revolt of black soldiers of the British West Indian Regiment in December 1918. The uprising at Taranto, Italy, was a protest against racist restrictions promulgated by the British War Office. From fifty to sixty men were arrested, charged with mutiny, and sentenced, and eight battalions—some eight thousand troops—were disarmed. Angered by differential pay for black and white soldiers and by restrictions on advancement, members of the Ninth Battalion of that regiment attacked their officers and severely assaulted their unit commander. The rebellion continued for several days; men refused to work, a shooting and a bombing occurred, and a "generally insubordinate spirit prevailed." One hundred eight sergeants sent a petition to the secretary of state for the colonies protesting military racial discrimination. White troops were finally sent in and the Ninth Battalion was disbanded and its personnel distributed among other units.[9]

(Colonial officials thought the "mutinous spirit of Taranto" was behind the disturbances in Trinidad and British Honduras the following year. They charged that the systematic attack upon colonialists' businesses and residences in Belize, British Honduras, in July 1919, had been planned at Taranto and on the voyage home. However, as no black troops from British Honduras had been present during the Taranto rebellion, it might be more accurate to equate their later action with a desire to "get a piece of the action" they had missed in Italy.)[10]

Within the United States, wartime conscription created a labor shortage in northern industrial centers, and well over a quarter of a million southern blacks, encouraged by the black press and by the advertisements of northern businessmen, deserted their rural cabins for jobs in the northern cities. Within the South itself, a sizable number moved from rural to urban centers. In general, these movements broadened the migrants' outlook and political consciousness.

The war was only one of many factors stimulating migration. In the first twenty years of this century, half a million West Indians moved back and forth across the Caribbean Basin, while close to a hundred thousand others came to live in the United States or Canada. Most of these migrants were displaced when U.S. investors bought out small farmers and developed huge agricultural combines.

In Africa, thousands upon thousands of blacks left rural villages for new urban centers and mining districts. Despite centuries of exploitation through the slave trade, almost all of black Africa had remained free from outright colonial rule until the 1890s. A generation of militants then fell fighting the conquerers from Europe, and the first years of this century—the first years of mining and plantation exploitation—were indeed bleak. But by 1910 a new generation of Africans had emerged, and from it came a group of leaders—skilled workers and the small but increasing number of civil servants—who would define the terms of the struggle which culminated in rebellion and independence forty or fifty years later.

These migrations from farm to city and from nation to nation helped develop race consciousness and camaraderie between black spokesmen throughout the world. The struggle against oppression based on worldwide race unity became a central feature of an emerging black radical movement. Migration also brought expectations of opportunities in skilled jobs and the professions, ambitions common to people on the rise. As the masters of the system thwarted these aspirations, frustration turned many toward militancy. The move from rural settings opened new opportunities to express this militancy: a black farmer who dared attend a protest meeting in Alabama risked eviction or even lynching, but in New York City the black man's landlord and his employer knew (and cared) less about what he did in his free time. A militant would have had great difficulty finding a meeting place in small-town Alabama, but buildings could be rented in New York and, in lieu of a hall, there was always the street corner.

* * *

With the creation of large urban concentrations of blacks, there emerged new social and political groups which addressed themselves to the new problems of urban life. Life in the ghettoes needed explanation: it was filled with contradictions between the promises of a better scene, and the realities of ghetto conditions. At first there were jobs in heavy industry, but few of these lasted after the white troops returned. Any improvement in living conditions was debatable—in fact, twelve people living in a one-room Alabama shack probably enjoyed some advantages over twelve living in a two-room tenement apartment. The very closeness which was to prove an asset in political action was often detrimental to individual well-being: food in the local store was often moldy, street lighting inadequate, and garbage almost never collected. Those fortunate enough to find work were rarely paid enough to escape to a better neighborhood—if any other area would have allowed a black person in.

Urbanization had a somewhat different impact in the Caribbean and Africa. Kingston, Jamaica, though founded in the mid-1600s, typified the sprawling growth of the Third World. Between 1910 and 1920 huge collages of cardboard and flattened water heaters, with names like Trench Town and Denham Town, mushroomed around the outskirts of central Kingston. Unlike the American migrants, who left the farm willingly, and usually against the wishes of white owners, blacks in the Third World had often been forced to leave their rural setting. Some found jobs in the city, many did not; but, as in the United States, urban existence required initiative and cunning, and there were leaders who directed these energies into political struggle.

Changes in social and economic conditions, then, provided part of the impetus for a new self-confidence. But not all: the "New Negro" who appeared during the war also reflected generational differences. Most of the new militant leaders were in their twenties or early thirties. Some merely shouted loudly about injustice, but the more thoughtful were seriously considering black nationalism and socialism. Political disagreements among blacks in this period basically reflected varying evaluations of what it meant to be black. These differences were determined not only by socio-economic background but also by national origin, travel, and experience with whites. Some tried to minimize color and to live according to the norms of white society. "New Negroes" rejected this pattern. Black socialists adopted the "un-American" notion of working-class solidarity; nationalists the even more "un-American" notion that black people had a worthwhile culture of their own, distinct from and equal to that of whites.

One cannot distinguish Old Negroes from New by saying the former despaired and the latter had hope. Old Negroes in the academic community had high hopes for substantial social and economic change, but these hopes were grounded in faith in the white-ruled system. The New Negro, in contrast, based his faith on the potential power of black people to change the system. Black socialists hoped to effect such change with the aid of white comrades; the nationalists hoped to do it independently.

Many New Negroes, including some who became high officials in the Garvey movement, entered political struggle through the fight to end white machine politics in the new urban ghettoes. Many who joined the revolt against organized religion and founded new church denominations during the war were attracted to Garveyite and other social protest groups. Garveyites and other New Negro groups also drew many whose first interest had been the protection of immigrants. The New Negroes' interest in peoples from different parts of the world, stimulated by migrations and wartime travel, was sustained by lecturers such as the Jamaican Gabriel Stewart, the Guianese Rudolph Smith and the American Henrietta Vinton Davis—three world travelers who later became able recruiters for the UNIA.

Only one journal which could be described as a New Negro publication appeared until late in the war: the *African Times and Orient Review*. First published in London in 1912 by the Egyptian nationalist Duse Mohammed Ali (who originated the phrase "Africa for the Africans"), the *Review* advocated the study of African cultures, independence for colonial peoples, and the building of international business connections between Africans, Asians, and the colored peoples of the Americas. Marcus Garvey, half a dozen of his leading lieutenants, and numerous other New Negroes contributed articles to the *African Times*. The NAACP journal *Crisis*, founded in 1910, did make important contributions to the development of new ideas, but its editor, Dr. DuBois, was ostracized by New Negroes because of his endorsement of the war; in the summer of 1918 Dr. DuBois presented in *Crisis* an article entitled "Close Ranks" in which he urged blacks to support the war effort. However, DuBois's thorough and intelligent critiques of America's racist institutions continued to be admired by many who decried his moderate politics.

In 1917, two socialists, A. Philip Randolph and Chandler Owen, brought out the first issue of the *Messenger*, a monthly journal of "scientific radicalism." The next year saw the first publication of Garvey's *Negro World,* "the indispensable weekly," which by 1920 had the largest circulation of all black weekly newspapers in the United States. In 1918 Cyril Briggs inaugurated his monthly *Crusader,* advocating black nationalism, Leninism and violent revolution. Two militant magazines emphasizing cultural and literary developments also appeared that year: William Bridges's *Challenge* and Hubert Harrison's *Negro Voice*. None of these journals could have been published in the South, the Caribbean, or Africa,* and all were cited as seditious in state and federal reports on revolutionary activity. The United States Post Office refused to handle the July 1919 issue of Randolph's *Messenger* because of its militant content—though it was not appreciably different from other issues, this one did carry a drawing depicting a burning lynch

* By 1920 Garvey's *Negro World* was banned in many parts of colonial Africa and the West Indies.

victim with the flames forming an inverted American flag, the waving stripes seeming to burn the seared flesh. Printed boldly across the picture was the legend "A Glorious Desecration." [11]

The New Negroes publicly endorsed the militant self-defense of black communities and many participated directly in such actions. Claude McKay, a Jamaican immigrant who wrote for the *Negro World* and many white socialist publications, summed up this new determination in his poem "If We Must Die."

> If we must die, let it not be like hogs
> Hunted and penned in an inglorious spot
> While round us bark the mad and hungry dogs
> Making their mock at our accursed lot.
> If we must die, O let us nobly die
> So that our precious blood may not be shed
> In vain; then even the monsters we defy
> Shall be constrained to honor us though dead!
> . . . Like men we'll face the murderous cowardly pack,
> Pressed to the wall, dying, but fighting back. [12]

Printed publications were not the only carriers of new ideas, however. Harlem streetcorners became free platforms for spokesmen advocating innumerable social and economic alternatives to the status quo. Almost all the prominent New Negro militants built their reputations through street oratory, as Malcolm X did later and as the leather-jacketed Black Panthers and Carlos Cooks and his nationalists (clad in the uniforms of the UNIA's African Legionnaires) do today.*

* * *

Marcus Garvey had something of a head start over the others who

---

* The man most responsible for building the tradition was Hubert H. Harrison, "the first professor of Street Corner University." Harrison, a self-educated immigrant from the Virgin Islands, also taught "Contemporary Civilization" at New York University, lectured on such subjects as "Literary Lights of Yesterday and Today" for the New York Board of Education, and served as professor of comparative religion at the Modern School, professor of embryology at the Cosmopolitan College of Chiropractic, and instructor in English and economics at the Harlem School of Social Science. Before the war, he had worked with the socialists around Max Eastman and John Reed, helping to edit the *Masses* magazine.

wanted to build New Negro organizations. He had established the Universal Negro Improvement Association and African Communities League, generally known as the UNIA, in Jamaica in August 1914. (The general offices were transferred to New York in 1917.) The Association's ambitious objectives were set out in a manifesto calling upon "all people of Negro or African parentage" to join in a great crusade to "establish a Universal Confraternity among the race; to promote the spirit of race pride and love; to reclaim the fallen of the race; to administer to and assist the needy; to assist in civilizing the backward tribes of Africa; to strengthen the imperialism of independent African states; to establish Commissionaries or Agencies in the principal countries of the world for the protection of all Negroes, irrespective of nationality; to promote a conscientious Christian worship among the native tribes of Africa; to establish Universities, Colleges and Secondary Schools for the further education and culture of the boys and girls of the race; to conduct a world-wide commercial and industrial intercourse." [13]

Garvey's manifesto shows that he had decided upon the general direction of his movement by the eve of World War I; it also shows that he still had much to learn. In a 1920 version, when Garvey understood the meaning of "imperialism" more clearly, that word was dropped from the part of the manifesto referring to actions of African states. As an attack upon organized Christianity had become a part of Garveyism, he replaced the phrase "Christian worship" with "spiritual worship." The later manifesto also reflected the group's growing political emphasis with a call "to establish a central nation for the race."

It is not surprising that the Garvey of 1914 lacked the political finesse of the Garvey of 1920. For Garvey, as for many other black militants, the war years were a vital period of ideological experimentation, and during these years there was an unusual camaraderie between militants of nationalist and socialist persuasion. Later, when ideological differences were clarified, new ideas were suspect merely on the basis of their source; but until then various black militants often wrote for each other's magazines and shared speaking platforms and insights.

Garvey's first appearance before a large Harlem gathering, in the summer of 1917, illustrates such an exchange. The socialist Hubert Harrison had taken a liking to Garvey, and introduced him at a rally to launch Harrison's anti-war Afro-American Liberty League. [14] Association with the League was no light matter; its call for peace came at the height of patriotic pro-war hysteria. (Nor did Harrison stop at pacifism: in a Boston speech he suggested blacks should rise up against the government—as the Irish were then rising against the British government—if they were not given their rights.)[15] His maiden speech earned Garvey enough notoriety for him to go forward with plans for his own organization, in which Garvey was soon joined by Harrison himself.

With the UNIA and other New Negro organizations based in Harlem, that community emerged as the international center for black liberation struggles, and an entire generation came to think of America as the sanctuary from which to launch the struggle. This helped foster the view that blacks in the United States were significantly more radical than their brethren elsewhere. But while blacks in this country were more literate and enjoyed a higher standard of living than those in the colonial world—and thus read more radical magazines and contributed more money to radical causes—they were not necessarily more radical. Harold Cruse argues that Garvey moved his headquarters to New York because of the "apathy in Jamaica." [16] But people in the West Indies were not apathetic. Urbanization and mass migration within agricultural areas had unleashed hopes of a better world, and Jamaicans flocked to the Garvey movement: by 1920, the Association had branch divisions in every sizable town on the island.

It is somewhat ironic that Harlem should have become the center for this global struggle. In one sense, the United States was the worst of all places for blacks—its lynchings and other barbarities were unequaled anywhere else in the world, with the possible exception of the Belgian Congo, and American blacks suffered the disadvantage of being only ten per cent of the population. On the other hand, black militants in the new urban communities had more freedom than their brothers in the Third World. The United States guaranteed freedom of press and assembly, at least nominally, and blacks could thus hold organizational meetings, set up offices and begin publishing magazines and newspapers. Whites in the United States had failed to make plans for controlling blacks in the new urban setting. Attempts to apply the traditional Southern approach of "pacifying" black communities with lawless citizen mobs only spurred the militants.* But in Third World colonies the government could simply ban public meetings or periodicals.

By 1918—two years after his arrival in America—Garvey had gathered several thousand followers. Most of these were in New York, but through speaking tours and the *Negro World* he had developed a broad base of support, enabling him to build his movement so rapidly after the Armistice that the UNIA could claim two million followers by the end of 1919. (The black left had also made an impact: one out of four Harlem voters chose the Socialist ticket in the 1920 elections.)

During the summer of 1919, numerous rallies were called to denounce the white mob actions and to raise money for the homeless and injured. The mood of the people at these meetings was unmistakably radical. At a rally protesting the white-inspired carnage in Omaha, Nebraska, Marcus Garvey pronounced: "The best thing the Negro of all countries can do is to prepare to match fire with hell-fire. No African is going to allow the Caucasian to trample eternally upon his rights. We have allowed it for five hundred years and we have now struck." Blacks were told to prepare for a great day, "the day of the war of the races, when Asia will lead out to defeat Europe, and Europe and the white man will again call upon the Negro to save them as we have often done. The New Negro has fought the last battle for the white man, and he is now getting ready to fight for the redemption of Africa. With mob laws and lynching bees fresh in our memories, we shall turn a deaf ear to the white man. . . . Let every Negro all over the world prepare for the new emancipation. . . . Our forces of industry, commerce, science, art, liberation, and war must be marshaled when Asia or Europe strikes the blow of the Second World War. Black men shall die then and black women shall succor them, but in the end there shall be a crowning victory for the soldiers of Ethiopia on the African battleground." [17]

Garvey expressed this view again at Madison Square Garden in a speech unnoticed in the American press but reported in the London *Times* for November 1, 1919: "Four hundred million black men are beginning to sharpen their swords for the war of races . . . and it will

---

* That Harlem itself escaped major violence may be attributable to the peculiar cultural character of New York City, where each segregated ethnic community fears every other ethnic community.

be the bloodiest war the world has ever seen. It will be a terrible day when the blacks draw sword and fight for their liberty. . . ."

In 1919 this determination to fight was considered respectable by major Negro newspapers which usually criticized Garveyites and other activists. Both the Chicago *Defender* and the Washington *Bee* quoted a black man in Chicago: "It is the duty of every man here to provide himself with guns and ammunition. I myself have at least one gun and at least enough ammunition to make it useful." And *Bee* editor Calvin Chase added, "We are only fighting for our rights." The Pittsburgh *Courier* commented, "As long as the Negro submits to lynchings, burnings, and oppression—and says nothing, he is a loyal American citizen. But when he decides that lynchings and burnings shall cease, even at the cost of some bloodshed in America, then he is a Bolshevist." [18]

Amid the fervor of 1919, even the meetings of respectable black middle-class organizations were taken over by militants and turned into rallies for revolution. That July the National Equal Rights League, a civil rights organization composed primarily of professionals and academicians, called a meeting in New York to welcome its president, William Monroe Trotter, home from France. In a hall crowded to suffocation, speaker after speaker fought his way to the podium to denounce America, and in the near-hysteria the purpose of the meeting was all but forgotten.[19]

At least until 1919, a major part of the New Negro struggle was simply to become recognized. The uninitiated public did not differentiate nationalists from socialists; rather they distinguished those who wished to upset the status quo from those who did not. For example, A. Philip Randolph was called the "most dangerous Negro in America" in 1918 when he was hauled off a speaker's platform in Cleveland and thrown into jail for talking about racism in America's war involvement.[20] News coverage of this event aided all militants, whose very existence had been largely ignored in the regular press, black or white. When Garvey shared the platform with Randolph at a protest rally in 1919, the audience doubtless included some future Garveyites drawn by Randolph, and vice versa.

In this period, all radicals shared a desire to end discrimination and forced segregation, lynching and disenfranchisement. A well-put phrase of righteous indignation from whatever source carried the message. In the suppressed July 1919 *Messenger*, columnist William

N. Colson, a former Army lieutenant, wrote of the fight to be waged by the returning black GI: "Remembering the pleasantness of French life, he will not rest until he has caused to be ushered into the United States a state of complete and uncompromising economic, political and social equality. This program will call for the benefit of every enjoyment, privilege, and immunity which the white race does or will possess in America." Colson himself looked forward to a thoroughly integrated America. Even though the issue between integration and independence remained unresolved, his statement stood as a straightforward call for action.

Garvey's speeches rang with calls to organize and prepare for an imminent rebellion of the oppressed races. In the December 1919 *Messenger* Randolph wrote favorably of current rebellions in Ireland, Bulgaria, Hungary and Germany, and a host of strikes, demonstrations and uprisings in Asia, Africa and America. Of course, Randolph was thinking of a white-led revolution for America, while Garvey had in mind a black one, and both eventually softened their talk of open rebellion. But the white agents of the United States Justice Department who investigated "radicalism and sedition among Negroes" saw little difference between Garvey's *Negro World* and Randolph's *Messenger*.[21]

For a time the two men did cooperate closely. In 1918 Randolph and Garvey joined to form the short-lived International League of Darker Peoples, which was to draw up a list of demands upon the European powers concerning the treatment of colonized peoples. After the war, Garvey announced that the UNIA had chosen Randolph to head a delegation of blacks to the Versailles Peace Conference. Garveyites held a mass meeting to raise passage money for Randolph, but Randolph declined.*[22]

In 1919 the *Messenger* and the monthly *Crusader* exchanged lists of agents, "with mutual profit and fraternity," as Randolph explained.[23] Three years later Randolph and *Crusader* editor Cyril Briggs were bitter enemies. The latter's endorsement of international communism contrasted sharply with Randolph's support for the American Socialist Party. Briggs had discovered Marxism during the war years, and added it to a volatile black nationalism. Early in 1919 he formed the African Blood Brotherhood, which he hoped

---

* "Needless to say, I never went," commented Randolph sarcastically some years later, during the height of his feud with Garvey.

would become a tightly knit paramilitary cadre within the UNIA. A number of Brotherhood members went to work in the Garvey Association; one, W. A. Domingo, was even the chief editor of the *Negro World* through most of 1919. Briggs's own journal, the *Crusader*, rang with endorsements of the Industrial Workers of the World, the Socialist party and the Russian Bolsheviks. During the war, Briggs lent his support to any and all radicalism, while spewing venom on anything smacking of "American mobocracy," as he called the bourgeois democratic process. The early *Crusader* was an important source of the nationalist ideology Garvey helped foster. One of its first issues carried a "Race Catechism," a classic definition of black nationalism arguing the superiority of the Negro race. The catechism went as follows:

Question: How do you consider yourself in relation to your race?

Answer: I consider myself bound to it by a sentiment which unites us all.

Question: What is it?

Answer: The sentiment that the Negro race is of all the races the most favored by the muses of music, poetry and art and is possessed of those qualities of courage, honor and intelligence necessary to the making of the best manhood and womanhood and the most brilliant development of the human species.

Question: What is one's duty to his race?

Answer: To love one's race above one's self and to further the common interests of all above the private interest of one. To cheerfully sacrifice wealth, ease, luxuries, necessities and, if need be, life itself to attain for the race that greatness in arms, in commerce, in art, the three combined without which there is neither respect, honor, nor security.

Question: How can you further the interest of the race?

Answer: By spreading race patriotism among my fellows; by unfolding the annals of our glorious deeds and the facts of the noble origin, splendid achievements and ancient cultures of the Negro Race to those whom alien education has kept in ignorance of these things; by combatting the insidious, mischievous and false teaching of school histories that exalt the white man and debase the

Negro, that tell of the white man's achievements but not of his ignominy, while relating only that part of the Negro's story that refers to his temporary enslavement and partial decadence; by helping race industries in preference to all others; by encouraging race enterprise and business to the ends of an ultimate creation of wealth, employment and financial strength within the race; by so carrying myself as to demand honor and respect for my race.

Question: Why are you proud of your race?

Answer: Because in the veins of no human being does there flow more generous blood than in our own; in the annals of the world, the history of no race is more resplendent with honest, worthy glory than that of the Negro Race, members of which founded the first beginnings of civilization upon the banks of the Nile, developing it and extending it southward to Ethiopia and westward over the smiling Sudan to the distant Atlantic, so that the Greeks who came to learn from our fathers declared that they were "the most just of men, the favorites of the Gods." [24]

In the early 1920s, black militants were divided over the question of whether or not a pro-black bias was legitimate. Through 1919, however, the few blacks who publicly objected to such a bias were the conservative leaders of the middle and upper classes. Black leaders especially showed their willingness to share ideas and programs in their general support of cooperative businesses as a solution to the shortage of capital in the black economy. Briggs and his Brotherhood promoted cooperatives; DuBois founded a Negro Cooperative League in 1919; Randolph supported the idea in the *Messenger*; and even the black bourgeoisie's Robert S. Abbott, editor-publisher of the Chicago *Defender*, endorsed the idea. Garvey himself (though he talked in the jargon of free enterprise) built a network of cooperatively owned and managed businesses.

By the end of 1919, the period of cooperation was drawing to a close. The UNIA had become a distinct branch of black militancy, and—though concerted opposition from other black radicals did not come until 1922—opposition groups were encouraging Garvey supporters to leave the UNIA. The Garvey movement took a separate course during the 1920s, establishing its own social and political context. As distinct factions developed within the UNIA itself, differences over tactics and ideology were confined to the separate world of Garveyism. By the mid-1920s, the term "New Negro" was barely used in a political context, either by Garveyites or others who had once coveted the title. The world of Garveyism is the subject of most of this volume, but what follows now is a brief account of the various approaches to liberation taken by blacks outside the UNIA.

3

ALTERNATIVES TO GARVEYISM

BLACK POWER IS NOT a new concept; black Americans have always suffered oppression and lacked group power and the black man has long demanded his "fair share." However, in the past much of his struggle was directed toward winning a more equitable share of what white America had to offer, while today the emphasis is on winning the right to create independent economic, social, cultural and spiritual power.

There are many shades of black power. In the middle of the black power continuum are those who believe that the injustices of discrimination and forced segregation can be successfully challenged if blacks join with disadvantaged whites and reform the system through interracial cooperation. This group has led the fight for integration and assimilation. At one extreme are those who believe that since racism is endemic to America the black man must accommodate himself to the segregated world that has been forced upon him, avoid any challenge to white authority, and build power within the segregated world through a combination of capitalist economics and white philanthropy. At the other extreme are those who believe the system is simply unworkable, so far as the rights of black people are concerned. People who hold this latter view refuse to accept forced segregation, but they do seek the right to build a society of their own. Independent black power, on a par with white power, is their goal.

What freedom means to an advocate of black power varies along the same continuum. The accommodationists, exemplified in the past by black businessmen and professionals, have conceived of freedom in a narrowly individualist context. The integrationists have been more willing to see the struggle of the black American in a class context. The advocates of independent black power, while recognizing that most black Americans are part of an oppressed economic class, see the overall racial struggle as far more significant than the class struggle.

To understand Garveyism and the actions of Garveyites, one must view them in relation to the wider struggle for black power, and to do that one must know something of the alternative types of struggle among black people during the post–World War I era, the prime years of the Universal Negro Improvement Association. In large part, Garveyism developed as a critical response to the programs of other black organizations, especially those in the United States.

* * *

One discernible approach to the question of power, taken by black professionals, academicians and businessmen, was developed after the Civil War and was modeled directly on the ideology of the white establishment. Committed to free enterprise in economics and individualism in social affairs, the middle-class blacks were wary of mass action politics. To them, security for black people differed little from that of the stereotype "mammy," who gained food, lodging and "totin' privileges" in return for submission to white authority. Social struggle meant winning occasional civil rights legislation or philanthropic handouts from benevolent whites through quiet negotiation.

The growth of large urban communities during and after World War I gave the black bourgeoisie high hopes for booming business and professional class opportunities. Robert S. Abbott typified the enthusiastic middle-class leader of this period. Born into poverty in the rural South, Abbott, who had worked nights to put himself through college and law school, came to expect other poor blacks to find success as he had—through propriety, perseverance and a move to the freer climate of the North.[1]

When World War I halted the inflow of European laborers and took thousands of white workers off the job to "save the world for democracy," Abbott was among the first to see an opportunity for Negroes to escape the horrors of the South. His Chicago *Defender* became the major promoter of the "great migration" of hundreds of thousands of blacks to Northern urban centers. He pioneered a "national edition" to reach Southern readers, and other papers later followed suit. Abbott told Southern blacks of opportunities for jobs and schooling, of freedom from lynching and legal segregation. The *Defender* carried weekly stories of lynchings, beatings and sexual exploitation in Dixie, accompanied by shocking photographs—stories which often required bravery and creative sleuthing from *Defender* reporters.

For those who came North, the *Defender* urged sobriety and hard work—the white, middle-class virtues. Thus a *Defender* cartoon strip in 1920 chronicled the life of George Smith, who pushed a broom all day and studied accounting at night. Each week he deposited part of his earnings in the bank. His strong will power enabled him to overlook life's frivolities and walk briskly past the sleazy dance hall. When opportunity finally knocked, George and a friend who also had "business qualities" began a small mail order enterprise. Only "after careful consideration" did he give up his porter's job for the new venture. George, now wearing a suit and white collar, worked diligently, eventually hiring a stenographer. Years went by and growth continued until finally, with dozens of young Negro men and women in his employ, "Smith's desire to help elevate his race" was realized.[2]

Such thinking led the black establishment to urge ghetto residents to "buy black" and "support race business." Black businessmen made no attempt to enlist the political radicals in their efforts; little capital was available to them and the businessmen did not want to jeopardize their tenuous ties to white money sources. Yet the black businessmen, forced to deal with the most powerful of white racists—American capitalists—failed miserably. From one-half to two-thirds of the black-owned businesses listed in the 1920 census had disappeared by 1930. Of more than two hundred thousand manufacturing establishments in the United States in 1930, only fifteen hundred were black-owned—half of them making hair straighteners and skin whiteners. After a decade of hard work, America still had only 25,701 black-owned stores, with black retailers doing only two per cent of black retail business.[3]

Between 1900 and 1930, blacks started eighty-eight banks; only forty remained by 1930—and only two of these had resources of over $1 million, while five had reached $500,000 in resources.[4] Over and over, whites stole ideas for new businesses from black businessmen, then ran the black businessmen out of business or bought them out. Harry Pace, for example, noting Chinese success with marketing ethnic foods, decided soul music could be a financial gold mine. Using the profits of his small insurance company, and with much fanfare in the Negro weekly press, he launched the Black Swan recording company in 1920.[5] One year later, Paramount Records—whose vast marketing apparatus could sell more records more cheaply than could the struggling black entrepreneur—bought Black Swan's jazz line. (Pace took out his frustration not on the whites but on the UNIA, contributing much money and time to a 1922 "Garvey Must Go" campaign.)[6]

The programs and goals of the black bourgeoisie had first been formulated by the National Negro Business League, black Greek-letter societies, college alumni associations and professional organizations, largely in the South. Booker T. Washington, founder of the National Negro Business League, had been the leading figure in the black middle and upper classes from 1895 until his death in 1915. "A conservative man, shrewd, hard working and, some say, devious, Washington essayed a program of conciliation and racial submission. He refused to attack Jim Crow directly and urged Negroes to subordinate their political, civil and social strivings to economic advancement. By implication anyway, he accepted segregation and concentrated on a program of 'industrial education,' " wrote Lerone Bennett in his version of the usual appraisal of Washington.[7] After World War I, the important promoters of middle-class goals were to be found in the North. These new leaders began to support civil rights agitation as part of their program for race advancement. This began the merging of two previously opposed middle-class factions—civil rights activists, represented by the NAACP, and business-oriented blacks; it continued during the fifteen years between Washington's death and the coming of the Depression, the period of Garveyism's greatest growth. The press played a major role in establishing middle-class unity. Both black business groups and civil rights organizations were promoted vigorously in many leading weeklies.*

The trend toward joint membership in both the NNBL and NAACP had appeared even earlier; in 1915 Charles Henry Parrish was president of the Louisville branches of both organizations, and

*Such as Fred Moore's New York *Age,* George Harris's New York *News,* Carl Murphy's Baltimore *Afro-American,* Carl Vann's Pittsburgh *Courier,* Harry W. Smith's Cleveland *Gazette,* and Abbott's *Defender.*

Andrew F. Hilyer took a leading role in the Washington, D.C. branches of both groups.[8] During the war, the Reverend Hutchins C. Bishop, owner of three-quarters of a million dollars worth of real estate, became a director of the New York NAACP. In 1918 Dr. DuBois and Robert R. Moton, the successor to Booker T. Washington as head of both Tuskegee Institute and the NNBL, were joint vice presidents of the Circle for Negro War Relief, an organization formed to fight for equal rights for black Americans in the armed forces.[9] In the first years of the Depression, DuBois eagerly supported Albon Holsey's Colored Merchants Association, the movement organized by the National Negro Business League.[10]

Thus by 1920 a revitalized black establishment had emerged, led by Northern optimists who wanted to forget old feuds and proceed with the modernization which would bring business and professional growth in urban centers. But the cooperative spirit did not extend to those supporting independent black power: both businessmen and professionals, with their need for white money, and civil rights groups, with their need for white political support, saw black nationalist proposals as a threat to racial harmony.

Leaders of the black establishment mirrored the optimism of the white middle class; similarly, civil rights fighters followed their white counterparts by falling in with the bourgeoisie. Many white reformers and liberal and left-wing leaders were trying to become more "respectable" in the age of Prohibition and Republicanism, isolationism and the revived Ku Klux Klan. Trade union membership declined during the 1920s from three million to two million. White leftist groups suffered a similar decline, and blacks connected with them shared the loss. The alienation from mainstream America promoted by Garvey may have saved his movement for a time and helped it reach a prominent position in black society. Thus the less conventional alternatives to Garveyism—the Pan-African Congress movement, Randolph's trade unionists, the African Blood Brotherhood, and the Abyssinians (who tried to start a war of liberation in the summer of 1920)—must all be considered in this context of declining radicalism.

* * *

The Pan-African Congress movement was conceived by the eclectic Dr. W. E. B. DuBois. When he sailed for France in the spring of 1919 to convene his first congress in Paris, DuBois hoped that the delegates would approve some declarations of policy for the world's ignored black people which could be sent to the new League of Nations. The congress, he noted, planned "nothing spectacular" or "revolutionary": "If in decades or a century they resulted in such world organization of black men as would oppose a united front to European aggression, that certainly would not have been beyond my dream." [11] Nonetheless, the U.S. State Department refused passports to blacks bound for Europe, probably to thwart investigation of ugly reports that black American soldiers had been badly mistreated there. DuBois had promised to check these reports, as had William Monroe Trotter—who, after first being refused a travel permit, finally shipped out disguised as a ship's cook, and missed the Pan-African Congress.

Once in Paris, DuBois met further difficulty: hotel after hotel refused to rent him a meeting place; finally one agreed, then forced him out at the last minute. George Padmore described the preparations for the congress as "a race against time, for at any moment the U.S. officials in Paris might have protested to the French Government . . . and have the Congress banned." [12]

To obtain a quorum of delegates, DuBois cornered unaware black soldiers on leave, black students from Africa and the United States, and black functionaries in the French colonial system. The congress proved an impressive assembly. Its fifty-seven delegates represented the United States, the West Indies and various parts of Africa. They proposed a set of amendments to the League of Nations Charter calling for civil rights guarantees, abolition of servitude, native African participation in colonial governments, and setting aside Germany's African possessions as a League of Nations trust. The League incorporated much of this final demand in its mandate system, giving the Pan-Africanists a significant victory. Mandate colonies were to be run under the League, so that indigenous African peoples could eventually attain their independence. When the first congress adjourned, a loose organization was formed to promote its ideas.* Its membership communicated through correspondence; the organization lacked an official journal until World War II, when the Pan-

---

* Notable members included Professor W. H. Jernigan of Howard University, Charlotta Bass of California, "negritude" theorist Blaise Daigne of Senegal, M. Camdare, delegate to the French parliament from the island of Guadeloupe, and J. Bellegarde, finance minister of Haiti.

African movement received fresh blood from a new generation (and from the cooperation of many older Garveyites). Congresses were held in 1921, 1922 and 1929 (with some small conferences in the years between) and never included more than a hundred delegates until the fifth congress, in 1945.

How did DuBois's Pan-Africanism compare with Garvey's concepts? First, Garvey, with more idealism than reason, demanded an immediate end to colonial rule, and explicitly asked the League of Nations to turn over Germany's African territories to the UNIA. DuBois, with a more pragmatic appraisal, was content to demand improved conditions for Africans under continued European control, and to work for a future of self-rule under a federated association of African states. Second, DuBois saw his congresses as general sessions for the exchange of ideas: "What I wanted to do," he said of his first congress, "was to sit down hand in hand with colored groups and across the council table learn of each other, our condition, our aspirations, our chance for concerted thought and action. Out of this there might come not race war and opposition but broader cooperation with the white rulers of the world, and a chance for peaceful and accelerated development of black folk." [13] In contrast, UNIA conventions discussed "legislation for the future independent African nation" and sought to obtain a national foothold for use as a base in the struggle for self-determination. However, Garvey was no more eager than DuBois to engage in violent revolution.

Third, the membership of the Pan-African Congress movement was, in its early years, almost entirely middle class, whereas the UNIA membership was primarily working class. The composition of the 1945 Pan-African Congress would be far more representative, including among its delegates numerous trade unionists and other spokesmen of the laboring masses. In earlier congresses, particularly the second and third, DuBois relied heavily on blacks who were acceptable to colonial rulers; in contrast, a number of UNIA officials in the Third World lost their jobs and were exiled and even imprisoned for their allegiance to Garveyism.

In its formative years, the DuBois Pan-African movement lacked programs for reaching the African masses. The Garveyites, their organization suppressed throughout much of Africa, also failed to reach the masses in an effective way aside from religious reform movements and a few trade union struggles. However, Garvey's nationalist rhetoric and organizational tactics, displayed more successfully in the Caribbean and in the United States, were borrowed by many of the Africans who led the independence struggles of the post–World War II era. Most of these African leaders were no less inspired by the vision of a united free Africa, as promulgated in the Pan-African vision of DuBois.[14]

During the 1920s the Pan-African Congress movement, though lacking the numerical strength of the UNIA, was vital in broadening the outlook of many black Americans who had been reluctant to identify with their brothers overseas. Some NAACP leaders opposed DuBois's congresses: James Weldon Johnson, NAACP national secretary, criticized efforts to engage black Americans in the affairs of Africa,[15] and objections to "diversionary activities" continued to come from leading blacks throughout the 1920s. *Negro World* columnist Samuel Haynes defended the Pan-Africanists after a derogatory attack by satirist George S. Schuyler. Haynes applauded the "internationalism of the Pan-African idea" and identified it as ideologically in league with the UNIA, the African National Congress and the West African Student Union.[16] The DuBois Pan-Africanists did not acknowledge ideological connections with the Garveyites; the 1921 congress publicly condemned Marcus Garvey and his organization.[17]

The most important contrast between DuBois and Garvey was in their social positions. Their now famous feud pitted an introspective scholar trained at Fisk, Harvard and Berlin against a gregarious, virtually self-educated, mass leader. As a social analyst, DuBois made critical evaluations of all leading blacks; most could accept it in good spirit; Garvey could not. During the 1920s, in addition to fighting with Garvey, DuBois was on poor terms with black and white leftists—his allies in earlier and later years—perhaps because he was struggling to win support from business and professional people who had opposed him in Booker T. Washington's era.

However, the verbal brawl which developed between DuBois and Garvey was by no means inevitable. In 1915, the UNIA honored DuBois and acted as his host on a trip to Jamaica.* [18] When DuBois first began commenting on the Garvey movement in the *Crisis* it was

---

* DuBois had gone to Jamaica to vacation and to conduct historical research.

with thoughtful, constructive criticism. DuBois found "the main lines" of Garvey's plans "perfectly feasible." Garvey, said DuBois, was arguing that "American Negroes can, by accumulating and administering their own capital, organize industry, join the black centers of the South Atlantic by commercial enterprise, and in this way ultimately redeem Africa." To DuBois, this was "feasible . . . in a sense, practical." [19] But Garvey would not accept qualified endorsements, and once the battle had begun both men lost all decorum. Discussing the UNIA leader in one *Crisis* editorial, DuBois described Garvey as a "little, fat, black man; ugly, but with intelligent eyes and a big head." Another opined, "Marcus Garvey is, without doubt, the most dangerous enemy of the Negro race in America and the world . . . either a lunatic or a traitor." [20] DuBois objected to Garvey's interpretation of the racial situation in the United States, the "unreality" of the Back-to-Africa idea, UNIA business methods, the pomp and pageantry of UNIA conventions, Garvey's dogmatic animosity toward the American labor movement, and the Jamaican's apparent dislike for light-skinned Negroes—a group which included Dr. DuBois.

DuBois was no stranger to conflict: throughout some seventy years of political involvement he was consistently at odds with the dominant mood of the day—and rarely without good reason. DuBois was virtually alone among black Americans when he joined the Socialist Party in 1903, but he pointed to a future growth of militancy along socialist lines. In forming the Niagara Movement with Monroe Trotter in 1905, to fight for civil rights, he presented a critical alternative to Booker T. Washington's policy of avoiding political struggle. In 1912 DuBois again ran against the tide of black opinion by endorsing Woodrow Wilson. He asked readers of *Crisis* to recognize that the Democrats' new urban liberal wing might transform the party of the dixiecrats into a force for change which could benefit black people [21] —a speculation which proved a decade or more premature. During the 1920s he called for a black and white liberal coalition. During the Depression, when this coalition was actually being forged, DuBois turned to black nationalism and formulated theories and practical programs which would have been extremely valuable to Garveyism in the 1920s. In *Crisis* and in his philosophical treatise *Dusk of Dawn,* published in 1940, DuBois suggested separate black trade unions (as "watchdogs" over white unions) and separate black communities; he argued that black colleges should be financed without white money, and that the race must unify its political and financial resources under one economic collective. He bitterly denounced the emptiness of New Deal integration programs, particularly in one book which was paid for and set in galleys but never issued because the publishers feared it would inflame the prevailing liberal coalition of blacks and whites.[22] Thus DuBois, once champion of the NAACP as an alternative to Garveyism, found himself in 1933 denounced as a segregationist by the NAACP. Finally, though he later joined the Communist Party, the DuBois of the 1930s described American communists as "men of pitiable mental equipment." They in turn labeled DuBois "an arch race mis-leader."[23]

DuBois's many scholarly works and criticisms deserved serious consideration, but he was not the leader of a movement. As Robert Poston, UNIA assistant president general, said of the fight between Garvey and DuBois, "To the credit of Dr. DuBois [he was] not responsible for his position. As a literary man, as a lover and maker of books, he is great. I often look upon it as a tragedy and a crime that this man should be trotted from the holy sanctum of books out into the wild rush of the mob, to assume any leadership. Dr. DuBois is not rugged enough for the task. His very soul rebels against the thought. I firmly believe he has accepted leadership because some few misguided people have thrust it upon him and will not take it off him. . . . But this has been done, and the genial Doctor sometimes feels called upon to justify himself before that public which expects it of him, by attacking Marcus Garvey, when to do this is to rebel against his own conscience."[24]

Even at the height of his opposition to Garvey, DuBois criticized Garvey's opponents, explaining daily events in a manner favorable to the nationalism of the UNIA. Thus, while he argued for trade union integration and greater black support for unions, DuBois was no less eager than the Garveyites to expose the racism of white labor. For example, in Alain Locke's anthology *The New Negro,* DuBois describes a trade union struggle in South Africa. At the time, white trade unionists had staged a series of violent strikes against the mine owners. For what end? For the right to exclude native South Africans from all skilled jobs in the mining industry. The Bantu were forced to appeal to the Imperial English government for assistance from their immediate oppressor, the white laborer. DuBois argued, from this and other examples, that simple class analysis alone could not explain oppression in the modern world. "The problem of the twentieth century is the problem of the color line, the relations of the lighter to the darker races of man in Asia, Africa, in America and the islands of the sea." DuBois claimed he was as convinced of the validity of this thesis in the mid-1920s as he had been when he first formulated it a quarter century before.[25] Whether borrowed from DuBois or not, the definition was an axiom of Garveyism.

Again, in *Darkwater,* published in 1920, DuBois offered substantial backing for the assumptions of black nationalism, which he skillfully juxtaposed with his emphasis on interracial cooperation. These essays included one on the labor struggle and race riot in East St. Louis, which showed that blacks could protect their jobs only by uniting against white trade unionists who had accused blacks of scabbing but refused them entry into the unions. This essay provides a convincing explanation of the conditions which led East St. Louis community leader LeRoy Bundy to move from his post in the integrationist NAACP to the UNIA.[26] *Darkwater* also includes an elaborate theoretical justification for building black economic cooperatives as an alternative to black capitalism. Cooperative principles were incorporated into the UNIA businesses.

DuBois did not see his many political twists and turns as inconsistent. He always attempted to analyze social and political issues from a black perspective, and this often put him at odds with traditional Western European thinking. As early as 1893, when he was a twenty-five–year–old graduate student, DuBois had written in his diary that he would soon move out into the world at large and "work for the rise of the Negro people, taking for granted that their best development means the best development of the world."[27] It was out of his conviction that "belief in humanity is a belief in colored men" that he formulated the basis of "Negro Socialism" in *Dusk of Dawn.*[28] Again and again, he showed that independent black power would best assure the liberation of his people.* Ideo-

* Especially in *Darkwater, Dusk of Dawn, The Ordeal of Mansart* (the first part of DuBois's trilogy *The Black Flame* [Mainstream; New York, 1957]) and in his essay in *The New Negro.* Significantly, DuBois's theoretical writings provide an ideological framework for the leading contemporary black power philosopher, Harold Cruse.

Ideologically, he differed from Garvey in believing that interracial cooperation could play a major role in this struggle.

DuBois's ties with the "man in the street" came primarily through the monthly magazine *Crisis,* which under his editing amassed a regular circulation of one hundred thousand copies. He pioneered the single-paragraph news story later used successfully by *Jet* and other black magazines. A number of Harlem Renaissance writers obtained their first public exposure in the pages of *Crisis.* Through his journal DuBois attempted to obtain support for the NAACP from the average citizen. However, membership in the Association remained essentially middle class. Aside from *Crisis,* DuBois was not in a position to reach the man in the street. His friends and contacts were in black academic and professional circles. He became a popular commencement speaker at black universities and colleges, but was not associated with the street-corner lectern.

Throughout this century the black scholar has been torn between the need to contribute in movements for mass action and the need to separate himself from the mainstream and concentrate on the development of the theoretical basis for action. DuBois's career reflects this dilemma. As a theorist and scholar he holds a place of immortality in the history of black liberation, but as a political figure in the 1920s he offered little in the way of a viable alternative to the mass movement of Marcus Garvey.

* * *

A. Philip Randolph was more directly a competitor of Garvey than was DuBois. The trade union movement and the UNIA both claimed to be militant, mass-based alternatives to the status quo.*

Randolph was a moderate throughout most of his career. Though he fought to increase the power and self-sufficiency of black laborers, he opposed most of the basic ideas behind independent black power. As late as 1966, Randolph described black power as "an unfortunate combination of words. It has overtones of black

---

* Randolph, who helped organize the Brotherhood of Sleeping Car Porters in 1925, was the most widely known black labor organizer during the Garvey era. Others of note were Ben Fletcher and R. T. Sims of the Industrial Workers of the World, Frank Crosswaith of the International Ladies' Garment Workers Union, Randolph's close associate Chandler Owen, and Lovett Fort-Whitman and James W. Ford, organizers for Communist Party–sponsored trade unions.

racism." For Randolph "this concept is linked up with Negro salvation through racial isolation." While the "idea of Negroes developing power is certainly sound," the question is, "How do you develop power?" [29] The evaluation was typical of Randolph's distrust of ideological "overtones." Yet, ironically, Randolph made these remarks as he was attempting to organize the National Negro Labor Congress, a black pressure group acting within the AFL-CIO. Twenty-five years earlier he had organized the all-black March on Washington, and by 1966 he had presided over the all-Negro Brotherhood of Sleeping Car Porters for over forty years.

Randolph's disagreement with contemporary black power recalls his dislike of Garveyism. As a devotee of the reasonable alternative, he consistently denounced programs emphasizing cultural, psychological or political unity at the expense of economic gains. His active support of the Socialist Party for more than half a century has been based on its essential concern with practical economic programs; he has zealously opposed Communists as extremist visionaries who mix economics with notions of revolution and nationalism. He was deeply influenced by sociologist Frank Lester Ward, who emphasized "scientific" programs and passionately rejected metaphysics and system-building in the social sciences. Randolph had joined the Socialist Party in 1911 when he was twenty-one, five years after his arrival in New York. By the time he began his career in the labor movement during World War I, he was far from his "roots" in rural Crescent City, Florida.[30]

In his personal life, Randolph did not conform to the conventional image of a trade unionist. He was an avid reader, deeply interested in theater, particularly Shakespeare. Randolph might have become an academic intellectual had he been able to afford such leisurely pursuits. But he had to work, and where he worked he organized: first among the waiters on a Hudson River excursion boat line, where he was soon fired; then among black elevator operators in New York. Within three weeks, six thousand of the more than ten thousand so employed had joined Randolph's union. He then called for a walkout but without a strike fund the attempt failed and Randolph was fired again. Undaunted, he found a job as hotel waiter—and began to organize the Headwaiters and Sidewaiters Society of Greater New York, this time joined by a young renegade from the black upper class, Chandler Owen. Together they brought out a few issues of a union magazine, the *Hotel Messenger,* and—after both were fired—they obtained enough money from Randolph's white friends to bring out the *Messenger* monthly.[31]

This memorable journal, which proudly proclaimed itself to be "the only radical Negro magazine in America," was, in its first years, a clarion call for total racial equality in a collectivist society. The historians Spero and Harris summarized the *Messenger*'s radical socialism: "They attributed race prejudice to capitalism. They held that in an individualistic economic system, competition for jobs and the profitable use of race prejudice to the capitalist class were incentives to race conflict; therefore, the removal of the motive for creating racial strife was conditioned upon the elimination of economic individualism and competition through social revolution."[32] It mattered not that Randolph had failed in three attempts to unionize blacks, nor that membership raids by established white AFL unions —which subsequently ignored blacks—hastened two of these failures, nor that white socialists never gave sufficient funds to these efforts. To Randolph, the need for socialism and trade unionism was an economic axiom.

The bitter results of his three organizing drives may have driven Randolph to adopt a revolutionary position for a time. In its first years, the *Messenger*'s revolutionary rhetoric had an intensity rarely equaled in American journalism. In issue after issue, Randolph and his associates played on themes of bitter anger and imminent cataclysmic change. For "Thanksgiving," the December 1919 *Messenger* had a prayer: "First, we are especially thankful for the Russian Revolution, the greatest achievement of the twentieth century. Second, we are thankful for the German Revolution, the Austrian Revolution, the Hungarian Revolution and the Bulgarian Revolution. Third, we are thankful for the world unrest which has manifest [sic] itself in the titanic strikes which are sweeping and have been sweeping Great Britain, France, Italy, the United States, Japan, and in fact every country in the world. Fourth, we are thankful for the solidarity of labor and the growth of industrial unionism." Thanks were also given for the Seattle General Strike, for the militant "New Crowd Negro" and the waning influence of the "Old Crowd Negro," and finally "for the new day dawning when we can celebrate a real thanksgiving in a world of labor, with peace and plenty for all."

The *Messenger* extolled the Socialist Party, the Industrial Workers of the World and the Russian Bolsheviks. "Soviet government proceed apace!" said one mid-1919 editorial. "It bids fair to sweep over the whole world. The sooner the better. . . . " The *Messenger* sought "an industrial commonwealth" which would "end slavery and oppression forever, and in its place would be a world of workers, by workers and for the workers . . . a world where the words 'master' and 'slave' shall be forgotten, and children of men shall live as brothers in a world-wide industrial democracy." [33] Blacks were urged to join the IWW as "the only labor organization in the United States which drew no race or color line," and because it dealt chiefly with unskilled workers, and "most Negroes are unskilled laborers." [34]

But Randolph's radicalism was short-lived. By the mid-1920s he had dropped his support of the militant IWW, denounced the Communists and announced open opposition to Marcus Garvey and black nationalism. What had happened? Garvey had the UNIA membership; DuBois had the NAACP, the Pan-African Congress and his ideas; but Randolph had no mass movement, and his ideas were borrowed from whites. Yet he did have connections. Randolph had emerged from the war as a statesman, mediating between militants and traditional black leaders. For instance, in January 1920 Randolph was the key speaker at a meeting of the American Negro Academy, an organization of black academicians and intellectuals. The Negro press noted the event with much fanfare, as if it were a momentous step for that august body to stoop to listen to a labor agitator. [35] Any radical approach would have cost Randolph many close friendships he formed with members of this group. He ran for New York State office on the Socialist ticket twice (for controller in 1920 and for secretary of state in 1921), and in appealing for votes, again cultivated the friendship of moderates. Late in 1920, Randolph endorsed James Weldon Johnson for the post of NAACP executive secretary, even though Johnson had consistently criticized "street radicals," the Pan-African Congress movement and militant causes in his weekly column in the New York *Age*. True, Johnson had earned respect for helping expose brutal American intervention in Haiti, but Randolph would never have endorsed an opponent of socialism a few years earlier—during the war the *Messenger* had regularly criticized the NAACP and even Dr. DuBois, whose brand of socialism was too bland for Randolph and company. [36]

With the collapse of the IWW only the segregated AFL remained, and organizing blacks for entry into the federation became a major task for Randolph. He formed an interracial organization, the Friends of Negro Freedom, to promote "unionization of the Negro migrant, the protection of Negro tenants . . . and the organizational forums for publicity educating the masses." [37] The Friends actively recruited blacks into "colored federal unions" (that is, separate black locals) with the encouragement of AFL leadership. These federal unions not only had less bargaining power and provided fewer jobs than white locals; they were also given less than half as many voting delegates as comparable white unions at AFL conventions. Such practices led more militant blacks to denounce the AFL in its entirety, and Randolph again had to seek support from moderates,* from civil rights leaders and, finally, from conservative blacks.

The *Messenger* mirrored these changing alliances, giving more and more space to general news and features and less and less to politics, ultimately arriving at the November 1923 "Negro Business Achievement Number," which included articles on "Marketing Problems of the Negro Farmer," "The Negro and Fire Insurance," and the "Future of Negro Business." The latter two articles were written by C. C. Spaulding and Robert R. Moton respectively, two of the most eminent reactionaries in twentieth century Afro-America. Randolph could still sound militant, but mostly in criticism: "Negro Communists are a menace," he wrote in 1923, who "with irrational and romantic zeal break down the morals and confuse the aims and ideals of the New Negro Liberation Movement. So utterly senseless, unsound, unscientific, dangerous and ridiculous are their policies and tactics that we are driven to conclude that they are either lunatics or agents provocateurs, stool pigeons of the United States Department of Justice. . . . Negro Communists seek to wreck all constructive, progressive, non-Communist programs." [38]

Randolph was no less harsh with Garveyites. In fact, Randolph held an especially deep animus for the Garveyite nationalists because their ideal of economic reorganization contradicted his call for black and white cooperation. The Friends of Negro Freedom expended much of its energy in attempts to discredit Marcus Garvey

* Including William Pickens, NAACP national field secretary, and Robert Bagnall, NAACP leader in Detroit.

and the UNIA, and during 1922 and 1923 the *Messenger* conducted a relentless and withering attack on Garvey—"the supreme Negro Jamaican Jackass," "clown and imperial buffoon," "monumental monkey" and "unquestioned fool and ignoramus."[39] The UNIA's vast following made it more difficult for Randolph to denounce Garvey in public; at one Harlem rally, Randolph was loudly booed when he denounced Garvey as a "little half-wit Lilliputian."[40]

Not all of Randolph's criticisms were so scurrilous. At one of many mass anti-Garvey meetings at Harlem's Shuffle Inn Music Hall, Randolph urged the audience to beware Garvey's alleged empire-building. "People now are fighting for the creation of democracies, not of empires. The Negroes don't want to be the victims of black despotism any more than white despotism. One gets no more consideration from black landlords than from white landlords." Randolph suggested Garvey use his fund-raising abilities to "set about freeing Haiti," or to raise "$5,000,000 so that Liberia wouldn't have to sell her freedom to the United States by accepting a loan of that amount."[41] (In 1921 the UNIA had indeed conducted a fund drive for Liberia, but little money was raised.)

Randolph's support for the Socialist party proved especially ill-conceived, not because collectivism would have hurt the black cause (on the contrary, various types of collectivism could have been most useful) but because, as the Socialists admitted proudly, they were "color blind." They were unable to see the special difficulties facing blacks, and offered them no more than equal rights in a white-led movement. This followed the dictum of the party's founder, Eugene V. Debs—"freedom for all, special favors for none." The monthly journal of the League for Industrial Democracy, an unofficial organ of the Socialist Party, contained only one reference to black people from 1925 through 1934: a cartoon accompanying an advertisement for a fund-raising dance in Harlem which showed three stereotyped, smiling black musicians.[42] Journals of the independent left, and of anarchist and communist groups, showed more interest in blacks.

The Socialist Party acknowledged that blacks occupied "a peculiar position in the working class and in society at large," but minimized the importance of racism: "All social and race prejudices spring from ancient economic causes which still endure. . . . The only line of division which exists in fact is that between producers and the owners of the world—between capitalism and labor."[43]

Black workers were officially "welcomed" as Socialist Party members, of course. Party leader Norman Thomas often spoke proudly of his long friendship with Randolph, and Eugene Debs himself, while in the Atlanta federal penitentiary during and after World War I, went on a hunger strike and in other ways protested the prison's discriminatory policies. (Just before his release in 1921, black inmates gave Debs a rousing going-away party.)[44] But personal friendship and declarations of class unity did not entice many black Americans into the Socialist fold.

Those who were attracted to the Socialist Party often exhibited a narrow-minded economism and an unwarranted confidence in the militancy of white workers. For example, W. A. Domingo, an early convert to socialism (though his outlook changed often over the years), urged white socialist leaders to increase their efforts to attract blacks in a 1918 private report. Domingo argued blacks should be recruited not so much because they needed the Socialist Party but because they threatened white labor as potential scabs and strike breakers so long as they remained outside the fold. Domingo categorized Afro-Americans as an incipient "lumpen proletariat," an ignorant "Black Guard," ready for use by capitalists to divide and wreck the labor movement. Domingo told his fellow socialists to present the wisdom of whites with tact: "intelligent Negroes" were to be induced to attend meetings so they could see "that Socialists are their friends," but recruiters were told not to sound all-knowing ("Give Negroes more prominence in the discussion; they like that") and to "avoid stressing problems of race and emphasize the advantages to all of the cooperative commonwealth."[45] The May-June 1919 *Messenger* included an article by "the editors," titled "The Negro—A Menace to Radicalism," which covered many of the arguments presented in Domingo's private report, but omitted the patronizing section on how to recruit black support.

Ironically, the Socialist Party's most significant contribution to blacks was a $10,000 grant to Randolph for organizing the Brotherhood of Sleeping Car Porters—a clear example of black, rather than integrated, power.[46] * BSCP members were instrumental in forming

* The money for starting the union—for three decades a black power base within the AFL—was made available through the Socialist-controlled Garland Fund to the Trade Union Committee for Organizing Negro Workers, a Socialist Party–sponsored attempt to aid the growth of the federal unions.

black labor conferences in 1929 and 1930 and in the March on Washington in 1941.

The Brotherhood was founded early in 1925 when a delegation of Pullman porters asked Randolph to assist them in creating a union. With the help of Randolph and organizer Frank Crosswaith, the BSCP was chartered in August of 1925.[47] But the Brotherhood was not admitted to the AFL until 1929, and then only with segregated "federal" status. However, the BSCP differed from other colored federal unions in that it was not a subsidiary of a larger white international.

The Pullman company refused to talk with the porters until the government compelled it to do so in 1935, and the first contract was not signed until August 25, 1937—twelve years to the day from the formative meeting of the Brotherhood. In the intervening years the union had overcome Pullman company efforts to form a company union and fire Brotherhood members, and attempts to foment racial antagonism by hiring large numbers of Filipino porters to replace blacks.

For blacks, the Brotherhood became a racial rather than a purely union movement. Its success would bring a measure of pride to all black laborers; its methods were considered models for future organization. Randolph, realizing this, did his best to win support from the black community. To attract the churchgoer and minister he used biblical passages in organizational appeals (most Brotherhood bulletins were headed, "Ye Shall Know the Truth, and the Truth Shall Set You Free"). Virtually every black leader expressed an opinion on the porters' struggle, and conservative Negro newspapers—some tied financially to the Pullman company—opposed the Brotherhood (often through paid advertisements from Pullman).[48]

Whatever his critics said, Randolph did not consider his efforts particularly radical. Writing on the porters' union in the Urban League's *Opportunity*, he commented, "This movement is not radical, except in the sense that the whole trade union movement is fundamentally radical. ... The porters also want a voice in the determination of the conditions under which they work, the abolition of the Pullman feudalistic paternalism, a relic of the old master and servant relationship. They want to maintain their manhood, their self-respect." For Randolph, the BSCP was a model of the struggle for racial uplift, through which black people had "reached the point in their development . . . where they will act deliberately, soberly, coolly and dispassionately to adopt a course of action which is calculated to protect and advance their social, economic and political interests." [49]

For all his concern with labor, Randolph's greatest following came from the activist wing of the black establishment. This group, differed from other businessmen and professionals in its impatience with the gradual progress of blacks: whereas the typical member of the black bourgeoisie avoided struggle and was reactionary, the minority activist wing showed a willingness to organize and to protest racial injustice openly. This elite corps (from which DuBois sought support for his Pan-African congresses) included intellectuals, artists, writers and editors for leading black weeklies, trade unionists, and functionaries of civil rights organizations. In general, these blacks were willing to form coalitions with liberal and left-wing whites. During the past half century, while this group has dominated black society, blacks as a group have fallen relatively farther behind whites economically, lost much of their land and the security that went with it, failed to gain a fair share of expanded governmental authority, and failed to neutralize white race hatred. What caused these failures?

Establishment activists talked of following the American pattern in which various blocs—representing labor, farming, business, or specific regions—have first organized internally and then turned to make demands upon the larger society. In actuality, these blacks sought to win freedom through a coalition with whites. Thus many refused to work with the UNIA during the 1920s when it represented a sturdy mass organization.

It is wrong to define this disagreement in terms of civil rights versus separatism, as did establishment activists from the Garvey era through the New Deal. They equated separatism with escapism and refused to acknowledge that the UNIA demanded every civil liberty and constitutional safeguard sought by the NAACP. A classic expression of the activist viewpoint is presented in *The Negro Americans: What Now?* by James Weldon Johnson, who served as NAACP national secretary for a decade. Johnson defined separatism as "the making of the race into a self-contained economic, social and cultural unit; in a word, in the building of an *imperium in imperio*"; the alternative to this lay "in the making of the race into a component part of the nation, with all the common rights and privileges, as well as duties, of citizenship." [50] Johnson's (and his colleagues') failure to see the black American struggle in an international setting may have led to their fetishism concerning American citizenship. Garveyites sought the rights of citizenship while holding loyalty to both the international black community and the American political system.

In addition to relying on white allies and ideals, establishment activists also developed a debilitating relationship with reactionary black businessmen and professionals—who offered even less of a power base than friendly whites. The few black bankers were at the mercy of the larger white banking establishment, and Negro businessmen usually relied on whites for supplies and capital. Black colleges were controlled by white philanthropy—a control which extended to curriculum and campus activities. Black civil servants worked for government offices run by whites, and the black press was indirectly censored by white advertisers. But—as Randolph discovered—connections with the white bourgeoisie offered status and prestige in black society. Although the activists and the reactionaries sometimes agreed (as in their rejection of Marcus Garvey), activists usually played the role of loyal opposition—criticizing the "Old Crowd Negro" for his fear of agitation and his failure to support the struggle for unions or civil rights. The old guard seemed more than willing to tolerate, even welcome, these critics. William Monroe Trotter, one-time arch-enemy of Booker T. Washington, solicited funds from black college presidents and had his political activities widely reported in the establishment black press, which was generally favorable to the NAACP. Harry Pace advertised his Black Swan record company heavily in the *Messenger* and in the left-wing *Crusader* magazine, and many black weeklies carried stories from the *Crusader*'s news service. In the late 1920s, labor leader Frank Crosswaith had a regular column in the Chicago *Defender,* a paper most antagonistic to Garvey.

This cooperation increased gradually during the 1920s. The *Messenger* showed conservative tendencies after 1921, when Randolph lost most of the votes he had won in 1920 (one out of four Harlem voters had chosen the Socialist Party in that year). His associate, Chandler Owen, lost confidence in socialism, and by the late twenties he was condemning all radicalism. *Messenger* columnist

George Schuyler, in 1919 a Socialist Party official in Syracuse, New York, began to offer biting satire of all camps (and eventually allied himself with white reactionaries).[51] The Socialist W. A. Domingo, one-time editor of the *Negro World,* maintained ties with the left, but became politically inactive while he developed a thriving import-export business.[52] Economist Abram Harris, an early writer for the *Messenger,* withdrew into the academic world; Floyd Calvin, another early *Messenger* writer, became a gossip columnist for the Pittsburgh *Courier.* Carl Murphy of the Baltimore *Afro-American,* and William N. Jones, who had worked in the Maryland Socialist Party during World War I, remained critical of the narrow-minded black bourgeoisie, but after 1922, when Murphy took over editorship from his father, the paper offered no particular praise for the Socialist Party or for Garvey. Murphy and Jones became simply left-liberals of the loyal opposition.*

The black left-liberals thought their respected position would make their arguments more attractive to the masses, and also thought their white allies had constructive programs for all dispossessed groups in America. Time would prove the latter supposition a poor one, as the alliance with whites only restricted blacks from developing their own power base and ideology. Though many individuals sought to think and act independently, most were trapped in the liberal mold by circumstance.

The story of Dean William Pickens provides an interesting example. Pickens, son of a South Carolina sharecropper, did not see the inside of a school until he was eleven. Ten years later, in 1904, he was a Yale graduate. As a man risen from the grass roots, he became the NAACP's most able recruiter and eventually its national field secretary. He was attracted to the Garvey movement in its early years, was befriended by Garvey, and contributed to the *Negro World.*[53] Then, in 1922, the NAACP launched an anti-Garvey crusade and Pickens-the-dean got the better of Pickens-the-share-

*Others of the same persuasion included NAACP national field secretary and former college dean William Pickens and NAACP official and novelist Walter White, who contributed to left-leaning white journals and black weeklies; poet Countee Cullen, who endorsed the Communist ticket in 1932; poet and novelist Claude McKay, who quit the *Negro World* and became an editor of the white *Liberator* monthly; Charlotta Bass, editor of the California *Eagle;* poet and educator Sterling Brown; singer Paul Robeson; Langston Hughes; James Weldon Johnson; DuBois; and Randolph.

cropper's son. As with many intellectuals tied to whites, the logic of Pickens's political position forced him to denounce black nationalism—though he was one of the last NAACP officials to join the anti-Garvey bandwagon.* He wrote to Garvey. "I believe in Africa for Africans, white and black, and I believe in America for Americans, native, naturalized and all colors, and I believe that any of these Americans would be foolish to give up their citizenship here for a 1,000-year improbability in Africa or anywhere else." [54] In Pickens's view, "The best thing is to see how best the whites and the blacks here can get along together." [55] Some intellectuals with relatively few white connections chose an integrationist approach because of their ties to the black middle class. Historian Carter G. Woodson wrote briefly for the *Negro World* just after World War I, but needed money from the black bourgeoisie to support his *Journal of Negro History* and his scholarly publications on black people. He, too, eventually joined the crusade against Garvey.

Some intellectuals defy such categorization. The historian, sociologist and anthropologist Joel A. Rogers maintained an enviable freedom. He earned his academic honors in France, where he was elected to a number of learned associations, and taught at the Sorbonne. Rogers was free from the usual restrictions of the black educator and scholar, whose creativity was so often stifled in the black bourgeois milieu; he published his books with his own money, thereby avoiding the enticements of publishers who might have pressured him to adopt a more conventional style. Thus Rogers was both a respected friend of the UNIA (he gave many lectures to gatherings of Garveyites) and also a contributor to Randolph's *Messenger*. His studies of racism were cherished by black liberals during the 1940s when he was a columnist for the Pittsburgh *Courier*, and his books are in great demand among black power advocates and cultural nationalists today. On that most difficult subject, racial identity, Rogers's writings have unmatched clarity, humor and impact. In some two thousand pages, he proved conclusively that biological race is a myth, that all peoples share most human customs, and that the black man has made unique contributions in all areas of achievement. Some scholars have been deeply concerned with proving race a myth, others with demonstrating the uniqueness of blacks; Rogers does both with uncanny ease.

* In the New Deal he became a high-ranking government official.

Hubert Harrison, the "street-corner professor," was also free to work with all factions, and was part of the significant minority of the black intelligentsia which maintained strong ties with the Garvey movement. The short-story writer Eric Walrond and the author and educator William Ferris worked with the UNIA intermittently for twenty years. J. R. L. Diggs, president of Morgan State College in Baltimore, served as UNIA chaplain general from 1922 until his death in 1924, and the journalist and bibliophile John "Grit" Bruce was a regular *Negro World* columnist until his death the same year. All four had interests outside the UNIA which brought them recognition in *Who's Who in Colored America* and similar publications. The UNIA religious leader Bishop McGuire was certainly one of the important religious reformers of recent times, although he was unrecognized in establishment circles; *Negro World* columnists Samuel Haynes and Ernest E. Mair made significant—and similarly unacknowledged—contributions to the ideology of black nationalism. Marcus and Amy Jacques Garvey certainly qualify as intellectuals, even though they would rarely be considered part of the black intelligentsia. Until most recently black people have not been recognized as intellectuals unless they accepted white social theory; thus historians have been able to imply that no intelligent black man seriously espoused the concepts of black nationalism.

* * *

One small group, the African Blood Brotherhood, provided an early version of the revolutionary self-defense program favored by many militants today. The Brotherhood was the first left-wing black nationalist organization and one of the first organizations to consider seriously a separate black republic in the Southern United States.* Information on the Brotherhood is hard to come by, since so much of its activity was covert. However, the Brotherhood did admit its role in the Tulsa riot of 1921.

This last of the many white mob invasions of black communities which followed World War I began routinely enough—a black was arrested for allegedly bothering a white woman in an elevator. The

* At least three former leaders of the Brotherhood were active behind the scenes in black power movements of the 1960s—Cyril Briggs, Harry Haywood and Richard B. Moore. Otto Huizwood was active in the independence movement in Surinam and W. A. Domingo played an important role in forming the People's National Party, which led the fight for Jamaican independence.

arrest occurred in a tense climate: the local ABB had announced a few weeks earlier that it would stop any attempt at lynching in Tulsa—with physical force, if necessary. The threat was not an idle one; the ABB's monthly, the *Crusader,* often discussed "the necessity of the use of force to get our rights," [56] and ABB branches held weekly "Calisthenics Club" sessions. The Brotherhood, the *Crusader* reported, "worked hard and fast to protect Negroes at Tulsa when first it saw the war-clouds gathering over that Oklahoma city." [57] Shortly after the arrest of the man in the elevator, a contingent of armed blacks formed in front of the jail, where they met a gang of whites apparently bent on a lynching. One white man tried to take a black's gun from him. In the ensuing scuffle the white was shot, and the riot was on.

The blacks "made an orderly retreat," established defensive positions at the railroad tracks which separated the races in Tulsa, and repulsed repeated white charges. The governor of Oklahoma then called out the National Guard, purportedly to stop the riot. Guardsmen entered the black neighborhood during a truce, disarmed its residents, then withdrew so the white mobs could return.[58] A private plane was hired to drop dynamite bombs on the black neighborhood. Robert Abbott of the *Defender,* ever eager for good Dixie atrocity photographs, outdid himself on the Tulsa riot. His newspaper carried two large photos showing entire neighborhoods leveled by the aerial bombings and ground fire.[59] There was some consolation in this riot: the black defense action was to bear fruit for other black communities; white mobs never again attempted to invade a major black neighborhood (except in Detroit during World War II).

Government officials accused the African Blood Brotherhood of playing a leading role in the defense of the black neighborhoods. The ABB later admitted this, and went on to use the action to attract members. One fund-raising advertisement in the November 1921 *Crusader* stated, "As We Have Done by You—Do You by Us! Remember *Tulsa!* Remember the Bright, Untarnished Record of the ABB! What Other Organization Can Match that Brave Record?"

Tulsa was one of the many ABB branches spotted haphazardly across the United States. The largest membership was in the New York home office, but there were sizable contingents in Chicago, Baltimore, Omaha and West Virginia. Most recruiting was done through the *Crusader.* The head of the West Virginia ABB, a Mr. White, had been attracted to the ABB when he was shown a copy by a soldier who had returned from Europe via New York: White was sufficiently enthused to walk all the way to New York to arrange to become a Brotherhood official. The ABB also established groups in the Caribbean area; in Trinidad, Surinam, British Guiana, Santo Domingo and the Windward Islands.[60] At its height, the ABB had only three to five thousand members, most of them ex-servicemen, though a sizable contingent of immigrant West Indians also joined. The number was kept small, in part by design, but the possibilities of danger, and the Brotherhood's militantly nationalistic and left-wing ideology, undoubtedly alienated and confused many people.

The ABB saw itself as a tight-knit, semi-clandestine, paramilitary group which hoped to act for a "worldwide federation" of black organizations. The Brotherhood's official program stated, in part: "In order to build a strong and effective movement on the platform of liberation for the Negro people, protection of their rights to Life, Liberty and the Pursuit of Happiness, etc., all Negro organizations should get together on a Federation basis, thus creating a united centralized movement. . . ." In the United States, according to the ABB program, such a movement could exist openly in the North, but would have to work secretly in the South to forestall premature attack. Within this federation, a secret protective organization was planned which would admit only the best and most courageous of the race. This inner organization was to function under strict military discipline, ready to act at a moment's notice "whenever defense and protection are necessary." In colonized Africa, ABB agents were to rally "Africans in the hinterland" to a "great Pan-African army" which would eventually descend upon the colonial plantations of the coastal areas. In the United States, the Brotherhood would have black people consolidate all business ventures into large cooperatives; the proposed federation would, like "every big organization, develop certain property in the shape of buildings . . . farms, etc." But these would be the "cooperative property of all members of the organization, and administered by members elected for the purpose. Under no circumstances should such property be operated under corporation titles written over to a few individuals."

While it acknowledged that building a powerful federation would take time, the ABB program noted: "Until the Negro controls the rich natural resources of some country of his own he cannot hope to compete in industry with the great financial magnates of the capitalist nations on a scale large enough to supply jobs for any number of Negro workers." In the interim, "The only effective way to secure better conditions and steady employment in America is to organize the Negroes' labor power . . . into labor organizations." The program had an optimistic tone: "The home governments of the plantation capitalists are weakening day by day and are trembling under the menace of the Proletarian Revolution. The oppressed colonies and small nations are in constant rebellion, as witness the Irish, Turks, Persians, Indians, Arabs, Egyptians, etc." [61] For the rank-and-file member, the Brotherhood's recruitment advertising offered "protective, economic, educational, physical, social benefits" with "Sick and Death Benefit Department, Cooperative Business Industrial Units," as well as "Calisthenics Clubs." [62]

The Brotherhood program, and the creation of the organization itself in the spring of 1919, were the work of Cyril V. Briggs, a native of St. Kitts who became an important member of the Communist Party in the late 1920s. Unlike other black leftists, who held strong ties with whites, he entered political struggle as an ardent proponent of a race-first philosophy. In 1912 the twenty-three-year-old immigrant Briggs became a reporter for the New York *Amsterdam News,* and in two years he became editor of the paper.[63] In 1915 he began a cultural and business monthly, the *Colored American Review,* which displayed a strident race consciousness but gave no hint of his future left-wing attitude. The *Review*'s first issue chided blacks for not "patronizing our own enterprise"; the lead article in the second issue urged Harlem residents to use the economic boycott. Briggs admitted there were too many white-owned businesses to make a total boycott feasible and called on Harlemites to "discriminate" against white shop-owners who would not hire blacks and against those who "think to hoodwink the race by employing in minor positions a solitary colored man, or at times even investing in what . . . is commonly known as a Figure head." [64] The article included a list of white establishments which hired blacks, and a long list of black-owned Harlem businesses.

When Briggs began to display his nationalist opinions in the *Amsterdam News,* the publisher demanded the right to censor his writings. Briggs refused, and on October 17, 1917, under the glaring front-page headline, "Security of Life for Poles and Serbs—Why Not for Colored Nations?" Briggs noted that President Wilson called for self-determination for oppressed white national minorities, but said nothing of colonies in Africa, Asia and Latin America. The editorial cost Briggs his job. Because of a hopeless speech impediment he could not turn to the street corner, so in November 1918—with help from Anthony Crawford, a black Wall Street ship broker—Briggs started a new monthly magazine, the *Crusader,* which soon became the official organ of the new African Blood Brotherhood.[65]

Briggs had a very light complexion, which, as his writings (including an autobiography left unfinished at his death in 1966) indicate, concerned him so deeply that he may have tried to compensate by becoming a "super-black." Certainly the *Crusader* was filled with strong statements on the virtues of blackness: "Taken as a whole the Negro people are better looking than the whites. Take the colored women, for instance; they are much more beautiful, judging them by every physical measure that might be applied. They are better formed, of better carriage, and fuller of life and female vanity. . . ."[66] Briggs's complexion led to his one and only public speaking engagement. At a street rally of Garveyites, Briggs was called "that white man passing as a black." Irate, he rushed from the audience and—forgetting his speech impediment—delivered an impassioned three-hour lecture.[67]

From the first the ABB drew blacks with socialist views who recognized the mass appeal of Garvey and his nationalist rhetoric. One of these was Richard B. Moore, who worked with the Garveyite John Bruce as the American agent for Duse Mohammed's *African Times and Orient Review.* Brotherhood members who worked within the UNIA included J. Ralph Casimir, the West Indian poet and UNIA organizer; W. A. Domingo, the editor of the *Negro World;* Edgar Gray, who became an official in the UNIA Black Star steamship company, the biggest of many Garveyite commercial ventures; and Ben Burrell, who wrote the libretto to the official Garveyite anthem. Hubert Harrison, the *Negro World*'s assistant editor, worked closely with the ABB, although he was never openly a member. Harrison and Briggs were friends for many years, with Harrison helping Briggs on the *Colored American Review,* and Briggs working with Harrison in the Afro-American Liberty League.[68] The Brotherhood actually attempted to use the UNIA as its "World Wide

Federation" for a time. In the April 1920 *Crusader,* Briggs defined his criticisms of the Garvey movement as "friendly and constructive" rather than "destructive and malicious," and suggested how the UNIA might best prepare for a forthcoming convention. ABB members contributed to the development of Garveyism as individuals and, indirectly, through the writings of Briggs and others in the *Crusader.* Briggs's "Race Catechism," cited earlier, was an important statement of black nationalist principles. It called for great sacrifice—of life itself "if need be"—not in the name of the working class, or of humanity, but "to attain for the race that greatness in arms, in commerce, in art, the three combined without which there is neither respect, honor nor security." [69] The 1918–1919 *Negro Yearbook* almanac reprinted the catechism for those unfamiliar with it. The ABB helped intensify the revolutionary militancy in the UNIA—which, in turn, helped the Brotherhood maintain a nationalist position, although Briggs denied Garvey's influence. As he moved closer to the organized white left, the Brotherhood leader jeopardized his place as a spokesman of black nationalism, but late in November 1919 he could still argue sympathetically for numerous nationalist ideas, including emigration: "Existing as we are, in a hell on earth, where mob murders, court injustice, inequality, and rank, widespread prejudice, are the rule, it should be a comparatively easy matter for the American Negro in particular . . . to pull up stakes from out of the hellish soil of American mobocracy." [70]

Briggs's forced resignation from the *Amsterdam News* coincided with the Bolshevik Revolution, from which he was soon to take ideological guidance. As he wrote later, he was not inspired by Garveyism, "nor was I interested in socialism per se. My sympathies were derived from the enlightened attitude of the Russian Bolsheviks toward national minorities. . . . I believed then and still believe that the Russian Communists had successfully solved the national question." [71] Briggs was not troubled by the USSR's failure to fulfill Lenin's plan for autonomous ethnic and national groupings; that self-determination was proposed at all was sufficient. Briggs wrote historian Theodore Draper, "I was never a member of the Socialist Party. I did not consider the Socialist Party interested in the Imperialist struggle or offering anything in particular for the Negro. I wasn't in the *Messenger* crowd. . . . My interest in communism was for the national liberation struggle, not economic struggle." [72] In a 1919 *Crusader,* Briggs defined his policy as "Negro first," but, "If to fight for one's rights is to be a Bolshevik, then we are Bolsheviks and let them make the most of it. And for further information of the asses who use the term so loosely, we will make the statement that we would not for a moment hesitate to ally ourselves with *any* group, if by such an alliance we could compass the liberation of our race and the redemption of our Fatherland. A man pressed to earth by another with murderous intent is not under any obligation to choose his weapons. He would be a fool if he did not use any or whatever weapon was within his reach. Self-preservation is the first law of human nature." [73]

Briggs believed that thorough revolution was necessary for genuine black liberation. He had no patience with Randolph and other moderate blacks who were proud of their reasonable goals and methods, and rancorously denounced one *Crusader* reader who agreed with Brotherhood goals but suggested, "Our cause is just and righteous and I am sure can be won in a nice quiet way." [74]

Briggs began with a rudimentary race consciousness and eventually concluded that all liberation struggles should be supported to aid the "self-preservation" of the black race. This shift in his thinking is delineated in two articles on the Mexican revolution, one in the *Colored American Review* of 1915, the second in a 1919 *Crusader.* In the former a particularly gruesome lynching in Georgia prompted Briggs to describe that state as "rivaling Mexico in her turbulence," and then he equated the struggling Mexicans with both the Georgians and the "Kultured barbarity of Germany." [75] Four years later, he was deriding the American intervention in Mexico to chase Pancho Villa. "What's this?" asked Briggs, "Americans trying to preserve law and order in Mexico? The mob rule in the United States [will make] law and order in Mexico? The barbarous and benighted U.S. [raids the land] of a people who, by all indications, seem quite able to live together without engaging in race wars, mob violence, and the fiendish torture of human beings, which are so freely and heartily indulged in on this side of the Rio Grande, and which more than any other thing in contemporary American history are the salient and identifying features of the much vaunted American civilization."

Briggs saw the invasion as an attempt to seize Mexican oil and mineral wealth by American "capitalists and their junkers" who could justify their action because Mexico was "peopled by a colored race" whose independence white America saw no reason to respect.[76] Marcus Garvey also endorsed many national liberation struggles, but he never advocated coalitions with these peoples, nor did Lenin's thinking influence his views on self-determination.

Since the Brotherhood was never designed as a mass organization, it could function according to its plan only by joining a larger body. The group attempted to work out such a contract with the UNIA, but when Briggs wrote Garvey in 1921 to ask for recognition and cooperation, his letter went unanswered.[77] By this time there were few ABB members left in the UNIA. Domingo had been dismissed from the *Negro World* for his "socialist and allied leanings";[78] an ABB member on the Black Star Line staff had lasted only a few months; and Hubert Harrison, the ABB's strongest link to the UNIA, was soon to leave the *Negro World*. In short, a split between the left and the black nationalists was coming into the open. Such differences were less sharp in the Caribbean: a Trinidad UNIA division president reported to the *Crusader* as late as November 1921 that the UNIA and the ABB were jointly struggling for survival in his country. He added, "While admiring Garvey and Briggs and their respective publications we must also remember others who are doing much for the race in some way or other. Negroes in Africa know of the Hon. Casely Hayford and others; those in America know of Ferris, Eason and others too numerous to mention; those in England know of Duse Mohammed Ali." For the Trinidad UNIA chief, Briggs still qualified for a *Who's Who* in black nationalism.

Briggs and the Brotherhood became *persona non grata* with Garveyites in the United States after a disturbing episode at the 1921 UNIA convention. Having received no response from his letter to Garvey, Briggs decided to bring the question of alliance with the ABB to the convention floor. Printed copies of the ABB program were passed out and, to distinguish his group from moderates on the left, Briggs arranged for the white communist anarchist Rose Pastor Stokes to speak. The fiery Mrs. Stokes extolled the Bolshevik Revolution's work for minorities and asked the convention to endorse the international communist movement. Brotherhood supporters in the audience put forth a motion to that effect, which was tabled after a lengthy and bitter debate.[79] The ABB question was raised again at a later session, this time by opponents who put through a resolution officially expelling the Brotherhood from the UNIA, with Garvey's blessing. Unofficial cooperation was now replaced by official separation. Garvey had sought to oust the Brotherhood because its members were dangerous "Bolsheviks," as he termed them. (Ironically, that same summer the DuBois Pan-African Congress called Marcus Garvey a "Bolshevist," the current cant term for extremist, often used with no reference to communism.) [80] In Briggs's account, Garvey "felt it necessary to prevent them from officially presenting for the consideration of the delegates the program formulated by the ABB ... because he saw that program gaining favor in the eyes of most of the delegates who had given careful consideration to the printed forms distributed by the ABB." * [81]

Though the ABB was unquestionably communistic, it had no organizational ties with international communism. It was founded at least half a year before the Workers Party, the Communist Party in the United States. A handful of key Brotherhood leaders did join the Communist Party by 1925, but few, if any, of the lesser leaders or rank-and-file members followed them. [82] "The African Blood Brotherhood was never affiliated with the Workers Party," Briggs wrote in 1961, adding: "Leading members of our executive or Supreme Council had joined the Workers Party but the ABB retained its organizational independence." [83] The Communist Party had only twenty-four black members in 1927, and half of them had joined between 1925 and 1927 without participating in the ABB. [84] In other words, less than a dozen of the ABB's nearly three thousand members in the United States joined the CP. Though white political groups can often control black groups through monetary contributions, the comparatively impoverished CP was in no position to buy off the ABB.

True, a few leaders with Communist Party ties might have dictated a policy in an organization as centralized and disciplined struc-

---

* Rose Pastor Stokes was the wife of J. C. Phelps Stokes, the socialist philanthropist whose foundation donated money to numerous black colleges and universities. She was far more radical than he, but nonetheless was the wife of a man who had helped found the anti-Garveyite NAACP. The Garveyite rejection of Mrs. Stokes was probably influenced as much by this connection as by UNIA opinion on communism.

turally as the ABB—but at least one ABB leader, Domingo, remained a Socialist. Further, the Communists not only had no Negro policy to dictate, but in the ABB's early years two rival Communist parties existed, along with the Industrial Workers of the World, which had won the support of many revolutionaries, including Briggs. Thus the "Communist" policy of the African Blood Brotherhood was its own doing.

The Garveyites broke with the ABB, then, because of the Brotherhood's extremism, not because of white Communist Party influence. Without such a coalition, the Brotherhood was doomed, although it survived until the late 1920s. Yet Garvey also lost, as the ABB would have provided a most useful wedge in the UNIA's fight with its black American opposition. With a militant left-wing organization, the UNIA could have exposed the conservatism of Randolph, DuBois and others. But the Brotherhood left Garvey no choice; it wanted revolution now. At the 1921 convention, Garvey talked of the day when Japan would lead Asia against Europe in a second world war, and blacks would refuse to side with the white man. Unimpressed, Briggs scored Garvey for failing to state simply that "in the event of war between the United States and Japan, the American Negroes should form a Japanese and anti-American society."[85]

Briggs often threw caution to the winds. Writing on the Ku Klux Klan in 1921 he declared, "It is war, and war of the cracker element of the white race against the entire Negro race. Whether the Negro race meets the issue courageously, demonstrating its essential humanity, or in cowardly surrender to the enemy, it will be war just the same—war against the Negro race. Whether other elements of the white race will eventually be drawn into the cracker onslaught against our rights and lives remains to be seen. History indicates its extreme likelihood. The only certainties are (1) that it is war, (2) that the white government of the United States will take no effective steps to protect us in our rights, (3) that the white North and our so-called white friends will continue apathetic to our wrongs or at best maintain a benevolent neutrality...."[86] Certainly not the words of a man who has sold out to white radicals. Perhaps history should honor Briggs for his nerve. Yet while there can be no compromise with truth, there can surely be tact when it comes to strategy.

The Brotherhood also faced internal difficulties. Domingo, for example, saw the ABB as a means of spewing hatred at Garvey, his former boss and boyhood friend. Otto Huizwood, the only Brotherhood leader who had first joined the Communist Party, held strong hopes of radicalizing white workers—in contrast to Briggs's skepticism. Huizwood helped shift the ABB from nationalism toward that part of its program which said: "The class-conscious white workers who have spoken out in favour of African liberation and have a willingness to back with action their expressed sentiments must be considered as actual allies. The non-class-conscious white workers, who have not yet realized that all workers regardless of race or color have a common interest, must be considered as . . . potential allies." [87]

The program also called for an alliance with Russia, not on the "merits or demerits of the Soviet form of government, but on the outstanding fact that Soviet Russia is opposing the imperialist robbers who have partitioned our Motherland and subjugated our kindred." The ambiguities and radicalism of the ABB prompted Garvey to comment: "Communism among Negroes in 1920–1921 was represented in New York by such Negroes as Cyril Briggs and W. A. Domingo, and my contact and experience of them and their methods are enough to keep me shy of that kind of communism for the balance of my natural life. A group of men of any ism or party who would seek to kill or illegally or improperly dispose of a political adversary . . . are no associates for those who seek the perfection of Government. . . . The American Negro is warned to keep away from communism, as it is taught in this country; he should work, watch and wait for his own opportunity, which is largely of his own doing." [88]

During 1922 and 1923, the ABB fought Garvey hard, while trying to build a new federation among black liberals and leftists. Its efforts culminated in a large meeting in New York, called the Sanhedrin,[89] which quickly degenerated into a shouting match between moderates and radicals. By 1924 Briggs was trying to make amends with Garvey: posing as a white man, he secretly purchased a ship for the UNIA through his ship-broker friend Anthony Crawford.[90] But Briggs lost any chance for a rapprochement later that same year when Brotherhood members who had infiltrated the UNIA convention were rebuffed in their demand for a declaration of war on the Ku Klux Klan. Briggs then turned completely to the CP, officially leaving the ABB in 1925, though he continued to handle some of its routine work. Harry Haywood, a compatriot of Briggs and a World War I veteran who found Garvey too reformist, said that leaders dropped out of the ABB because "it was wrong to think twelve million Negroes could obtain freedom on their own, when they were such a minority in the nation as a whole." [91]

The Brotherhood itself has now been dead for nearly half a century, but contemporary black revolutionaries have African, Asian and Latin American models, while Briggs and his followers had only the Soviet Union as a convincing example of successful social revolution. This obscured the valid, revolutionary aspects of Garveyism which the African Blood Brotherhood had helped to create.*

* * *

One early rival to the UNIA stands out beyond all others—the Star Order of Ethiopia and Ethiopian Missionaries to Abyssinia, commonly known as the Abyssinians. Centered in Chicago, with branches in Detroit, Washington, D.C., and New York,[92] the Abyssinians first came to the attention of the nation in the summer of 1920, when their leader, Grover Cleveland Redding, headed a procession through Chicago's South Side. Redding rode a white stallion which set off his multi-colored toga. The parade, designed to recruit new members, ended in the heart of the black community. After a brief ceremony, Redding produced an American flag, poured gasoline over it and set it afire. He and an associate each took a corner and walked up and down the street with the blazing Old Glory flapping in the wind. Perhaps somewhat carried away, Redding then produced a pistol and put a few bullet holes in the charred remains.

Two white policemen tried to restrain the Abyssinians, but left to seek reinforcements when threatened with revolvers. One black policeman who remained tried to remove a second flag before Redding could ignite it, only to be shot and wounded along with a white sailor who also tried to interfere. An Abyssinian then shouted to the onlookers, "Join us, brothers, we are forty million strong!"

---

* Years after Ben Burrell had joined (then left) the communist movement, Garveyites continued to sing his Universal Ethiopian Anthem (see appendix 1).

(Garvey's slogan). They took a number of high-powered rifles from inside a limousine which had accompanied the parade. More police arrived and further shooting broke out; in all, two were killed and half a dozen wounded, but the Abyssinians got away—for the moment.[93]

The Chicago incident was probably the most extreme expression of post–World War I black radicalism. The Abyssinians had been formed in the spring of 1919 and most of their members came from the Garvey movement. Where Garvey had asked for money for ships to return to Africa, Redding secretly sought funds for an "armed train" to ride into Dixie and herald the battle for freedom. [94] Redding proposed that black Americans immediately take out citizenship under the Ethiopian flag, which he thought was legal and binding under a 1904 Ethiopian-American trade agreement. His organization raised money by selling Abyssinian flags and certificates of citizenship. Though born in Georgia, Redding told his followers he was a native of Ethiopia. The Reddings were known as a family which had difficulties dealing with the realities of life (which meant getting along with the racists); some members of the clan spent time in the Milledgeville, Georgia, insane asylum. Grover had moved North some time before World War I, and his political activities began through friendship with the white J. D. Jonas family, which lived in the same apartment house. Redding, who was out of work, would drop in for a free meal now and then, and Mrs. Jonas suggested to her husband that Redding might aid in his community work. Dr. Jonas worked in black ghettoes, speaking at street corners and attempting to organize poor blacks around a variety of economic improvement schemes. For a while he ran a cooperative store in the Chicago black community and tried to sell shares to his customers. In 1917 he was active in collecting food and clothing for the relief of black victims of the East St. Louis race riot.* [95]

Jonas formed the Abyssinian order, but Redding became its leader. The black man was a far more effective street-corner organizer than the white, and the many ex-Garveyites drawn to the order

*In the opinion of Garveyite John Bruce, Jonas was "a confessed British spy, working among Negroes in this country to stir up trouble." In a *Negro World* editorial Bruce concluded, "We always suspected him of being a spy, and he was kicked out of one of our meetings in Liberty Hall for this reason." [96]

thought Jonas out of place in a black organization. Attempts to form branches outside of Chicago showed that other cities were far less interested in Redding's brand of militancy. In the hot-bed of Chicago he could sell the Abyssinian flags for one dollar each, but in Detroit they brought only eight to fifteen cents. [97] The actual size of the movement was secret, as was the planned "armed train"—a scheme which did not become known until Redding's murder trial.*

After the flag-burning and shooting, Redding and seven of his followers, including two women, barricaded themselves inside a hideaway. Informers led police to arrest them, though two men identified as ringleaders at the shootout were never apprehended. Redding and Oscar McGavick, the secretary of the order, were tried for murder. The disdain for American society which Redding had shown by burning the flag carried over into his trial. He pleaded guilty to murder and refused to sit politely during the proceedings, throwing books at prosecution witnesses and calling them names. Upon hearing the verdict he stood up and said, "I do not want a new trial, judge; if they are going to hang me, let them do it now, so the worry will be over." [99]

Redding received considerable amounts of money during his imprisonment, but he tore it into tiny shreds and cast it about his cell. When the governor of Illinois issued a two-month stay of execution for him and McGavick, there was wild rejoicing on death row. But Redding held fast until the end. The Chicago *Defender* reported that at his execution "he walked to his death with a firm tread." [100] His thirty-seven years of life may have ended in failure; nonetheless, for one summer day in 1920, he experienced a liberation from America. Many thought Redding was insane. If so, such insanity is hidden in the hearts of many a black American.

---

* A certain "Bill Briggs" was identified in a *Negro World* article as a member of the order, a William H. Briggs was a contributing editor to the *Crusader,* and one of the most active ABB branches was in Chicago, but if there was any connection between the Abyssinians and the African Blood Brotherhood, it was never made public.[98]

4

THE
ORIGINS
OF THE UNIA

IN THE FIVE YEARS from its founding in 1914 through the end of 1919, the UNIA became a dominant force among blacks in the United States and established outposts throughout the world. The next five years, 1920 through 1924, were critical: the success of the movement now hinged not on winning a wider following, but on achieving real economic and political victories. By 1925, opposition from blacks and whites had effectively blocked the Garveyites' political and economic program; the UNIA, however, remained the largest mass organization for blacks into the early 1930s, while a variety of splinter groups attempted to carry on what each considered the essence of Garveyism. By the time of Marcus Garvey's death in 1940 and the advent of World War II, the UNIA to all intents and purposes had ceased to function.

* * *

Marcus Garvey visited and worked in nearly a dozen countries on three continents before founding his association, and many of his followers had similar histories. Their broad experience helped dispel racial myths and prepared them to develop original ideas and programs. The typical UNIA leader had become disillusioned about the possibility of working through accepted channels: journalists who had been fired for telling the truth, ministers excommunicated for attempting to reform the church, politicians who had tried in vain to work through traditional processes all joined the movement. Garvey had at first espoused the liberal arguments for friendly interracial cooperation, and a surprising number of his comrades came to the movement after similar efforts (as many of today's black power spokesmen began by trying to achieve freedom through the moral suasion approach of integrationists). The black power element in the thinking of Garvey and most of his followers increased over the years, and when the movement reached its peak they were working out a new definition of humanism from this perspective.

Although Marcus Garvey was a man of unique talent, his background was in many ways similar to the backgrounds of many of his followers. An outline of Garvey's early life is therefore informative, not only because it helps explain an important historic figure, but also because it shows the experiences which influenced others to join him. Garvey was born, the youngest of eleven children, in the small coastal town of St. Ann's Bay on the island of Jamaica, August 17, 1887. He was said to be descended from the Maroons, who had governed a virtually independent black nation in the mountains of Jamaica from 1664 to 1795, and who remain a distinct group to this day. Their glory lives in the minds and hearts of black Jamaicans and Garvey carried their spirit beyond his island to the entire world of colored peoples. Perhaps because of his Maroon heritage, he was always proud of his full-blooded blackness.[1]

During Garvey's youth, around the turn of the century, many large sugar plantations were being shifted to banana cultivation, which required relatively few workers. Thousands of jobless Jamaicans became contract laborers on new plantations in the coastal areas of Central America: some forty thousand migrated to Cuba alone, and thousands more emigrated to the United States.[2]

St. Ann's Bay felt the squeeze. Garvey abandoned his formal education at fourteen and took a job in the printing trade with a relative in Kingston. His family could only afford to send him through the few years of education provided in the Jamaican public schools, but the headmaster, impressed with Garvey's grasp of world events and his artistic abilities, had been tutoring him without charge. The young Garvey's artistic and social interests echoed those of his father, a skilled stonemason whose sizable private library and broad general knowledge won him community respect.*

In Kingston, young Garvey learned the printing trade and

---

* According to his widow, Garvey's personality is best reflected in a picture of the young Marcus hiking into the lonely mountains of Jamaica to sit for hours looking out to sea, meditating on visions of greatness for his people. Others close to Garvey describe him as alternating between delivering extemporaneous speeches and being lost in deep contemplation.

watched through six troubled years as the city swelled with unemployed refugees from the farms. At twenty, he had become a master printer and the youngest foreman printer in Kingston. Two years later, in 1909, he sided with his workers in a strike and was elected their leader. The employers carried on with imported scab labor and eventually broke the strike by importing linotype machines. Worse, the union treasurer had run off with the funds—an experience which may have left Garvey skeptical of the value of trade unionism. The next year he traveled to Costa Rica to work as timekeeper on a United Fruit Company banana plantation. Most of the workers were immigrant Jamaican blacks who were paid less than the indigenous white Costa Ricans. This time Garvey avoided a labor union struggle, and instead complained to the British consul in Costa Rica that British subjects were being mistreated by local employers. The consul proved indifferent, leading Garvey to state that no white would ever "regard the life of a black man equal to that of a white man." [3]

Yet Garvey was only beginning to interpret the workers' oppression in terms of color. Between 1910 and 1911, Garvey traveled and worked in Panama, Nicaragua, Honduras, Colombia, Venezuela and Ecuador and observed injustice based on color in each country. These experiences influenced his later emphasis on an international solution to race problems.

* * *

Garvey went to London in 1912, where he became associated with the dark-skinned Egyptian nationalist Duse Mohammed Ali, editor and publisher of the monthly *African Times and Orient Review*. Historians have ignored Mohammed or made only a passing reference to his connection with Garvey, but Mohammed was instrumental in arousing the consciousness of blacks the world over and deserves to be examined in some detail.

Born in a country where rigid class distinctions prevailed, Mohammed was something of an anomaly: his father was of the generally fair-complexioned upper class and his mother from the lowly *fellah* peasantry. Mohammed inherited his mother's darker hue, which made him stand out among his father's well-to-do friends. His father sent him to England for schooling—to acquire the proper Western veneer and a distaste for the culture of his native land, the culture of the *fellah*. But he did not follow the usual pattern. England may have helped Mohammed develop his demeanor of "haute culture," but it was the culture of Egypt to which he looked, not that of the West. He failed to be impressed with so-called "superior" English ways, just as he had previously learned to stand aloof from the prejudices of upper-class Egyptians toward their lower-class countrymen. His return to Egypt in 1882 coincided with an uprising against England's unofficial colonial rule. The revolution was suppressed after a few months, but it led Mohammed to the view that modernization in the colonial world could proceed only on terms decided upon by the subject peoples themselves.

Mohammed expounded a new type of humanist philosophy in his *African Times and Orient Review*. On the one hand he called on Africans and other colonized peoples to fight for brotherhood independently of whites, and his magazine provided a worldwide forum for this view. On the other hand, the magazine was dedicated to the awakening of that "touch of nature which makes the whole world kin . . . that bond of universal brotherhood between White, Yellow, Brown and Black." Mohammed believed that white misunderstanding of "African and Oriental has produced non-appreciation, and non-appreciation has unleashed the hydra-headed monster of derision, contempt and repression." [4]

The monthly magazine was started in 1912 with funds Mohammed had received from the sale of his lengthy history of late nineteenth-century Egypt, *In the Land of the Pharaohs*. In this volume he presented a strong case for an independent Egypt with a representative government built upon Egyptian political and social traditions. Mohammed described himself as beyond the European mode of thought and stated: "I have no axe to grind, nor am I identified with any political party." [5] He argued that Western political thought was corrupted to its core with "colour prejudice"—Africans and Asians who adopted Western values were ignored, and Westerners refused to acknowledge the values of the African and Asian world. "I have patiently awaited the death of colour prejudice for many years, and I have a rather large spade in readiness wherewith to expedite its interment," [6] he wrote.

In the Land of the Pharaohs gives a glowing account of the thoroughly Egyptianized government which ruled Egypt for a few months after the 1882 uprising. Mohammed describes well-attended meetings of the ruling "council" which included instructors at the

Al Azhar University, "the Turkish Grand Cadi, the Grand Mufti, the Sheykh of El Islam, and the heads of the four orthodox sects. Also among the overwhelming number of representative Moslems in attendance were four princes of the reigning House who had publicly avowed their nationalistic principles; a goodly number of the provincial governors; and the chief country notables. Among the non-Mohammedan representatives of the population were the Coptic Patriarch and the Chief Rabbi." According to Mohammed, the council "comprised all sections of political opinion and class divergency." Though there were few representatives of the working class (the *fellah*), the council's very existence hinged on military support—*fellah* from officers to privates—commanded by Ahmed Pasha Arabi, a man of the "peasant class . . . [and] faithful follower of the Prophet." [7] Mohammed longed for the return of such a government to Egypt and for similar systems in other colonized areas.* To the British, who had overturned the 1882 government on the grounds that Egyptians were incapable of self-government, he replied that Europeans were incapable of evaluating such a government "unless the obscuring cobwebs of prejudice are swept aside . . . There is no system of political economy extant which is so perfect in construction that it may be universally applied to all communities of the human race." [8]

Mohammed's magazine applied his social and political views to every oppressed ethnic group, with articles on American Indians, Chinese, Arabs, Jewish culture, Zionism, and African culture and politics. Numerous anthropological studies described the customs and value systems of non-Western peoples: for example, a contribution entitled "West African Marriage Customs" told how the people of Sierra Leone have "more and better law and legal morality than have Europeans, it is simply different." [9] The journal's anthropological articles often mixed apparently contradictory cultural chauvinism and cultural relativism.

Though the magazine did much to build self-respect and unity among the darker peoples of the world, Mohammed himself was neither a social activist nor a radical in his economic views. He could praise the American socialist weekly *Appeal to Reason* because it

---

* The short-lived government of 1882 was the first headed by ethnic Egyptians in nearly three thousand years. Gamal Abdul Nasser's would be the second.

dared to "seek to destroy the profit system" and "because it stands for what the people believe is right,"[10] but he was never a socialist: his solution to the economic problems of oppressed ethnic groups called for building their own businesses. Almost every issue of his journal told of some new business venture started by a man of color in some part of the world. Nor was there anything particularly socialistic in Mohammed's denunciation of "the hand of the exploiter" in Trinidad, where Englishmen were trying to intimidate "colored people" and buy up their oil-rich property.[11]

Mohammed thought he could awaken his readers to the similarity of conditions facing all oppressed minorities simply by distributing his journal. Like a classic liberal, he thought injustice would be rectified simply by the spread of information. As he said in his history of Egypt, "It is because I believe the people of Great Britain to be, not only a freedom-loving race, but possessed of a genuine desire to see other nations as free as themselves, that I am emboldened to pen these pages."[12] But militant Africans, West Indians and Afro-Americans who read Mohammed's writings would interpret them as a call to action.

Marcus Garvey learned from Mohammed and, in turn, contributed to some early issues of the *African Times,* as did a broad range of black leaders and future UNIA officials. In one article, Garvey ventured "that there will soon be a turning point in the history of the West Indies, and that people who inhabit that portion of the Western Hemisphere will be the instruments of uniting a scattered Race, who before the close of many centuries will found an empire on which the sun shall shine as ceaseless as it shines on the Empire of the North today."[13]

A frequent contributor to Mohammed's journal was William Ferris, a college professor and later a leading UNIA official. Ferris foresaw an end to "the arrogance and presumption of the Anglo-Saxon, who was indebted to the Jews for his religion, to the Ethiopians, Egyptians and Greeks for his philosophy and theology, to the Romans for his law and colonial administration . . . and much from India in philosophy."[14]

Among the many who were moved by such statements was the young African George O. Marke. Marke had gone to Oxford from a missionary school in Sierra Leone and returned to his homeland to work in the civil service, eventually to be discharged for his militancy. After some unsuccessful attempts at a journalistic career in Freetown, he joined the "Duse Mohammed crowd," through which he came to know Garvey. By 1920 Marke was a ranking official in the UNIA.[15]

James B. Yearwood was another future UNIA leader influenced by Mohammed's magazine. An itinerant laborer and part-time school teacher from the British West Indies, he had helped dig the Panama Canal. Some years later, while working on a banana plantation, Yearwood argued with a white man who had made a racial slur upon him. The man (unknown to Yearwood) was the plantation owner; impressed with Yearwood's courage, he hired him to tutor his children. On the strength of his notoriety from the exchange with the owner, Yearwood became a leader among the workers in Panama; he built a protective association for British Commonwealth blacks in Central America, which later became part of Garvey's UNIA.[16] Similarly, Rudolph Smith read Mohammed's journal in his native Guiana. Smith became highly respected for his speeches on the need for brotherhood, first in Georgetown, and then, during the First World War, throughout Europe. He, too, became prominent in the Garvey movement.[17]

Among the many associates of "Mr. Duse," as he was called, were four men—Hubert H. Harrison, Arthur Schomburg, John "Grit" Bruce and Richard B. Moore—whose attempts to preserve works by and about black people have given us the incomparable Schomburg Collection of the New York Public Library. John Bruce, later one of the UNIA's first members in the United States, had been in earlier years a key link in a chain of correspondence among blacks interested in international affairs and cultural exchange. Letters in his correspondence between 1907 and 1917 reveal connections with many future Garveyites.* Both Bruce and Harrison would later write for Garvey's weekly newspaper, the *Negro World,* while Moore became a leader in the African Blood Brotherhood. The Gold Coast nationalist Casely Hayford, author of *Ethiopia Unbound,* was a close friend of Duse Mohammed and later of Marcus Garvey. A

---

* Including Hubert Harrison; Henrietta Vinton Davis; Rabbi J. Arnold Ford, a leader of Harlem's black Jews; Theodore Stephens, who would head the Haitian UNIA; James J. Dossen of the Liberian UNIA; and Garveyites Casely Hayford and Akinbama Agbebe of the Gold Coast.[18]

number of other prominent blacks were associated with Mohammed, through his journal, his business dealings or his extensive
correspondence.*

* * *

Garvey first read Booker T. Washington's autobiography, *Up
from Slavery,* while working for Mohammed in London. Though he
later rejected Washington's conservatism, he then believed the autobiography symbolized the aspirations of the race. Years later Garvey
could still acknowledge, "I read *Up from Slavery* . . . and then my
doom—if I may so call it—of being a race leader dawned upon me.
. . . I asked: 'Where is the black man's government? Where is his king
and his kingdom? Where is his president, his country, and his ambassador, his army, his navy, his men of big affairs?' I could not find
them, and then I declared, 'I will help make them.' " [20] When he
returned to Jamaica, Garvey gathered some of his friends and, on
August 1, 1914, established the organization which was to occupy
all his energy until he died: the Universal Negro Improvement and
Conservation Association and African Communities League—the
UNIA.†

The new organization issued a general manifesto of purposes, but
it had no definite program. Its tactics developed gradually through
trial and error. In the UNIA's first year or two, Garvey's activities
included speaking engagements, giving flowers to the orphans of
Kingston at Christmas time, welcoming DuBois to Jamaica, and
soliciting the support of the Jamaican Federation of Labor. [21]
Garvey hoped many whites would cooperate and urged blacks in
one early speech to "move together for the one common good, so
that those who have been our friends and protectors in the past
might see the good that there is in us"; he continued, "[the white
man] of Europe is longing to see the Negro do something for himself." [22] But by the end of World War I, Garvey had been disap-

---

* Including Gabriel Johnson, mayor of Monrovia, Liberia, and holder of one of
the highest offices in the UNIA; E. S. Beoku Betts, a Fellow of the British
Royal Anthropological Institute and president of the African Students Union
of Great Britain and Ireland; Harlem Renaissance personality and NAACP
official James Weldon Johnson; and the noted educator and compiler of the
Negro Yearbook, Monroe Work of Tuskegee University. [19]

† By 1917 the word "conservation" had been dropped from the title, and
"African Communities League" was rarely used.

pointed so often that he had little hope of dealing fruitfully with whites except from a position of black power. Garvey's stand on the war itself shows the shift in his thinking in these years: the UNIA first received international attention in October 1914 when the London *Times* carried a UNIA statement supporting England in the war effort.[23] A few years later Garvey was condemning the use of black men in the white man's war.

Garvey's opinion of light-skinned members of his own race also shifted: the "Universal Confraternity among the race" was to include any person of African descent. In one early speech he said, "I am pleading, yea, I am begging, all men and women within the reach of the Blood Afric to wake up to the responsibility of race pride and do something to help in promoting a higher state of appreciation within the race. Locally, we are suffering from a marked shade prejudice, among ourselves, which is foolish and destructible. The established truism reigns the world over . . . that all people with the African blood in their veins are Negroes. It is so disgusting to hear some foolish people talk sometimes about their superiority in shades of color."[24] But Garvey was rebuffed, first by the fair-skinned bourgeoisie of Jamaica, then by a similar group in the United States, and later he had many bitter words about the "treachery" of light-skinned Negroes.

Garvey came to the United States in 1916. He hoped to visit Booker T. Washington, but his specific mission was to talk to one of Washington's aides, the head of a recently established African-American trading firm which Garvey had learned of through Duse Mohammed. When he reached New York, Garvey found Washington had died, and his aide was unwilling to cooperate. Lest the trip fail altogether, Garvey decided to build a UNIA chapter in Harlem. At first he had no more success than one might expect of an unheralded twenty-eight-year-old immigrant from the West Indies. John Bruce has sketched Garvey as a new arrival in America: "I was among the first American Negroes on whom he called. He was a little, sawed-off hammered down black man, with determination written all over his face, and an engaging smile that caught you and compelled you to listen to his story. . . .Mr. Garvey is a rapid-fire speaker [and when he delivers a speech] two stenographers are necessary to keep up with him." Bruce sympathized with Garvey's plans, and gave him a list of "our leading men in New York and other cities who I felt would encourage and assist him."[25]

People like Bruce helped Garvey deliver the UNIA message to America—not that Garvey himself was idle: by the summer of 1917 he had lectured in Boston, Atlanta, Washington, Philadelphia, Chicago, Milwaukee, St. Louis, Detroit, Cincinnati, Indianapolis, Louisville, Nashville, and other cities. He had gathered eight hundred to one thousand followers in Harlem, a considerable number in view of the fact that the New Negro movement was just beginning and Garvey himself had yet to refine his program and his appeal to the masses.[26]

In its first two years in America, the UNIA faced two divisive splits of the sort which can ruin new organizations. The first fight involved Duse Mohammed, who, in a letter to one of Garvey's opponents, made serious charges against Garvey's character. The letter was read at a meeting of the New York Association and started a power struggle which resulted in the loss of all but fifty members.[27] Contributing to their fight in 1917 was the fact that Garvey had aligned himself with anti-war groups, while Mohammed chose to accommodate the British government. Pro-war hysteria in England reached even into the ranks of the far left and the anarchists, and citizens of the Third World living in England were pressured to encourage colonial peoples to support the allied effort. (Mohammed was rewarded for his loyalty in 1919 when the British Colonial Office appointed him to investigate charges of floggings and murder of Nigerians.) But in opposing black involvement in the war, Garvey had gone beyond Mohammed's cultural nationalism, and this was an important step in the development of the Garvey movement. In the long run, the split between Garvey and Mohammed was inconsequential for the growth of the UNIA. The two later reconciled, and Mohammed became a UNIA official.

The second split also involved a group with a narrow conception of the movement. Most of Garvey's early followers in New York came from among the thirty thousand immigrant West Indians residing there: thus some members thought the UNIA should function primarily as an immigrant aid society, like the protective associations begun by other immigrant groups. Samuel Duncan, president of the New York chapter, held this view, and used his control of the Association's funds to declare himself head of a separate UNIA which, for a time, held the allegiance of a sizable percentage of

Garvey's recently rebuilt following. (Duncan later renamed his organization the West Indian Protective Society of America.) While Garvey held a place open for Mohammed's possible return, there was little reason to hold a place for Duncan, whose actions included warning British authorities of the UNIA's "pernicious propaganda"; listing strikes and demonstrations in the Caribbean involving Garvey-ites; and saying the movement "is not only anti-white and anti-British but it is engaged in the most destructive and pernicious propaganda to create disturbances between white and colored people in the British possessions." [28]

Despite these disruptions, membership in the Garvey movement soared into the hundreds of thousands, with much of this growth a consequence of the race wars of 1919. In the spring of that year, Garvey followed his earlier nationwide tour with a whirlwind excursion through thirty-eight states, issuing calls for racial unity through one great organization—the Universal Negro Improvement Association. Events had clarified his ideas, sharpened his oratory and enhanced his appeal. The many hours he had spent in his youth studying the speeches and techniques of great orators of the past were now paying off. He told his listeners they should be "New Negroes," that a "Renaissance of the Negro race" was coming, when "Africa for the Africans" would be a reality and all black people of the earth would share proud citizenship in a free African nation. He had the appeal of a man with supreme confidence and an eagerness to share his inspiration with all who would listen. "Up, you mighty race," shouted Garvey; and the masses rose to respond.

One reason for the amazing success of this tour was unexpected: while in Pittsburgh, Garvey spoke of a plan for a fleet of black-owned steamships to carry Afro-Americans back to their homeland. The suggestion was well received and was repeated in other cities. Garvey saw the fleet principally as a way to coordinate black commercial enterprises throughout the world, but his listeners found the prospect of returning to Africa more attractive and the UNIA office in New York was flooded with ticket inquiries. When his tour ended Garvey moved hastily, and the Black Star Line was incorporated under the laws of the State of Delaware in May of 1919. Shares in the company sold at five dollars each (in an attempt to keep it a joint venture of the race, no individual could own more than two hundred shares).

As money for shares rolled in, so did applications for local UNIA charters and membership. Members paid a dollar initially and monthly dues of thirty-five cents, ten cents of which went to the international office in New York. New members seemed to think of the UNIA as something of a fraternal organization, and after many requests, Garvey installed a system of health and death benefits for members. (Many fraternal organizations were at first simply devices for obtaining insurance.) Within two months the UNIA had enough money to purchase a large auditorium at 114 West 128th Street (in Harlem) and rename it Liberty Hall—because, as members at the dedication services were told, this would henceforth be the black American's citadel of liberty, the recent bloody riot in Washington, D.C., having made the monuments to liberty in America's capital a mockery of freedom. The hall became a social center as well as a meeting place, and UNIA branches in other cities began raising money for their own Liberty Halls. Mrs. Amy Jacques Garvey described them: "Liberty Halls, wherever located, served the needs of the people: Sunday morning worship, afternoon Sunday Schools, Public Meetings at nights, and concerts and dances were held, especially on holidays and Saturday nights. Notice boards were put up where one could look for a room, a job, or a lost article. In localities where there were many members out of work there were 'Soup Kitchens' to give them a warm meal daily. Often there were portable screens for a corner of the Hall where men who could not be temporarily housed with fellow members could sleep on benches at nights. In the freezing winter days stoves had to be kept going to accommodate the cold and homeless, until they 'got on their feet' again." [29]

The UNIA was developing its own life-style, and sought to create its own social hierarchy, based on new measures of status and prestige. Members could hold rank in the African Legion, a paramilitary marching society, or work for the Royal African Motor Corps —fleets of moving vans in New York, Philadelphia and Pittsburgh, whose drivers could think of themselves as preparing to use their trucks in the struggle for African liberation. Large numbers of UNIA women joined the Black Cross Nurses. Few were trained nurses, but many were doing the work of nurses at servants' wages. In donning their Black Cross outfits, Garveyite women pointed the way to a much-needed uplift in status and pay for all engaged in housework and nursing. One little-publicized organ of the UNIA was its police force. There were also youth groups, choirs, bands, fire departments—in general, opportunities for all to find a sense of involvement.

In 1920 the organization created an international leadership comprising nearly two dozen titled offices, and in 1922 the Noble Order of the Knights of the Nile was created to honor leaders of the race both in and out of the movement. During 1919 the UNIA began to buy and rent property for what would become cooperative grocery stores, restaurants, laundries, garment factories, dress shops, a greeting card company, a millinery, a phonograph record company and a publishing house. Most of these businesses were made part of the Negro Factories Corporation, an economic cooperative whose directors were elected annually at UNIA conventions.

But the most important of all Garveyite business ventures was the Black Star steamship line. No mere service industry, this was one of the rare attempts by black Americans to deal with Wall Street on Wall Street's terms. In its first year the Black Star Line raised nearly three-quarters of a million dollars through stock sales. Holding a share in the Black Star Line gave the black American, at least vicariously, some connection with the world of international finance. On September 17, 1919, the company purchased its first ship, the *Yarmouth*. It was rather small (only 1,452 gross tons), and not new (built in 1887)—but the UNIA had difficulty purchasing any ship at all. Many brokers were reluctant to sell to blacks; others were willing, but charged exorbitant prices. One dealer said openly he knew Garvey had one dollar from every Negro in America and was therefore quite able to pay a steep price. The *Yarmouth,* obviously not the best buy on the market, cost a stiff $165,000 and set a pattern: during the next few years, repeated over-priced purchases would sap the company of funds needed to outfit ships, and the line eventually went bankrupt.

Moreover, Black Star was hounded by government agents from the start. Twice in 1919 New York's Assistant District Attorney Edwin P. Kilroe called Garvey into his office to warn that any promotion of stock through misleading circulars or improper procedures would bring a federal indictment for commercial fraud.[30] The line was indeed a risky business. It needed some good fortune in buying ships and in securing profitable cargoes, and at least five years of sustained high stock sales to meet payments on the high purchase prices. In large part, public confidence in the line depended on the success of the UNIA's emigration plans. Most stock purchasers were interested in the "Back to Africa" idea, but the Black Star Line first had to be primarily a commercial venture, connecting black business throughout the world. The chances for emigration hinged on securing territory, and this in turn presupposed a victory for the UNIA in the political arena.

* * *

Garveyite politics was complex and diverse because the Garveyites aimed at reconciling autonomous local struggles with international black unity. The ultimate goal was the liberation of black nationals in every country in the world. "The difference between the Universal Negro Improvement Association and other movements of this country," wrote Garvey, ". . . is that the Universal Negro Improvement Association seeks independence of government, while the other organizations seek to make the Negro a secondary part of existing governments." [31] However, the Garveyites did see the need to become involved in electoral politics—but on behalf of a group of blacks ignored by other black organizations. As one Garveyite wrote in the *Negro World:* "The NAACP appeals to the Beau Brummel, Lord Chesterfield, kid-gloved, silk stocking, creased-trousered, patent leather shoe . . . element, while the UNIA appeals to the sober, sane, serious, earnest, hard-working man, who earns his living by the sweat of his brow . . . the self-reliant yeomanry. [The NAACP leader DuBois] appeals to the 'talented tenth' while Garvey appeals to the 'Hoi Polloi.' " [32]

In short, Garveyite politics was for the black masses—those who had labored on slave plantations—while traditional politics was the province of the "house Negroes" who had worked within and around the master's house, and enjoyed better clothing and lodging, and often a close (if stilted) relationship with the master. During Reconstruction, the house Negroes had been grudgingly allowed to hold political office and push for minimal reforms. But the field Negroes sought the revolutionary "forty acres and a mule." In the 1890s, when most Negro politicians held fast to Republicanism, the "field Negroes" had organized their own Colored Farmers Alliance and joined the militant Populist Party. And in 1919, while the black bourgeoisie rallied around the NAACP, the black masses flocked to the Universal Negro Improvement Association. True, many UNIA leaders were of the middle class, but they were the young renegades of that class, those who had lost hope in the American way. As one black defender in the 1919 Chicago riot said, "God is with us, and he stamps world democracy a sham." [33]

Garvey's politics was in the tradition of the field Negro: he was concerned with organizing mass-based power, independent of the American system. Leadership and the program were to come exclusively from the UNIA, with its demands backed by international race unity. Where Negro politicians required acceptance by at least one segment of white America, Garveyite politics depended solely on black solidarity. To serve this end, in the fall of 1919 Garvey called for a giant world convention of the Negro race, to be held in August 1920. For almost a year, the Association engaged in a massive recruitment effort, granting many new charters and raising local money to send delegates to the convention.

5

THE
GARVEY
MOVEMENT
IN ITS PRIME

NEVER BEFORE AND NEVER SINCE has there been an assembly of black people to match the UNIA convention of 1920. Delegates came from twenty-five countries on four continents—two thousand all told—most of them representing the working masses of black people. Dr. DuBois's Pan-African Congress the year before had included fair representation of black people among its fifty-seven delegates, but nothing to compare with the UNIA gathering in New York. The UNIA planning committee had worked for months, selecting subjects to be discussed, establishing voting rules, and arranging parades and festivals and a number of affairs to build support and interest, including a rally at Madison Square Garden late in 1919.

For many delegates the convention was a first chance to meet leaders of the movement. Garvey's *Negro World* had been the only link with many distant UNIA chapters which sent delegates. The newspaper's success in recruiting was attributable in part to its content and in part to the hard work of its distributors. Sailors played a key role, taking bundles of the paper from New York to their ports of call—often smuggled under a shirt, because by 1920 the UNIA weekly had been banned in French West Africa, part of British Africa, and much of the Caribbean.[1]

The UNIA also sent official representatives abroad to promote the convention. Henrietta Vinton Davis, a stately and somewhat elderly woman who had worked for Frederick Douglass in her youth and subsequently became a noted Shakespearean actress, toured on the maiden voyage of the Black Star Line's *Yarmouth* to recruit for the UNIA. Miss Davis's contingent included a singing group, and meetings were advertised as combination variety shows and political gatherings. The delegation was received enthusiastically by large groups in Cuba and Jamaica.[2]

Other recruiters did not fare so well: the delegation to Panama, headed by Cyril Henry of Jamaica and Marie Duchaterlier of Haiti, was at first refused entry into that country. Panama had recently been swept by strikes and disturbances protesting the government's refusal to allow two white trade union organizers into the country. Miss Duchaterlier wrote to John Bruce in New York: "The United Fruit Company . . . had used their great influence with the Panamanian government and the Canal Zone authorities" to prevent the landing of the UNIA contingent. "As soon as the Negroes of Panama learned it they went wild, and together with the West Indians and led by Morales, a radical Spanish Panamanian, they threatened a strike of the workmen on the Canal and also that they would burn down the city of Colon unless I was permitted to land."[3] The government yielded, the recruiters landed, and a very sizable group of Panamanians came aboard to return to New York as convention delegates.

The UNIA also enlarged the Great Convention by absorbing groups and individuals who had been working toward similar ends. Dr. J. D. Gordon, a West Indian living in America who had tried to create an African liberation movement before the war,[4] and his friend and former college classmate, E. L. Gaines, were voted into leading positions at the 1920 UNIA convention. The Duchaterlier-Henry delegation had been invited to Panama by James B. Yearwood, who had formed the Universal Loyal Negro Association during the war. This organization of blacks in Panama and Costa Rica pledged itself to fight for England if the British government would increase its efforts to improve conditions for black Commonwealth citizens, many of whom were immigrant laborers in Central America. The ULNA was involved in strikes in Costa Rica and Panama. Impressed with Garveyism as presented in the *Negro World*, Yearwood had urged branch leaders of his own organization to affiliate with the Garvey movement. The delegation from New York had come to cement these ties, and Yearwood left Panama as a delegate to the convention in New York.[5]

Garvey himself traveled widely throughout the United States in the twelve months before the convention. He also went to Montreal, where he received a tumultuous welcome from the local UNIA. Canada had few black citizens, but a high percentage of them were Garveyites. Attending the 1920 convention were George Creese from Nova Scotia, T. H. Golden representing the Alberta UNIA, Richard Edward Riley from New Aberdeen, I. Braithwaite of Toronto, and Dr. D. D. Lewis, a native of Nigeria who had come to Montreal to study medicine and had set up a sanitarium there. Garvey's personal touch was felt in the Caribbean through letters sent to friends he had made during his travels from 1910 to 1912. As a result of all these efforts, delegates to the convention from the Western Hemisphere hailed from West Indian islands large and small; from most of the Central American countries, including Mexico; from Venezuela, Colombia, Guiana, Surinam, and Brazil; and from all forty-eight of the United States.

Recruiting in Africa proved extremely difficult. The French-language edition of the *Negro World* had been banned in the French colonies soon after its first appearance; prohibition in British West Africa followed quickly. White authorities everywhere in colonial Africa watched the movement closely. Garveyites from Sierra Leone who attempted to recruit in Dakar, Senegal, were quickly deported. Nevertheless, UNIA divisions eventually spread throughout Britain's African colonies and into Dahomey, Togo, and the Cameroons. Travel to the convention cost more time and money than all but a few Garveyites could afford, but the Sierra Leone division sent its leader, George O. Marke, and Prince Alfred McConney represented African royalty. Though he officially represented the Montreal division, Dr. D. D. Lewis worked in caucuses with African delegates. Among the prominent female delegates was Emily Kinch of Liberia, who brought African cuisine to UNIA banquets. Perhaps the most distinguished African was Gabriel Johnson, mayor of Monrovia, at that time expected to be Liberia's next president. Johnson's attempt to enter the United States for the 1921 UNIA convention illustrates one difficulty in finding African delegates: the quota system allowed precisely one-half of one Liberian to enter the United States in July of 1921. Only the most strenuous protest convinced officials this was insane.[6] (African representation at the conventions may have been more impressive than the official lists show, since many African UNIA members were forced to use false names and work clandestinely.)[7]

Beyond their geographical diversity, UNIA convention delegates represented a variety of religions and political persuasions. By 1922, delegates had been addressed by black Jews, black Hindus, black Catholics, black Muslims, and black Protestants of all denominations, and the conventions included black Marxist revolutionaries (mostly from the ABB),[8] free-lance socialists who never left the movement, and—especially in 1920—a sizable contingent of frustrated black participants in electoral politics. From Boston came William Monroe Trotter and that city's leading black Republican, attorney William C. Matthews, president and vice president respectively of the National Equal Rights League. These two wanted to be chosen as delegates to a proposed "Black House" to be set up near the White House in Washington, D.C., to represent the black nation in the white man's capital city.[9]

Delegates poured into Harlem all during July. Leadership in organizing the convention and running its first sessions was assumed by Garvey, Miss Davis, Dr. Lewis, the Reverend James W. H. Eason (a native of North Carolina and minister of a Philadelphia church), and Bishop George Alexander McGuire. The bishop's eclectic background was typical of the Garvey leadership. Born on the West Indian island of Antigua, McGuire had come to America to work in the Episcopal church. He preached in white churches in New York, and then moved to Arkansas, where he fell under the influence of the communist atheist "Bad Bishop" Montgomery Brown. On his return to New York in 1919, McGuire joined the Garveyites and became one of the movement's most distinguished representatives.[10]

Plans for the 1920 convention included drafting a list of grievances and a Declaration of Rights for the Negro People of the World. The convention was also to construct a political Constitution for the race and was to elect international officers. Special committees were to report on such subjects as "The Negro and Business Opportunities" and "The Negro in Electoral Politics." The convention was scheduled to run the entire month of August (the pattern for succeeding conventions), including two full weeks for deliberations on the Declaration of Rights and the Constitution, with each delegate given fifteen minutes to present ideas for the Declaration. Evenings were given over to speeches by various luminaries and to musical and other artistic presentations.

The social gatherings that accompanied the conventions were almost as important as the official sessions. Here, black people from different countries could learn first hand of problems common to all members of their race. The New York *World* reported heated discussions in the hallways over the prospects of war with Great Britain and the need for armed struggle to liberate Africa.[11]

Referring to the battle in the United States, one zealous delegate stated, "We are going to have democracy in this country if we have to kill every white man in it." [12] Whatever the contradictions in this statement, the convention itself was indeed committed to democratic processes. All officers were elected from the floor, and any delegate could make a nomination. Voting was conducted in the manner of the United Nations. Each country was given at least one vote; in countries with many UNIA divisions, geographical lines were drawn and each area was given one vote. This method distributed two hundred voting units among the two thousand official delegates. More than five thousand Garveyites participated in the convention in one way or another, since many delegations included unofficial representatives.*

The convention opened ceremonially on Sunday, August 1, with three religious services, followed by a silent march through the streets of Harlem. On Monday afternoon, a massive parade which stretched for miles brought business in Harlem to a standstill. Entire blocks seemed filled with people. Mounted African Legionnaires paraded under the direction of former U.S. Army Captain E. L. Gaines of Pasadena, California. A fifty-piece band—one of twelve in the parade—followed a platoon of police; then came more Legionnaires, marching in blue uniforms and red striped trousers. Behind the Legion marched neatly formed contingents from local branches and Garveyite business ventures. Two hundred Black Cross nurses in white uniforms marched by, as did squadrons of children and

---

* The UNIA convention voting system confused many—outsiders and members alike. On reading reports of votes at the 1921 convention, the president of the Los Angeles UNIA division suggested few delegates had actually participated, since there had been at most two hundred votes on any one issue. "Where were the other five thousand delegates—asleep?" she asked. A critic of the movement, attempting to prove the UNIA conventions were poorly attended, stated that the 1921 sessions never had more than two hundred delegates in attendance, "as revealed by a careful analysis of the vote, day by day, as given in the *Negro World*." [13]

choristers singing new songs of the homeland. Many men carried banners or signs proclaiming "Down with Lynching," "Uncle Tom's Dead and Buried," "Join the Fight for Freedom," and "Africa Must Be Free." Two marchers at the head of the Woman's Auxiliary bore a large banner marked "God Give Us Real Men!" (The feminist movement of the 1920s drew strong support from Garveyite women.) As one participant remembered it: "Hundreds of thousands of people took part . . . and watched the parade from windows (for which many had to pay) and sidewalks. The onlookers could not help but catch the spirit of the occasion; they clapped, waved flags and cheered themselves hoarse. . . . Here indeed were New Negroes on the march, with a goal to be reached, and a determined look in their eyes to achieve it." [14]

The first business session of the International Convention of the Negro Peoples of the World opened on Monday night, August 2, 1920, at Madison Square Garden. The *New York Times* reported a crowd of nearly twenty-five thousand, and thousands who could not get in gathered in the area to discuss the day's happenings. Inside, excitement reached its peak as Marcus Garvey mounted the platform to speak. An ovation lasting more than five minutes swept the hall before he could begin. Garvey finally quieted the crowd by waving a telegram which the UNIA had just sent to Eamon de Valera, the leader of the Irish fighters then battling for independence from England. Garvey read the telegram: "Twenty-five thousand Negro delegates assembled in Madison Square Garden, in mass meeting, representing four hundred million Negroes of the world, send you greetings as president of the Irish Republic. Please accept sympathy of Negroes of the world for your cause. We believe Ireland should be free even as Africa shall be free for the Negroes of the world. Keep up the fight for a free Ireland."

The message was answered by another five minutes of applause. Garvey then launched into a call for the liberation of Africa. He told the delegates to be prepared to shed blood for this ideal. "We New Negroes, we men who have returned from World War I, we will dispute every inch of the way until we win. We will begin by framing a Bill of Rights for the Negro race. . . . The Constitution of the United States means that every white American should shed his blood to defend that Constitution. The Constitution of the Negro race will mean that every Negro will shed his blood to defend his

Constitution. If Europe is for the European, then Africa shall be for the black people of the world. We say it; we mean it."

One man in the audience yelled at the top of his voice, "No more lynchings," but Garvey went on: "Wherever I go, whether it be France, Germany, England, or Spain, I find that I am told this is a white man's country and that there is no room for a nigger. The other races have countries of their own and it is time for the four hundred million Negroes to claim Africa for themselves."

Garvey concluded with a warning to the European colonialist: "We are going home after a long vacation and are giving notice to the tenant to get out. If he doesn't there is such a thing as forcible eviction." [15] This was a more militant echo of a statement which had drawn a prolonged standing ovation earlier.

Reverend James David Brooks said, "We're mighty grateful for all the white man has done for us; but we want to go home now. You brought us over; be manly and let us go back." [16]

The euphoric mood continued through later Liberty Hall meetings. One committee worked night and day to correlate the delegates' ideas on the Bill of Rights and Constitution. (Many found such discussions difficult—there were so many people to meet and so much to learn about the problems and activities of black people all over the world.) Delegates spoke on a variety of issues: a man from Norfolk, Virginia, took his allotted quarter-hour to explain that black people were treated better in his state than in any other state in the South; an Atlanta man asked the convention for help, telling of an attempt to press a version of a "grandfather clause" through the Georgia legislature.*[17] Finally, just two days behind schedule, the convention was asked to approve a final draft of the Declaration of Rights of the Negro Peoples of the World. As reported in the New York *Age,* the three thousand assembled delegates "jumped to their feet and many held high their right hand as if taking a solemn oath when it had been moved and seconded that the 'Bill of Rights' of the Negroes of the World . . .be adopted and Marcus Garvey . . . asked that all in favor of the motion stand. . . . It was said to be the Magna Carta of Negro freedom, the signers of

---

* "Grandfather clauses" exempted persons whose grandparents had been eligible to vote from the poll tax and from literacy tests. These were then used to prevent black people from voting.

which, like patriots of old, pledge their last drop of blood for its maintenance."[18]

This UNIA declaration is now half a century old, yet its twelve points of grievance and its fifty-four demands might well pass for the pronouncement of a contemporary black power organization. Garvey republished it periodically in the *Negro World,* in a series on the Garvey movement in the Pittsburgh *Courier* in 1930, and in his *Philosophy and Opinions.*[19] The demands call for social and political separatism, and ask recognition of the UNIA as sovereign representative of the race. Interestingly enough, a number of demands concern civil rights and equal opportunity in business and the professions.

The first demand reads, in part: "We, the duly elected representatives of the Negro peoples of the world, invoking aid of the just and almighty God, do declare all men, women and children of our blood throughout the world free citizens, and do claim them as free citizens of Africa, the motherland of all Negroes." This call for political recognition is backed up by demand number thirty-seven: "We hereby demand that the governments of the world recognize our leader and his representatives chosen by the race to look after the welfare of our people under such governments." And number forty-three states: "We call upon the various governments of the world to accept and acknowledge Negro representatives who shall be sent to the said government to represent the general welfare of the Negro peoples of the world." Number fifty-two adds: "We demand that our duly accredited representatives be given proper recognition in all leagues, conferences, conventions or courts of international arbitration wherever human rights are discussed." Immediate recognition for the Universal Negro Improvement Association would give it the formal status of the national states, and agreements between the UNIA and recognized white governments would take the form of treaty agreements. Demand thirteen includes the Garveyite slogan, in this instance expanded to read "Africa for the Africans at home and abroad," in an attempt to tie the struggle for worldwide race solidarity to battles for national sovereignty within Africa.

The Garveyites, recognizing that many blacks would become involved in the affairs of white nation-states where they lived, stole the integrationists' thunder by asking for full political rights within the white political structure: point four of the Declaration of

Rights demands that black communities in white countries be represented "in legislatures, courts of law, or such institutions as may exercise control over that particular community."

The Garveyites' Declaration of Rights added to the concept of black nationalism the idea of a parallel struggle for separatism protected under the law. Demand number twenty reads: "We protest against segregated districts, separate public conveyances, industrial discrimination, lynching, and limitations of political privileges of any Negro citizen in any part of the world on account of race, color, or creed, and will exert our full influence and power against all such." This demand exemplifies the Garveyite view that separatism is consonant with the struggle for civil liberties. A *Negro World* editorial commented that the Fifteenth Amendment to the United States Constitution "is like the Ten Commandments and the Sermon on the Mount. It proclaims a principle of justice and righteousness applicable to men everywhere. It is a necessary corollary to the Declaration of Independence and to Lincoln's Gettysburg Address." The UNIA wanted civil rights and also "complete control of our social institutions without interference by any alien race or races." Integrationists had long pleaded for an end to segregation so blacks could freely enter and work within white institutions; Garveyites asked for a pluralistic society.

One prerogative of nationhood is the control of military affairs, and point forty-seven of the Declaration states: "We declare that no Negro shall engage himself in battle for an alien race without first obtaining the consent of the leader of the Negro people of the world, except in a matter of national self-defense." And for blacks in white armies, point forty-eight protests "the practice of drafting Negroes and sending them to war without proper training," and demands "in all cases that Negro soldiers be given the same training as the aliens."

Some of the demands strike a threatening note. Demand number two states that "all things are created and given to man as a common possession," and the black man is now deprived of his equitable share; hence Garveyites "believe it right that all such things should be acquired and held by whatsoever means possible." Point sixteen is equally uncompromising: "We believe all men should live in peace one with the other, but when races and nations provoke the ire of other races and nations by attempting to infringe upon their rights, war becomes inevitable, and the attempt in any way to free one's self or protect one's rights or heritage becomes justifiable."

With so many demands, some apparent contradictions are almost inevitable, but on closer examination they appear to be subtle distinctions. "We believe in the inherent right of the Negro to possess himself of Africa," states point fourteen, adding, as a conciliatory note, that such possession "shall not be regarded as an infringement on any claim or purchase made by any race or nation." No conciliatory tone, however, appears in point fifteen: "We strongly condemn the cupidity of those nations of the world who, by open aggression or secret schemes, have seized the territories and inexhaustible natural wealth of Africa, and we place on record our most solemn determination to reclaim the treasures and possession of the vast continent of our forefathers." Apparently, legitimate white business would be allowed in free Africa, but extortionist imperialism would be stopped.

Modern nationalism has shown a cynical and fascistic side, but the UNIA declaration of 1920 shows a positive concern for "free speech universally for all men" (point twenty-five); "the self-determination of all peoples" (point twenty-seven); and for "freedom of religious worship" (point twenty-eight); and calls on "all men to do unto us as we would do unto them, in the name of justice; and we cheerfully accord to all men the rights we claim herein for ourselves" (point forty-six).

Garveyites saw black nationalism in both regional and international terms. Thus, the UNIA sought to establish bases in Africa and in Caribbean countries with black majorities, but where blacks were a minority, a form of dual citizenship would suffice. Many Garveyites in the Americas were already immigrants holding British Commonwealth citizenship. Marcus Garvey often denied he was attempting to establish a separate government in the United States, though he declared that all black people would "share in the proud citizenship" of a free Africa. Increased movement of blacks had already promoted the idea of black international sovereignty, and the 1920 declaration demanded free immigration of black people everywhere, an "unfettered commercial intercourse with all the Negro people of the world," and "freedom of the seas for all peoples." And while some demands pertained exclusively to one region (e.g., the protest against "the atrocious practice of shaving the heads of Africans"), most were international in effect. The call for teaching Negro history was as pertinent to the islands of the Caribbean as to the cities of the United States or to Africa. And the UNIA claimed that blacks had "no obligation" to pay taxes to governments which denied representation on account of race.

This was indeed a "Declaration of Rights for the Negro Peoples of the World." It was also an action program for the Universal Negro Improvement Association, and a ringing answer to critics who dismissed the UNIA as merely a "Back to Africa" movement. The *Negro World* analyzed the declaration under five banner headlines which provide a capsule view of the way Garveyites were expected to relate to the complex manifesto. The lead headline ran: "Declaration of Independence of the Negro Race"; the second, "The Negro Emancipates Himself and Has Become Really Free"; the third, "All Negroes to Obey Declaration of Rights and Not to Allow Any Other Race to Infringe upon Same"; the fourth, "31st of August Each Year an International Holiday for the Race"; and the fifth, "No Negro Will Go to War Except with the Approval of the World Leader of the Race."[20] Historians who have discussed the Garvey movement have paid little attention to the Declaration of Rights. David Cronon mentions it only in passing in *Black Moses;* others neglect it entirely. Yet Garveyites discussed the Declaration for many years after, and the 122 delegates who signed their names to the document came to hold a privileged and honored position in the movement. No other statement from the period comes close to encompassing so many divergent nationalistic and civil rights goals. Though the declaration omits any endorsement of socialism per se (or of capitalism, for that matter), the eloquent demands for social, political, and cultural equality could be the envy of any democratic socialist.

Today's black militants who are desperately trying to reconcile the embittered factions of nationalists and socialists, separatists and integrationists, should be able to find solace and inspiration in the achievement of the Garveyites of 1920. Their program fixed, Garveyites set about electing an international leadership, including a "Supreme Executive Council." The leadership comprised more than two dozen administrative positions. Critics of the Garvey movement would ridicule the UNIA's elaborate structure because they confused the many honorary titles and grants of nobility in UNIA fraternal orders with the jobs necessary to run a world-wide organization with roughly one million members. Unfortunately for the UNIA's reputation, the two top offices in the hierarchy were the only two that could be considered "honorary." The position of potentate—"titular head of all black people of the world"—was reserved for an African residing in Africa. Mayor Gabriel Johnson of Monrovia, Liberia, was selected. (The UNIA hoped to make Liberia a home for emigrants to Africa, and may have granted Johnson their top position to create good will.) The office next in rank—deputy potentate—went to George O. Marke, the Oxford-trained civil servant from Sierra Leone, who would work many years for the UNIA, never returning to his native country. Although they had few official duties, Johnson and Marke traveled extensively on diplomatic missions to spread the image of UNIA internationalism.[21]

Marcus Garvey was elected both president general and provisional president of Africa, positions ranking just below the potentate and his deputy. He won the latter office over stiff opposition from Dr. Lewis, who argued that he, as a native Nigerian, had better claim to the position. (Serious contests characterized elections for officers throughout the many UNIA conventions—in fact, the first convention was unable to fill many minor offices because no one had obtained the needed two-thirds majority. Opponents of the UNIA called Garvey a dictator, but these battles for office belie this assumption—for instance, Garvey himself nominated attorney Vernal Williams "assistant president general" in 1920, but the Panamanian delegate J. B. Yearwood won the election.)[22]

Ranking just below Garvey was the "leader of the American Negroes." This post went to the Reverend James Eason, who spent virtually all of his three years on the job traveling through the United States, organizing branch divisions and handling local problems. Eason—who was also chosen delegate to the "Black House"—saw himself as a representative of the UNIA "nation-at-large" and also as a lobbyist for the black citizens of America. Eason promised to use his position to help build a "pro-Negro party" that would become a power in the political life of racist America. "We should have colored Congressmen and colored Senators," said Eason, who never found time to establish a base in Washington.[23]

The Reverend J. D. Brooks was elected secretary general, an office charged with organizing conventions and conducting Association fund drives. Brooks turned much of his work over to James Yearwood, claiming the job was impossible for one man. The UNIA's banker was High Chancellor Clifford Bourne of Guatemala. Lady Henrietta Vinton Davis held the office of international organizer for a decade. Other offices included surgeon general, a post regularly given to a medical doctor, who would manage UNIA health and death benefits, and ministers of industries and of labor to oversee the Association's cooperative businesses.

A dominant figure throughout the 1920 convention was Bishop McGuire, who chaired many sessions and was a member of the organizing committee. After his election as chaplain general he told the crowd: "The white race is the most avaricious of races. Not content with Europe, they took part of Asia and Africa. Then they came over here and took America from the red man, and because he would not work for them, they brought members of our race from Africa. They call us the white man's burden, and I hope that the burden will keep him down until we get back to our homeland. We don't want anything from the white man except what is ours by divine right. The white people say they want humility from the Negro, but what they really seek is servility. We must go as missionaries among the whites, and teach them the everlasting brotherhood of man." [24] Early in 1922 McGuire founded the African Orthodox Church, an attempt to develop a religion for militant blacks. He had himself ordained as first bishop.

The counsel general and his assistant were leading lawyers in the movement who coordinated the work of the Association's legal staff. Similar in function to the office of leader of the American Negroes were the positions of leader of the eastern province of the West Indies–South and Central America, and the post of leader of the western province of the West Indies. Captain E. L. Gaines served as minister of legions for many years, traveling around the country training UNIA drill teams and parade units. The post of auditor general was held for a time by Eli Garcia, a UNIA diplomat and official of the Black Star Line who had been exiled from his Haitian homeland for political reasons. Other major offices included high commissioner, registrar general, assistant secretary general, and speaker of the convention.

It was the consensus of the 1920 convention "that its officers would, by their fitness and extraordinary ability, earn their salaries by active remunerative service," and a section of the UNIA constitution specified that these salaries would be determined by periodic review of the individual's work record. The Association's opponents would have a field day publicizing the maximum payment for a single year, but most UNIA officers took only a fraction of their allotment—due mostly to the innumerable fund drives to which all Garveyites were urged to contribute part of their salary. In addition to dues, each member held a ledger book which recorded loans and contributions. In effect, these were a form of taxation and functioned as do some governmental income tax systems.

The much-publicized maximum salaries were: for potentate, $12,000 annually; for Garvey's dual positions, $10,000 each (but in 1921, for example, he received only $1000); for leader of American Negroes, $10,000; for assistant president general and half a dozen other offices, $6,000; with the rest moving down the scale to the $3,000 paid yearly to the minister of legions and speaker of the convention.[25]

The most controversial offices connected with the UNIA were those of the Black Star Line. To sell stock and purchase ships and insurance, the UNIA was forced to establish the line as an independent corporation. Thus its affairs were often conducted without being discussed by the UNIA leadership, even though only Association members served as company officials. Only two of Black Star's directors—Garvey and Eli Garcia—held leadership positions in the UNIA International. The company was in serious financial trouble by the time of the 1921 convention, but Association members received only a most perfunctory report. This error was not repeated at the next convention, but by then the line was near bankruptcy. Promoters of the line were selling stock at a satisfactory pace, but the use of money received from stocks should have been discussed—especially since Black Star had to negotiate for ships and provisions with magnates of Wall Street, who were eager to exploit the slightest error in judgment.

The line's affairs were usually discussed at the annual stockholders' meetings, held just before international conventions. And these huge affairs were more like membership meetings of an economic cooperative than those of a capitalist corporation. The rule forbidding any individual to own more than two hundred of the five-dollar shares did give a semblance of membership control, and some five thousand stockholders attended the first annual meeting in 1920. Marcus Garvey, who presided, and other BSL officials turned that meeting into a rally rather than a deliberative session— perhaps because deliberation was difficult with such a large gathering. "We entered as a people with but little experience in the running of steamships," Garvey declared, hence "we were satisfied to purchase small boats so as to show that we can run them. We have much to be thankful for in that no unfortunate accident has befallen us." Though no large profits had yet been earned, he argued that the line had greatly benefited black people by "its recognition to us as a race—it has elevated our men." Loud cheers greeted Garvey's declaration that the Black Star Line had closed its first year "as solvent and as intact as any corporation can be."[26] George Tobias, a former railroad clerk and treasurer of the line, presented a financial report: during its first year the Black Star Line had garnered $610,860 in capital; assets, including real estate, equipment, and three steamers, totaled $328,190.38. His report overlooked a great deal—for example, $280,066.27 cryptically listed as "organizational expense." Nor was there any discussion of whether the ships had been worth the prices paid.[27] Such matters were overlooked in the general rejoicing; the summer of 1920 was not a season for questioning among many Garveyites.

* * *

The summer convention periods continued to be the high points of Garveyite activity, with month-long sessions in New York during August of 1921, 1922, 1924, and 1926, and in Jamaica in 1929. Reports in the white press, the NAACP magazine *Crisis,* and most Negro weeklies pictured the UNIA conventions as revels of merry-making, pageantry, and pompous speeches. It is true that Garveyites had a good time at their conventions. Each session opened with a musical or dramatic presentation, anticipating the present-day use of "soul" in political struggle. The musical director for the UNIA conventions was Rabbi J. Arnold Ford, a black Jew from Barbados who had played with the James Reese Europe military band, which with its avant-garde music had created a sensation in France during the war. Ford's UNIA band performed at fund-raising events around the country, as well as at the conventions.

Outside musical celebrities and talented members appeared regularly at the conventions. The UNIA's acceptance of "soul music" distinguished it from traditional black groups, which acknowledged the worth of spirituals only grudgingly and bitterly denounced the "debauched" strains of jazz. Black concert performers such as Roland Hayes and Marian Anderson were also sponsored by the UNIA at Carnegie Hall. Concert sopranos Marie Barrier Houston and Ethel Houghton Clarke were stalwart Garveyites and regular attractions at UNIA conventions. Black opponents of Garveyism struggling to acquire the emotionally bleached "respectability" of bourgeois America found the UNIA's color and pageantry an inexcusable affront. Others were honestly impressed with Liberty Hall during convention time.

"As you enter, your first impression is that of patriotism, for dangling from the low-hung rafters is a bewildering array of flags. flags, flags; interspersed here and there by silk banners with the names of various states and foreign countries worked in gold and other colors." [28] The patriotism was for Africa and African peoples. Pride was the theme sounded in the convention—even in the food served. A banquet menu listed "African Punch, Liberia Chicken, Sliced Cold Shoulder à la Monrovia," salads with "tropical dressing," and desserts including "Liberty Special Ice Cream" and "Lady Vinton's Black Macaroons." The idea was evidently more important than the authenticity of the concoction; one guest at this banquet remembers African Punch as a "mixture of a little bit of everything available." [29]

This willingness to be black was a militant act in and of itself. Popular white conceptions of Africa saw ignorant cannibals whom the white man had to lead towards civilization by the rings in their noses. And many black Americans were reluctant to think about Africa or Africanism. Garveyism, coming when it did, performed an immeasurable service in breaking down the lies of whites and uplifting the image of the African.

The conventions also offered more tangible programs. Delegates formed committees to work on such problems as the role of women, better relations within the Negro race, economic opportunities for the Negro, how to prevent lynching, discipline within the movement, etc. What the critics called petty haggling was in fact serious debate. Nor were the issues discussed trivial: at the annual Women's Day session in the 1922 convention, every speaker noted that black women "were willing to work side by side with men, but they were unwilling to follow any longer." UNIA women vigorously protested the double standard of morals, and one commented, "A bold statement and a pair of trousers do not make a man."[30] In the many discussions on lynching, some delegates argued for the use of self-defense tactics, others defended the efficacy of a federal anti-lynch law, and still others called for a complete withdrawal from conventional politics in favor of emigration to Africa. After years of discussion about a world-wide black political party, the 1924 convention inaugurated a Negro Political Union to raise money for and otherwise support black political candidates. Discussions on the nature of black nationalism and the feasibility of creating a separate black republic in the United States took place through the conventions.[31]

The UNIA International took no formal action on many issues in an attempt to avoid factional disputes and to leave local divisions free to make policy decisions responsive to local needs. For example, Garveyites worked within trade unions in the Caribbean and opposed them in the United States on the grounds that conditions for black labor differed in the two areas. The International consequently took no position on labor unions. Nor did the black nationalist UNIA endorse the Dyer anti-lynch law of 1922, since most delegates considered the measure useless verbiage.[32]

At the same time, the International was always ready to endorse active struggles for national liberation. The first note of support was to de Valera in 1920; it was followed at the 1921 convention by enthusiastic backing for the Indian revolt against Britain (later Gandhi would correspond with Garvey)[33] and by "wild applause" for a dispatch claiming "the Moors in Morocco had massacred twenty four thousand Spaniards."[34] Few Americans—black or white—were even aware a war of liberation was then being waged in Spanish Morocco.

A full-page advertisement in the Garvey weekly in 1924 suggests the broad scope of the conventions: "All divisions, branches, chapters, and churches, lodges, fraternal organizations, civic and uplift bodies, and newspapers are invited to send delegates." An elaborate outline of the topics to be considered starts with religion: "(1) Discussing the Deification of Jesus as a Black Man of Sorrows; (2) The Canonization of the Virgin Mary as a Negress; (3) The Idealization of God as a Holy Spirit without physical form, but a Creature of . . . resemblance of the Black race." Political subjects included formation of the Negro Political Union, educating Negroes in communities where they form the majority population to rise to the responsibility of self-government, and "conferring with the white nations and with the League of Nations for an amicable adjustment of the race issue, and for a rearrangement of the system under which Negroes are governed." There was also to be a discussion about petitioning the president and Congress of the United States, and the Parliament and king of England, to consider the universal desire of black people "to peaceably build up a country of their own in their motherland Africa."

Industrial growth covered: "(1) The development of Liberia, Abyssinia and Haiti as independent Black nations, and other countries where Negroes form a majority of the population, i.e., Jamaica, Barbados, Trinidad, British Guiana, British Honduras, and other Islands of the West Indies and Africa. (2) Ways and means of adjusting the race problem of the Southern States of the United States of America to the satisfaction of all concerned. (3) Ways and means of correctly educating white people to the needs and desires of the Negro race."

Social topics: "(1) Discussing the educating of the Negro race as to the real meaning of society, and laying down the principles that should guide those who are desirous of becoming socially distinctive. (2) Creating an atmosphere around the young generation of the race, to better prepare them for a high social life."

On commerce: "(1) Discussing the linking up of all Negro communities in a trade and commercial relationship. (2) Promotion of exchange business enterprises in all Negro communities. (3) Encouraging travel among and between Negroes of commercial and industrial professions."

Education: "(1) Discussing the formulation of a code of education especially for Negroes. (2) The censoring of all literature placed in the hands of Negroes. (3) Educating the race to discriminate in the reading of literature placed in its hands. (4) The promotion of an independent Negro literature and culture."

Propaganda: "(1) The tabooing of all alien propaganda inspired to destroy the ideals of and enslaving the minds of the Negro. (2) The disseminating of education among the race for the promotion of its own ideals."

Constitutional questions: "(1) Amending the Constitution of the

Universal Negro Improvement Association as found necessary. (2) Discussing the annual business of the Universal Negro Improvement Association."

And under the heading "Humanity": "(1) Discussing the promotion of a closer bond of fellowship between the black and white races of the world. (2) Discussing, without prejudice, the aims and objects of the Ku Klux Klan. (3) Discussing the intra-racial problems of the white race as they affect the Negro. (4) Discussing the progress of a white Canada, a white America, a white Europe, and a white Australia, as enunciated by white leaders. (5) Discussing the sincerity of the League of Nations as a clearing house for the ills of the world. [Items 6, 7 and 8 concerned the policy of France, England and America toward the Negro.] (9) Discussing the Negro's share of the spoils of the war 1915–18. (10) Discussing the new German demand for the return of certain colonies in Africa that were robbed from the natives and taken from the Germans during the last war. (11) Discussing the honesty of diplomacy in dealing with the lands, liberty and rights of weaker peoples. (12) Discussing the forwarding of an appeal to His Highness the Pope of Rome, His Grace the Archbishop of Canterbury and the heads of the American churches, as leaders of Christianity, for an honest and human settlement of the problems of humanity, especially as such problems affect the Negro. (13) An appeal to the kings of England, Italy, Spain and Belgium and their parliaments for a square deal for Negroes in Africa and the colonies. (14) An appeal to the Presidents of America, France and Portugal for a square deal for Negroes in Africa, America and the colonies. (15) Discussing the Negroes' attitude in the next world war [this subject was discussed at all UNIA conventions]. (16) Discussing the petition of appeal of the Negro peoples of the world to the League of Nations for the turning over to them of certain mandatories in Africa now being exercised by alien peoples over the natives." [35]

For the many Garveyites who never attended a convention, the weekly *Negro World* was a vital source of nationalist ideas. The *Negro World,* published continuously from late 1918 to the fall of 1933, stands as one of the UNIA's proudest achievements. Managed and staffed entirely by blacks, it became the world's most widely read black weekly in the early 1920s, with circulation reaching nearly two hundred thousand—far ahead of its nearest rival, the

Chicago *Defender.* In its first years, the *Negro World* was published in English, Spanish, and French editions, and in many West Indian and African colonies possession of the *Negro World* could lead to a jail sentence as surely as possession of a UNIA membership card.[36]

Edicts prohibiting the *Negro World* often helped rally support for the movement. In 1919, for example, the right to read the weekly became a cause célèbre in the British West Indies, most sensationally in British Honduras, where the governor banned the paper after reading the Garvey editorial declaring the former German colonies of Africa to be "the property of the Blacks and by God, we are going to have them now or some time later, even if all the world is to waste itself in blood."[37] Garveyites in Guatemala and Mexico smuggled the paper into the colony, but the governor would not lift the ban—a grievance which contributed to the uprising at Belize in July 1919. This revolt caused $100,000 in damage, and a British Navy shore party was needed to put it down when the local (and largely black) police force proved uninterested in maintaining the governor's law and order. By 1922, the British had rescinded their bans on the weekly in most of the Caribbean colonies.[38]

The *Negro World* was also an important part of meetings at UNIA divisions throughout the world. It was customary to read the paper's front page editorial and lead stories aloud to assembled members. The tactful explanation for this was that not all members could afford their own copy; the more vital reason was that some members could not read. The *Negro World* allowed members to follow the growth of the movement week by week. A "News of Divisions" page carried a running account of new outposts of Garveyism.*

The *Negro World* also served as an open forum for many political viewpoints, and offered news coverage of a depth matched by few newspapers anywhere. The weekly was remarkably open about its sources. Editors would borrow from the "enemy" NAACP *Crisis* or from the *Daily Worker* ("U.S. Capitalists Have New Way to Free Ethiopia Slaves;" "Are the Philippines a Chinese Problem?"; "Sacco-Vanzetti Petitions Signed"). The editors subscribed to papers around the world, and often re-used material from the *Gold Coast Leader, Gold Coast Times,* Belize, Honduras, *Independent,* Panama

---

* The October 22, 1921, edition, for example, carried stories on new divisions at Moron in the Camagüey province of Cuba, and at New Bern, Connecticut. It also carried a long account of UNIA organizing in Syracuse, New York.

Daily Star, South African *Worker,* Johannesburg *Star, Rand Daily Mail, Abantu Batho* (an English- and African-language paper), the Kingston, Jamaica, *Daily Gleaner,* and numerous other white or black papers in the United States. Analysis of important events was featured. One H. H. Weed, for example, discussed the U.S. Marines' invasion of Haiti shortly after World War I, and noted that American financial pressure after 1910 had brought the very monetary crisis which was the main excuse for the invasion.[39]

The Garveyites attracted a whole generation of journalists who could not work with the establishment press. W. A. Domingo was an early editor of the *Negro World.* Ulysses Poston, co-founder of the militant *Detroit Contender* before going to the *Negro World,* became publisher and editor of the *New York Contender* in the late 1920s. This was the first Democratic Party–connected paper for blacks in New York.[40] Short-story writer Eric Walrond worked on newspapers in Panama and in Brooklyn before joining the *Negro World.* Later he was with *New Masses* and was also managing editor of the Urban League's *Opportunity.* Walrond also worked on Garvey's daily *Negro Times,* published from late 1922 to early 1924 under the editorship of the elder statesman of black journalism, T. Thomas Fortune, founder of the New York *Age* in the 1880s and chief editor of the *Negro World* during the mid-1920s. William Ferris, author of the voluminous historical and anthropological study *The African Abroad,* inaugurated a poetry section in the *Negro World.* The paper's foreign correspondents included the poet Claude McKay, and Garvey's mentor, Duse Mohammed Ali. One of the many columnists was the historian John "Grit" Bruce, who had earlier started his own newspaper in Washington. Born of slave parents, Bruce rose from poverty to become, through his "down home" editorial columns, one of the most popular figures of early twentieth-century black America.*

Another columnist, Samuel Haynes, was dubbed a "Black Ku Klux Klanner" by anti-Garveyites because of his many hostile editorials on white injustice.[42] During and after World War II, Haynes was active among the Pan-Africanists in London. Hubert H.

---

* Active in lodge work and in scholarly pursuits, Bruce was nonetheless first and foremost a journalist. In the words of a contemporary: "Every time I see John E. Bruce, he is on the streets. He looks like any other ordinary man, except that he always has a newspaper under his arm or in his coat-pocket."[41]

Harrison, one of Garvey's earliest allies in America, worked for the *Negro World* until 1922. He, too, had edited his own journal before working with the Garveyites. For many years the paper was blessed with Amy Jacques Garvey's feminist column, "Our Women and What They Think."

Though Marcus Garvey was editor-in-chief of the *Negro World,* he usually wrote only lead editorials, giving other duties to various members of the staff. In its last years the UNIA weekly was edited by Hucheswar G. Mugdal, who came to the United States from Hubli, India, by way of Trinidad.[43]

Women played a significant role in the growth of the Universal Negro Improvement Association. They enjoyed equal status with men at conventions and in divisions, and participated freely in the debates and voting. True, women attended their own group meetings and each branch had a "lady president" to handle "those departments of the organization over which she may be able to exercise better control than the male president." But the recognition of femininity, the special clubs, etc., did not create sexual apartheid in the UNIA as it did in many other organizations. The lady president was often as important as the branch president. The Constitution allowed "each local division" to arrange the department organization "that shall be especially controlled or supervised by the male and female presidents, respectively." The Los Angeles division deemed its male and female leaders "the presidents," and they made policy decisions as equals in the best sense.

The international organizer Henrietta Vinton Davis ("Lady Vinton") was one of the few women to hold a key position in any major political organization at that time. Beyond this, the UNIA's progressive stand earned support from leading women in all walks of life. America's most prominent and richest black businesswoman— Ledia Walker, daughter of the inventor of the nation's leading hair-straightening process—was an ardent Garvey backer. Charlotta Bass, later an important political figure in California, and the Progressive Party's candidate for vice president of the United States in 1952, served as one of the presidents of the Los Angeles UNIA for a time. Augusta Savage, whose sculptures adorn many public buildings in New York City, was the wife of the assistant president general Robert L. Poston. Mittie Gordon, lady president of the Chicago Division for many years, organized her own Back-to-Africa movement in the mid-1930s. Assistant international organizer Madame M. L. T. De Mena was an important political figure in Jamaica during the 1930s and '40s when she was active in the People's National Party.

The most important woman in Garveyism never held a position in the International, and her full value has never been recognized. The life and works of Amy Jacques Garvey, the president general's second wife, deserve attention from students of both women's liberation and black nationalism. The first-born in her family, she received the attention and schooling usually reserved for the first son, absorbing her father's deep interest in racial betterment and political issues. Shortly after World War I, Amy Jacques left her native Jamaica for America and further education, but she quickly became exclusively involved in the UNIA. Marcus Garvey, who had separated from his first wife late in 1919, developed a close intellectual friendship with Amy Jacques, then working as a secretary in the *Negro World* office, often asking her for criticism on his drafts of editorials.[44]

Amy Jacques was a woman of startling physical beauty, which she had found more a curse than a blessing. Beset with an endless procession of unwanted suitors, she developed a disarming technique of turning their small talk into political debates. She found most men would disappear when a woman competed as an intellectual equal, but Garvey accepted her terms. Amy Jacques and Marcus Garvey were drawn together in her respect for his creative genius and his admiration for her intellectual prowess. Early in 1922 they were married.

Garvey had broken with his first wife, Amy Ashwood, because, according to Amy Jacques, the first Mrs. Garvey offered him diversion rather than assistance.* The two Mrs. Garveys held contrasting views of the role of the rebellious female. For example, both worked for the radical Peoples National Party of Jamaica in the 1940s—Amy Jacques editing the party newspaper and Amy Ashwood running a political discotheque for teenagers. Amy Jacques' involvement in politics represented a deep moral commitment; Amy

---

* Though newspaper accounts and letters strongly suggest the first Mrs. Garvey was without principle, Herbert Hill, who worked closely with both women in the Jamaican PNP, believes Amy Ashwood to have been a sincere black militant, despite her idiosyncracies.[45]

Ashwood apparently saw politics as one way to assert her right to live a bohemian existence. After her divorce from Garvey, Amy Ashwood became an avid opponent of the UNIA. In the 1950s, however, she decided to capitalize on her name by representing herself as *the* Mrs. Garvey.

Amy Jacques Garvey compiled a book of her husband's poetry and edited and published the two-volume *Philosophy and Opinions of Marcus Garvey*. Her correspondence with Garvey shows they shared that deep understanding from which a true exchange of ideas can come.* But Amy Jacques Garvey's contributions to Garveyism went far beyond assisting her husband. Her woman's page in the *Negro World* called on every woman to use her mind to its fullest capacity; news of cocktail parties and bridge games was conspicuously lacking. Mrs. Garvey included accounts of how "women were faster workers than men," or quoted experts who urged women to develop their individuality or made suggestions for the "larger usefulness of women." Reports of women freeing themselves from male bondage in Africa and Asia often appeared. One told of the "liberation of Japanese women from old ways"; another was headlined "Egyptian Women Discard Veil." Mrs. Garvey suggested black women should be liberated from domestic jobs with white families so they could better care for their own, and chided black men for not providing more secure lives for their women: "Be honest enough to admit your laziness," she wrote. "Survey the intellectual, political and industrial groups of other races, and ask yourself if black men are measuring up to present day standards." Adjacent to this editorial was a report of how China was "in the birth throes of a new epoch" because its patriarchy was crumbling. Another article on the same page was headlined "Indian Ex-Queen Raps Mannish Women; Cultivate Womanly Spirit, Not Man's Role She Advises." [47] Equality, not female (or male) domination, was Mrs. Garvey's goal.

Though Garveyite women were expected to de-emphasize physical beauty, "We were taught that Black was Beautiful, long before the idea became popular," according to Ruth Beckford, who was

---

* Few Garveyites established such rapport with their leader, who was generally considered to be unpredictable. James Yearwood, UNIA secretary general, relates a typical scene in the Association offices in which he and Garvey were quietly sifting through paperwork when suddenly Garvey jumped up and began to expound on some new idea that Yearwood had never heard before. [46]

raised in a Garveyite household and is presently one of America's foremost instructors of African dance.[48] The Garveyites didn't go so far as to promote "natural" hair styles, but they did sport what they considered to be African dress, in the form of the robes and uniforms worn by UNIA dignitaries at convention times. The *Negro World* was probably unique among black newspapers in that it did not carry advertisements for bleaching creams. The only line of hair straighteners advertised was that produced by Ledia Walker.*

* * *

The UNIA also attracted blacks eager to reform Christianity or adopt a new faith. The Negro church, like many others, was undergoing profound changes. The other-worldly religion of deep Dixie was increasingly challenged by secular realities; it offered few constructive ideas for those facing the problems of urban life and was no longer the community's only social center. The Garveyites sought to make the church an agent for social change, and condemned dictatorial ministers who bullied their parishioners with references to damnation and sin. Such ideas threatened the well-to-do ministers of black society. Although many men with the title of Reverend held leading positions in the Association, all were from the lower ranks of black church hierarchies. Of some two hundred black ministers listed in the *Negro Yearbook* throughout the 1920s, only two—the heads of the UNIA's own African Orthodox Church— were connected with Garveyism. Ministers in the movement could sympathize with Garvey's pronouncement at the 1924 convention that "the Negro preacher is the curse of his race."[50] In 1922, Garveyite ministers had joined Garvey in fighting an attempt by the Bible Tract Society to present a free Bible to every delegate. The

---

* Ledia Walker, whose product served so many black women who wished to be white and accepted, was herself a dark-skinned child of poverty—until her mother discovered the process which would make her rich. Frantic promotion of the hair straightener drove the elder Madame Walker to an early grave in 1919. At the funeral, the bereaved daughter announced she was donating $5,000 to the NAACP campaign for a federal anti-lynch law. The *Negro World* promptly criticized the young heiress, suggesting her money could be better used as part of a UNIA "fund for the purpose of purchasing a house in which poor colored persons about to be evicted by autocratic landlords might receive shelter."[49] Madame Walker, who could have taken this as an affront, turned instead toward the UNIA, and soon became one of its few wealthy black supporters.

convention rejected the idea by a two-thirds vote "to let the whites know we disapprove of their brand of Christianity," in Garvey's words.[51]

For many Garveyites, the UNIA itself was a religion and Marcus Garvey "the Black Moses." William Ferris, speaking of the spiritual doldrums into which the black man had fallen, commented, "Then in the spring of 1918 Marcus Garvey appeared upon the scene like John the Baptist." The Reverend R. R. Porter, writing in the *Negro World*, described Garveyism as a religion: "I do not know whether or not Marcus Garvey is aware of the fact that he has given the world a new religion; nevertheless, he has. . . . To me true Garveyism is a religion which is sane, practical, inspiring and satisfying." As with any devout believer, a true Garveyite "holds fast to that which he believes is best—Garveyism. . . . He is true to himself, others and his religion—through the right understanding of One God, One Aim, One Destiny [the UNIA motto] he shall enjoy life and live abundantly in the Kingdom of Heaven on earth, and know that Africa shall once more become the land of the Good, Strong, and Wise." [52]

Garvey himself, though raised in a Roman Catholic family, rarely attended mass or confession; his funeral ceremony was presided over by religious representatives of several denominations. The UNIA leadership included a number of agnostic or only vaguely religious people, but the organization's followers were largely from that segment of black society most addicted to religion. For these members the UNIA had its own clericalism. Thus even the bitterly anti-church Samuel Haynes, president of the Pittsburgh division, found himself leading the singing of hymns at weekly meetings.

In Garveyite theology, blacks were the chosen people of God. "We are somewhat like the Hebrews. Like them we have left our native land and have no place to go," said Bishop McGuire. [53] Garveyites often noted their similarities with Zionists. The Jewish people could have Palestine, "why not the Negroes another Palestine in Africa?" ran an argument presented at the 1922 UNIA convention. (The Yiddish press, in turn, showed interest in the Garveyites and sent reporters to UNIA conventions.) A sizable minority of New York Garveyites were black Jews—some six hundred marched in a special contingent of the 1922 convention parade, and Rabbi J. Arnold Ford, the Association's musical director, had adopted Judaism long before he joined the Garvey movement, bringing most of his Beth B'nai congregation with him. Ford had hoped Judaism would be adopted as the official Garveyite religion; instead, the African Orthodox Church founded by Bishop McGuire in 1921 became the nearest thing to an official UNIA denomination. McGuire had himself ordained bishop of the new faith by an archbishop in the Greek Orthodox Church; this, McGuire said, gave him apostolic succession through Ignatius Peter III, the 126th successor of St. Peter as Bishop and Patriarch of Antioch, making his church purer and more "orthodox" than that of the Roman Catholics or the Protestant denominations of America.[54]

For McGuire this was the climax to a unique personal odyssey. The tall, deep-voiced, dark-hued prelate had come to New York from his native Antigua before the turn of the century. He preached primarily in Negro churches of the basically white Episcopal denomination, but also gave visiting sermons before white congregations— which on one occasion included J. P. Morgan. In 1903 McGuire moved to Arkansas to proselytize among the poor. There he ran into the ugliness of Jim Crow—and also into Bishop Montgomery Brown. This white communist preacher of revolution and brotherhood, "Bad Bishop Brown,"doubtless contributed to McGuire's militancy, but the latter's radicalism was to take a different course. When Brown was cast out by organized religion, McGuire concluded that the white Christian denominations in America were too infested with racism to benefit the black man. In 1919 McGuire returned to New York, hoping to be appointed bishop to Liberia. When the post was given to a white man, McGuire turned to Garveyism.[55] Next to Garvey himself, Reverend McGuire was the UNIA official most quoted in the white press and the man most often identified by outsiders who referred to radicalism in the Garvey movement.

On the question of God's identity, McGuire held the position that "God is not a Negro; a spirit is nothing physical. But in one's prayers one must vision someone to listen, and we can think only of someone in human form. I had the picture in my mind of a white God. Now came the picture of a black God." Again, in a somewhat different context, McGuire noted, "If God is a father of all He must have had black blood in His veins, and Jesus must have had black blood in His veins. So it is proper for the dark race to conceive of their spiritual Saviour as a Negro."[56] On one occasion the bishop predicted that Christ would have to live in Harlem should He visit

New York "because all the darker people live here in Harlem." [57] Garveyites studied historical texts and found that apparently the Essenes—the Jewish sect of which Jesus was a member—were a people with swarthy complexions and tightly curled hair. This, combined with biblical references to the Saviour's "feet of polished brass" and "hair of lamb's wool," convinced the researchers that Christ did indeed have significant African features.

Bishop McGuire's approach was less scholarly. Standing under a large oil painting clearly portraying a black Madonna and Child, he would demand that black people name the day when all members of the race would tear down and burn all pictures of white Madonnas and white Christs which adorn black homes. "Then let us start our Negro painters getting busy," declared the Bishop, "and supply a black Madonna and a black Christ for the training of our children." [58]

The question was not a trivial one. Black Muslims would later go a step further and declare the black God the only one, and the white man simply the devil. For Muslims, this undermined the entire moral basis of America. The more militant Muslims, such as Malcolm X and Eldridge Cleaver, would move from this break with America into a thoroughly revolutionary position. But it was the Garveyites who showed the way ahead.

By 1924, the African Orthodox church had twenty-one congregations, with two thousand five hundred communicants, spread throughout the United States and into Canada, Trinidad, Cuba, and Haiti. [59] The church remained an important institution in Harlem for two decades, and many congregations elsewhere survived into the 1930s. At present, it has a following of some six thousand members. Even at its peak, however, the African Orthodox Church never captured a majority of Garveyites. The elaborate ritual—a compound Roman Catholic and Episcopal masses—may have alienated prospective followers. Then, too, the black Jews and black Coptic churches in Harlem provided alternatives to white Christianity and drew many UNIA members. Many Garveyites refused to participate actively in any church. Some ministers within the UNIA sought to build an ecumenical movement in response to a committee report at the 1922 convention calling on them to seek out other religious leaders in black communities "for the purpose of embracing the Negro's faith into our own doctrine." [60]

Marcus Garvey, founder and president general of the Universal Negro Improvement Association, circa 1922

The Garvey ladies brigade, 1924

Black Cross Nurses parade, 1924

AMY JACQUES GARVEY

Marcus Garvey in the Atlanta federal penitentiary, circa 1926

a.

b.

. A UNIA protest parade, 1924

. The Garvey militia, 1921

. The Yarmouth, first ship of the Black Star Line. In 1920 the Yarmouth carried teams of UNIA recruiters around the Caribbean.

c.

a. The Garveyite *Negro World* carried the Declaration of Rights of the Negro Peoples of the World in its September 11, 1920, issue. The *Negro World* was the most widely circulated black weekly of its time. To the right of the Declaration is a suggested reading list for UNIA supporters; it includes books by Thomas Huxley, Kropotkin, Herbert Spencer, and the American socialist James O'Neal.

b. Outside Liberty Hall, the Garveyite headquarters in New York, during the 1921 UNIA convention

c. Rabbi J. Arnold Ford and members of his congregation

c.

UNDERWOOD AND UNDERWOOD

DECLARATION OF INDEPENDENCE OF THE NEGRO RACE

THE NEGRO EMANCIPATES HIMSELF AND HAS BECOME REALLY FREE

All Negroes to Obey Declaration of Rights and Not to Allow Any Other Race to Infringe Upon Same

31st OF AUGUST OF EACH YEAR AN INTERNATIONAL HOLIDAY FOR THE RACE

No Negro Will Go to War Except With the Approval of World Leader of the Race

THE UNIVERSAL ETHIOPIAN ANTHEM

Poem by Burrell and Ford

I.

Ethiopia, thou land of our fathers,
Thou land where the gods loved to be,
As storm cloud at night sudden gathers
Our armies come rushing to thee.
We must in the fight be victorious
When swords are thrust outward to gleam;
For us will the vict'ry be glorious
When led by the red, black and green

INDEPENDENT

a.

INTERNATIONAL CONVENTION OF NEGROES OF THE WORLD

INDEPENDENT

b.

Hubert Harrison, the "first professor of street-corner university" and an editor of the Negro World

William Ferris, UNIA assistant president general and literary editor of the Negro World

St. Ann's Bay in Jamaica, where Marcus Garvey was born

Marcus Garvey Jr.
(Mwalimu Marcus Garvey)

The remains of the black business district (above) and the wealthiest black residential area (below) of Tulsa after the riots of 1920. Both areas were burned by white rioters; the Chicago Defender reported they were also bombed from the air.

Grover Cleveland Redding, leader of the Abyssinian order, attempted to start a war of black liberation in Chicago in 1920. Redding was arrested and executed for murder.

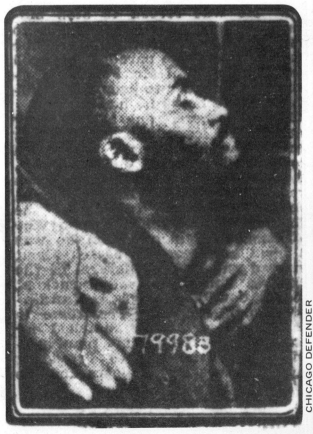

CHICAGO DEFENDER

A young Garveyite with her black doll. This photograph
was published in a pamphlet issued by the Cincinnati
UNIA in 1927.

6

PERSONALITIES AND MOTIVATIONS

ESTIMATING THE SIZE of a worldwide mass movement is obviously an extremely difficult matter. Does one consider only actual paid memberships, or the number—two or three times as great—of non-paying followers as well? In the UNIA, a sizable turnover within branches affected the count, and during the Association's strongest years, 1919 to 1925, there were probably half again as many members as there were paid memberships at any one time. An analysis of UNIA fund-raising contribution lists, *Negro World* "News of Divisions" reports, and outside press reports indicates the organization had about four hundred thousand active dues-paying members. But considering the turnover and the many poor blacks who moved in and out of the movement as their funds and time would allow, the UNIA probably had some three-quarters of a million members during the early 1920s. Even after membership began to decline, the UNIA attracted many new recruits, including some second generation Garveyites. Certainly well over a million black people were official UNIA members at one time or another; counting non-paying followers, two to three million people were in and around the movement and its activities. At its peak the Association could draw upon two hundred fifty thousand working members in more than four hundred United States divisions. Garveyite strongholds in the Caribbean and Latin America had roughly one hundred twenty thousand members. Surprisingly, divisions in Canada and Nova Scotia—areas with very small black populations—had some five thousand members. The UNIA's numerical strength in Africa is more difficult to estimate. Driven underground, African Garveyites found it dangerous to mail reports; those which did arrive at UNIA headquarters had often been censored by colonial authorities. Despite this handicap, the UNIA had sizable divisions in Liberia, Sierra Leone and the Union of South Africa, with smaller pockets elsewhere—in all, probably twenty-five to thirty thousand active followers throughout the continent, and many who sympathized with the cause while working through "safer" organizations.

Who assumed the task of organizing and holding together all of these followers? Among the UNIA's leaders—International officers, writers on the *Negro World,* officials of the Black Star Line and the Negro Factories Corporation, and heads of leading divisions—are seventy-two whose occupations can be identified. Of these, twelve were ministers, seven were lawyers, seven were teachers (two at the college level), four could be called professional artists or musicians, ten were skilled craftsmen or worked as clerks and civil servants, and eight worked in semi-skilled or unskilled occupations. The remaining twenty-four would have to be classified as politicians and journalists, though many worked at odd jobs to support their political activity.

A similar diversity is reflected in nationalities of some seventy-five leading Garveyites: thirty-six were from the West Indies (including fifteen from Jamaica and five from French-speaking areas), eight from Africa, and one from India via the West Indies. Afro-Americans whose birthplace could be discovered came mostly from the South (fifteen of nineteen). But, as we have noted, many Garveyite leaders were world travelers, and their places of national origin were of secondary importance.*

* J. D. Gordon, who was born in the West Indies and educated in Georgia (where he tried to institute an African Liberation Plan before World War I), moved to California during the war and joined the UNIA. He served as assistant president general in 1920–21, and later as president of the Los Angeles division. *Negro World* columnist Samuel Haynes, who hailed from British Honduras, served as a soldier in Mesopotamia, then returned to the West Indies and was UNIA head in British Honduras during the Belize uprising of 1919 before coming to America, where he headed the Pittsburgh division for some ten years. The Barbadian Rabbi Ford served in Europe during the war, settled in the United States and then, late in 1926, journeyed to Ethiopia, where his wife and children live today. J. J. Adams, official translator for the UNIA Mission to the League of Nations and then UNIA Ambassador to France, was born in Haiti, educated in Europe, and joined the UNIA in San Francisco, California. Cyril Henry, a Jamaican, was educated in Canadian and American agricultural colleges, discovered Garveyism while in New York, and returned to the Caribbean as an agent for the UNIA. UNIA high chancellor Gabriel E. Stewart, a very early associate of Garvey, traveled widely in America and the West Indies before settling in his native Jamaica.[1]

Of course many West Indians in the UNIA had simply migrated directly to America, but most Garveyite leaders had traveled widely. Most of the members within the Caribbean basin had done extensive island-hopping, and many of the prominent Garveyites born in the United States were war veterans who had seen Europe. Some had journeyed to that other world of California; most were former Southerners. The Africans who became UNIA notables—George O. Marke of Sierra Leone, Prince Kojo Tavalou of Dahomey, Justice Dossen of Liberia, Dr. Lewis of Nigeria, Emily Kinch of Liberia, and Duse Mohammed—had traveled abroad prior to discovering Garveyism.

Those who had not traveled learned the larger vision of race unity from those who had seen the light, particularly from Marcus Garvey. James H. Robinson, long-time Garveyite, told of how he came to join the movement: "Marcus Garvey captured the imagination of thousands because he personified the possibility of the fulfillment of a dream latent in the heart of every Negro. I remember as a lad in Cleveland, Ohio, during the hungry days of 1921, standing on Central Avenue, watching a parade one Sunday afternoon when thousands of Garvey Legionnaires, resplendent in their uniforms, marched by. When Garvey rode by in his plumed hat, I got an emotional lift which swept me up above the poverty and the prejudice by which my life was limited." [2]

William Sherrill, president general of the UNIA after Garvey's death, remembered his conversion in Baltimore just after World War I: "Here was I, a successful businessman with a family, member of a Church, a Lodge, and fully insured to protect them. I did not have to join anything else. I subscribed to the anti-lynching campaign every time a Negro was lynched. I did not like to hear people talk about conditions of my people, as I had overcome many of them: let everybody else do likewise. I argued this way against the persuasion of friends. . . . One night on my way to a show, I saw a huge crowd outside a Church. I went up and said, "What's going on in there?" A lady turned to me and said, 'Man alive, don't you know that Marcus Garvey is in there talking? Yes indeed, Garvey in person.' 'Shucks,' I said, 'I may as well see what he looks like.' I could not get near the windows, so I had to get a ticket for standing room only. I squeezed in, until I could get a good look at him; then suddenly he turned in my direction, and in a voice like thunder from Heaven he said, 'Men and women, what are you here for? To live unto yourself, until your body manures the earth, or to live God's purpose to the fullest?' He continued to complete his thought in that compelling yet pleading voice for nearly an hour. I stood there like one in a trance, every sentence ringing in my ears and finding an echo in my heart. When I walked out of that Church, I was a different man—I knew my sacred obligations to my Creator, and my responsibilities to my fellow men, and so help me I am still on the Garvey train."[3] Many of his followers saw in Marcus Garvey a living example of the aggressive self-assertion which they desired, but feared to express. At times, some wished him less direct. John Bruce wrote to Marie Duchaterlier, asking her to get Garvey "to bridle his language." (Miss Duchaterlier was an immigrant from Haiti, a domestic worker turned UNIA organizer.) She replied, "I had just as well stop the flowing waters of Niagara Falls. . . . All that you say is true and if Mr. Garvey was less radical it might be better, but you had just as well hope for the Ethiopian to change his skin, or the leopard his spots as to ask Garvey to change his method of procedure. I am convinced that it is the outpouring of the pent-up feelings of generations of his ancestors who have borne with oppression and injustice of the white man for centuries. The cry has come ringing down the ages, and he is giving voice to the cumulative agonies our people have suffered during their slavery and since their emancipation. . . . I cannot stop him even if I would."[4] The quality of Garvey's oratory was a constant topic: "My voice is great since my tonsils have been removed. I can bellow like Marcus in his happy moods at Liberty Hall," wrote one Garveyite to another.[5]

Oratory alone did not attract followers, however. The reasons for joining the Universal Negro Improvement Association were as varied as the rewards. For example, two prominent figures in the 1920 convention, Lionel Winston Greenidge and Charles Augustus Petioni, were immigrant West Indians who had encountered racial discrimination in New York. They turned to Garveyism as a defense against slurs and as an outlet for their anger. Petioni became a key figure in the New York division while working days as an elevator operator and attending the City College of New York at night. Eventually, he went to Meharry Medical School, became a doctor, and had a long and successful practice in New York. Greenidge traveled to Brazil during the early 1920s and became an electrical engineer.[6] Alfred Smith, a seaman by trade, joined the UNIA when he was hired on one of the Black Star Line steamships. Smith later became a prominent organizer for John L. Lewis's United Mine Workers and for the National Maritime Union.[7] Louis Campbell, an illegal immigrant from the Caribbean, was sheltered by friends in the UNIA, and during the 1930s emerged as an important community leader in left-wing political activities.[8] Fresh out of Yale Law School, J. Austin Norris of Philadelphia turned to Garveyism when he found himself facing the prejudices of the American court system. Through the years Norris fought his way to a position of prominence among the lawyers of his city, black or white. UNIA assistant counsel general Wilford Smith came to the organization after being rejected as the Reform Republican candidate for a state assembly seat in a Harlem district.[9]

The pattern of having tried to work within established channels for social change—and failing—characterized a number of leading Garveyites. The story of Dr. Leroy Bundy, a dentist and president of the local NAACP in East St. Louis, Illinois, is typical. In 1916, advertisements telling of job possibilities in the area drew large numbers of blacks to East St. Louis. These ads had been placed by the white owners of factories being struck by white workers—mostly poor immigrants from Europe who resented the incoming blacks and refused to allow them into the unions. The blacks were then offered jobs as scabs. As DuBois described the situation, "The Negroes had no intention of undercutting the gains of the white laborers, but they were determined to win a measure of security for their own."[10] Bundy was forced to take a stand, and he denounced the white workers for not allowing blacks into the trade unions. Tensions rose, inflamed by a racist local press, and eventually led to a riot and massacre of local blacks and the burning of their neighborhoods. Bundy was arrested for inciting to riot and escaped a lengthy jail sentence only through shrewd legal maneuvering.[11] Bundy moved to Cleveland, where three years later he heard Garvey and soon after became a leader in the UNIA.

Henry Vinton Plummer, who became UNIA publicity director, had faced a more extended series of disappointments. Son of a chaplain in a black cavalry regiment, young Plummer attended school in Wyoming and graduated from high school in Omaha, Nebraska, as valedictorian—and the only black—in a class of 125. In

1894 he was a Republican candidate for the Nebraska state legislature, but went down to defeat with practically the whole ticket. He was rewarded for his effort, however, with a position as tax clerk, making him the first black employed in the Omaha civil service. Around 1910, he joined the Reform Republicans, and two years later served as assistant sergeant-at-arms during the national convention of the Progressive Party—Teddy Roosevelt's reform GOP. He backed the Progressives because he believed their social reform package, though it offered no special program for blacks, would help blacks because it would benefit all laboring groups. But when he found the "progressive" Republicans recruiting lily-white and openly anti-Negro delegations from the South for their convention, Plummer bolted and became one of the few blacks to support Woodrow Wilson, in the hope that the Democrats' liberal program would provide substantial benefits for his people. Again he was rewarded, this time with a position on the Public Comfort Committee at Wilson's inauguration. And again he was let down as he watched the new administration institute blatant segregation in the civil service. (The Democrats had partitions built around the desks of those black civil servants who could not be readily fired.) With the wartime rise in black militancy and after his own bitter experience, Plummer might have been expected to turn to the left, as did many blacks with reform political views. But he was through with white politics, and took a militant turn toward black nationalism. He would remain an intimate associate of Garvey into the mid-1920s.[12]

William C. Matthews had established a sound reputation as a civil rights lawyer for William Monroe Trotter's National Equal Rights League when he was elected UNIA counsel general at the 1920 convention. Because the NERL was a civil rights organization which followed a nationalist principle and refused to be tied to white money or white political groups, Matthews could readily fit in with the Garveyites. He remained UNIA chief counsel until 1923, when he was fired after an argument with Garvey over legal strategy and quit the movement. During the late twenties he was a GOP national committeeman.[13]

Political interests drew the three Poston brothers to the UNIA— Robert Lincoln, an assistant president general; Ulysses S., minister of industries; and Arthur H., minister of labor. They brought a concern for justice instilled by their father, Ephraim Poston, who had been fired as president of Kentucky State College for exposing the corruption of certain trustees. Just after World War I Robert and Ulysses had published the weekly *Contender* to promote the liberal Democratic organization in Detroit. The newspaper had a short life: few black people were willing to deal with Democrats, even where the party was solidly liberal; for most, Democrats and dixiecrats were synonymous.*

After the *Contender* failed, Robert and Ulysses joined their brother Arthur in the UNIA. They worked with the Association newspapers, and were elected to important positions in the International. The amiable Robert became the unofficial UNIA "toastmaster general," regularly accompanying Garvey on tour, and always introducing him. His untimely death in 1924 was a major loss for the movement. His brothers left the UNIA leadership in the mid-1920s, but remained friendly to the movement. With money from Jim Farley, Ulysses brought out a New York *Contender* to promote the Democrats in 1928. Again the paper had a short life, and Ulysses joined the staff of the *Inter-State Tattler,* a pro-Garvey gossip weekly supporting the Democrats which was founded in 1926 by *Negro World* editor-in-chief T. Thomas Fortune.[15]

Outsiders were fond of criticizing many Garveyites' social lives. *Messenger* columnist Floyd Calvin said that Hubert Harrison worked with Garvey for the fun of it, and Calvin described William Ferris as a typical over-forty bachelor, "easygoing" and "without scruples." To outsiders, *Negro World* columnist John "Grit" Bruce was a comic wit (to Calvin, he was a "terrible writer") but his fellow Garveyite Ernest E. Mair found Bruce could provide penetrating analysis of social issues. Many critics confused sociability with a lack of principles.[16]

The UNIA did, in fact, attract people who felt at home in fraternities and lodges. James Yearwood is today as proud of having become a Grand Exalted Leader in the Negro Elks as he is of having

---

* Robert Poston's connection with the party of Woodrow Wilson seems rather odd. Poston had been a student at Princeton in 1909 when Wilson became president there and promulgated campus rules segregating blacks. Poston led an unsuccessful protest against these rulings and was forced to leave Princeton. Very few blacks enrolled in the university from the time Poston quit until the early 1960s.

been a leading UNIA official. Some UNIA members were active in the Masonic order, though this may have been a cover for secret UNIA activity in Africa. Masonic work is often mentioned in the extensive correspondence between African Garveyites and John Bruce.[17] Garvey himself had joined the Masons at the request of John Bruce; he did not attend Masonic meetings, and as he was at least a nominal Catholic, it appears unlikely that he was dealing with the Masons except as a method for furthering the UNIA.[18]

So much of the Garveyites' work in Africa was clandestine that little is known of how the African laborer related to Garveyism; the role of African notables is similarly clouded as many risked losing their position in society if they were too outspoken in support of the UNIA. These difficulties are exemplified by the story of Prince Kojo Tavalou, who came to France shortly after World War I. The prince established social and political ties with Frenchmen sympathetic to the African cause, becoming something of a darling of the Paris left bank in the process. Tavalou wanted to establish a giant federation of all French-speaking African states, and arranged to be a delegate to the 1924 UNIA convention. He was elected potentate, replacing Gabriel Johnson, who had resigned early that year. But connecting his cause with the UNIA proved quite different from hobnobbing with white bohemian socialists in Paris bistros: Tavalou was driven out of France by the authorities, and when he returned to Dahomey, he was pressured by the authorities into severing his ties with the Garvey movement.[19]

More typical, perhaps, was the experience of the Gold Coast nationalist Casely Hayford, a key Garveyite and a respected barrister in his home country. Hayford apparently never took office in the local UNIA, though he received packages of the *Negro World* smuggled into Ghana, and worked to spread Garvey's ideas in his own West African National Congress. (One UNIA dispatch from New York told of instructions sent to Hayford to help him combat the influence of Dr. DuBois in Ghana.)[20] Hayford was not exactly "underground," since he did attend one UNIA convention in New York, but was a philosophical rather than an activist Garveyite, as was the case with prominent Garveyite sympathizers in most of Africa.[21]

Duse Mohammed Ali cooperated with the UNIA in the early 1920s, reprinting many articles from the *Negro World* in his monthly magazine. With the Garvey weekly banned from much of Africa and the Caribbean, Mohammed's journal was often the only source of favorable news of the Garvey movement. In recognition, Mohammed was voted a position on the staff of the *World* when he attended the 1922 convention.[22] But the Garvey movement never held more than tangential interest for Duse Mohammed, who had become deeply involved in religious work among Muslims in Nigeria. Leaders of this group held a grudging, but real, loyalty to the British;[23] strong identification with the UNIA could have destroyed Mohammed's work by earning the enmity of either prominent Muslims or the British, or both. Mohammed had also developed extensive business connections throughout West Africa, and purchased goods for export to Africa from black businessmen in America—a practice which did not endear him to the Garvey movement.*

Despite their critical attitude toward black businessmen, only a few Garveyites were inspired by socialist ideals, and these were mostly West Indians who remained outside the organized political left in the United States. No socialists served in the international hierarchy, although many worked for the *Negro World,* or served as leaders of divisions, where their concern with immediate issues carried more weight than at the international level.†

Though most UNIA officials were attracted to the movement for political reasons, the cultural side of Garveyism was probably of equal importance in drawing members. Garveyites played an important role in the Harlem Renaissance of the 1920s. We have already noted the work of Hubert Harrison and John "Grit" Bruce, Rabbi Ford's involvement with jazz, and Augusta Savage's sculpture. Beyond this, Garveyites helped usher in the Renaissance. As early as 1915, William Ferris, in his encyclopedic historical and anthropological study *The African Abroad,* prophesied a coming brilliance in culture and politics for African peoples the world over. When Hubert Harrison published *When Africa Awakes* in 1920, he foresaw the coming of the Renaissance even as he contributed to its making.

* A letter from an Ohio Garveyite to John Bruce early in 1923 noted with derision Mohammed's fraternizing with the American bourgeoisie.[24]

†Local UNIA leaders Freeman Martin of St. Louis, Arthur Gray of Oakland, California, Charlotta Bass of Los Angeles, A. Bain Alves and J. Denniston of Jamaica, and J. R. Ralph Casimir of Trinidad involved their divisions in trade union work and other left-wing causes.[25]

Claude McKay, an essayist and foreign correspondent for the *Negro World* in 1919 and 1920, was the first Renaissance figure to produce a volume of his own poetry, *Harlem Shadows* (1922). *Negro World* editor Eric Walrond's book of short stories, *Tropic Death,* was one of the most widely heralded works of the Renaissance and earned him a Guggenheim grant.

A number of Harlem Renaissance figures worked with the UNIA, or expressed themselves favorably toward the Garveyites, without becoming UNIA members. In the introduction to his anthology *The New Negro,* Alain Locke pointed to the major role played by the *Negro World* in bringing the Renaissance to the masses. He also noted that the philosophy of Garveyism, with its emphasis on interchange between Afro-Americans and Africans, helped generate the spirit behind the Renaissance. Among outsiders who contributed to the *Negro World* were the NAACP's William Pickens (before his break with Garvey), historian Carter G. Woodson, essayist Dr. Harold Moody, theologian I. G. Steady, and Joel A. Rogers.

Though it attracted many artists and writers, the UNIA received almost no support from professors and administrators of Negro colleges in the United States. (J. R. L. Diggs, president of Morgan State College in Baltimore, was an exception.) West Indian academicians were far more willing to support the UNIA. The Association itself purchased the Smallwood-Cory Institute in Virginia, renamed it Liberty University, and ran it for three academic years under the presidency of the West Indian educator J. C. St. Clair Drake.[26]

The lack of support from black academicians and intellectuals in the United States may be attributed to the financial and social connections they had developed with their white counterparts. To maintain these ties, they tended to minimize the differences between the races and to claim that Garveyism was alien to American blacks. Intellectuals connected with the NAACP, for example, such as DuBois, James Weldon Johnson and Walter White, became Garvey's bitter enemies; such men used their influence with the white press and white organizations to spread the erroneous impression that all thoughtful blacks opposed Garvey.

Central to the critics' argument was their claim that Garveyites were uninterested in the civil rights struggle. That was not true. Just as the Garveyite journalists and political figures were concerned with civil liberties, so were the black intellectuals who joined the movement. J. R. L. Diggs was deeply involved in civil rights struggles in and around Baltimore; and J. C. St. Clair Drake was a noted civic leader in Pittsburgh prior to his joining the UNIA. Drake had worked with civil rights leader William Monroe Trotter and had accompanied him to Washington for the historic meeting between Trotter and President Woodrow Wilson, which ended in a shouting match. In 1919 Drake was a member of the Committee for the Defense of the Right to Organize, which had been set up to investigate alleged mistreatment of workers in the violent Pittsburgh steel strike of that year.[27]

The manner in which Drake joined the UNIA provides a poignant example of one major motivating force attracting Garveyite leaders and rank and file alike. Drake was a Barbadian who had been living in the United States since shortly after the turn of the century. In the immediate post–World War I period, when other West Indian immigrants were flocking to the Garvey banner, Drake remained aloof. In 1923 he visited his native Barbados, and it was this visit which convinced him to join the UNIA. While in his native land he became concerned over the plight of his countrymen and impressed with their display of devotion for Garvey. He had always considered himself a man of the world and had developed an interest in Africa while attending Virginia Theological Seminary in the years just prior to the World War.* But it took a visit to his homeland to see the connection between all black people, and the relevance of Garvey's internationalism. J. C. St. Clair Drake's son, the noted Africanist St. Clair Drake, co-author of *Black Metropolis,* considers the Garveyism of his father a major motivation for his career as a black scholar.[29]

---

* The seminary ran an African-American trading company in partnership with businessmen in Nyasaland, and had on its teaching staff the noted African John Chilembwe, who was to lead an uprising against the British in Nyasaland during World War I.[28]

7

A
WORLDWIDE
MOVEMENT

THE UNIA RESPONDED to the worldwide oppression of black people by engaging in diverse local and national actions rather than by formulating a uniform international policy. In 1922 these local programs were carried out through more than four hundred chartered divisions, and the Association had applications for four hundred more. The growth, activities, and problems of these local units had important effects on the Association. Each division was free to decide policy matters as long as it followed the procedures prescribed in the UNIA constitution. This freedom led to differing interpretations of Garveyism among divisions in various parts of the world, and even in parts of one country.

In Africa and the Caribbean, the immediate task was to build political movements which could fight for independence. In Canada and the western United States, the UNIA sought to unify the few black citizens through projects co-sponsored with other organizations, as it did in colonies where the UNIA itself was suppressed. In contrast, the UNIA took a decidedly separatist posture in the violently racist American South, neither receiving nor asking cooperation from other blacks or from whites. In Central America the Association worked mainly to improve conditions for immigrant farm laborers and to promote international ties among black people, while Garveyites in major U.S. industrial centers had the primary responsibility for raising money and working toward the long-range goal of economic self-sufficiency for the race.

Setting the pace for hundreds of smaller divisions within the United States were the Garveyite strongholds in New York, Philadelphia, Pittsburgh, Cleveland, Cincinnati, Detroit, and Chicago. These seven cities accounted for one hundred thousand UNIA members; each division was large enough to purchase its own Liberty Hall and engage in sizable business enterprises. The many fund drives for international causes relied heavily on these seven divisions. Large groups also developed in Baltimore, New Orleans, Los Angeles, and Washington, D.C., but they were never as successful. Significantly, there were divisions of one size or another in virtually every city in the northern United States; for instance, there were at least half a dozen divisions in Kansas alone.[1]

The seven larger divisions tried to present all Garveyites with working examples of economic self-sufficiency. Though none could provide employment for all its members, each had begun to move in this direction. As early as the summer of 1920, the Chicago division had established a moving firm, a laundry, and a hat factory. Pittsburgh had moving vans and a short-lived publishing company. Many Association-run businesses were opened in Cleveland and Cincinnati, but state law required them to incorporate as Ohio concerns rather than as part of the Negro Factories Corporation, which ran most Garveyite businesses elsewhere.[2] New York City was the home office for Universal Restaurants and Universal Chain Store groceries, which had branches in Philadelphia, Newark, and other cities. Another New York–based affiliate produced Garveyite items sold throughout the world, including Black Cross rosettes; red, black and green UNIA flags; a series of UNIA lapel buttons; framed photographs of UNIA officials, parades and conventions; and UNIA cigars with a picture of Marcus Garvey on the band. The New York division also owned a millinery, a chain of laundries, and a record company which produced a speech by Garvey and recordings of the UNIA orchestra and musical personalities in the Association.[3]

Only UNIA members could buy stock in Association businesses, and no one member could own more than two hundred shares. The Black Star Line had been formed under a standard corporation charter, but the Negro Factories Corporation was both more amorphous and more socialistic. The factories were, in effect, cooperatively owned, staffed by UNIA members, and directly responsible to the minister of industries, who was in turn accountable to the international conventions and the supreme executive council. While black socialists talked of building socialism, Garveyites created a working model. Insofar as the UNIA was a "nation," it was a nation with a collectivist economy.

The concept of nationhood lay behind many practices of big city divisions. All employees belonged to the UNIA civil service; divisions even had civil service commissions to examine job applicants. Some positions carried monetary rewards; others entailed service in the branch police force, as youth group leaders, or in some other service function. The Liberty Halls provided virtually all the members' social needs, from weddings to funerals—the latter prepaid under the Association's death benefit plan. There was also an Association court system. Members with a poor work record, or given to wife-beating, alcoholism or similar offenses, appeared before an Association judge, were provided with a defense lawyer, and were tried before a jury of the division members. Regular meetings in the larger divisions usually drew five to ten thousand members. A full-page photograph in the *Negro World* for December 17, 1921, showed Garveyites completely filling a double-tiered, chandeliered Liberty Hall for a "Sunday Meeting of Cincinnati Ohio UNIA." If such a photograph inspired a follower in a small town to move to the big city, he would probably write the secretary general's bureau of passports to obtain a UNIA passport, another of the trappings of nationhood adopted by Garveyites.[4]

* * *

In the American South, Garveyites led a more tenuous existence. Members had less money than their brothers in the North. Besides, starting a business or building a Liberty Hall would have proved next to impossible in many areas, whatever their financial resources. The UNIA nevertheless had strong appeal for blacks in the South, as the existence of roughly one hundred divisions in the thirteen southern and border states clearly shows. There were, however, many gaps. The *Negro World* "News of Divisions" pages reveal branches in Mobile, Alabama, and suburban Prichard, but none in Birmingham, Montgomery, or any other town in the state. Mississippi, on the other hand, appears often, with reports from Natchez, Biloxi, Jackson, Vicksburg, and sometimes from smaller towns— Sumner, Malvanes, Mound Bayou, Yancey, and Fayettesville. Active divisions sent news from Nashville, Chattanooga, and Knoxville, but none came from Memphis or elsewhere in heavily black areas of western Tennessee. Divisions reported from many large and small towns in Florida, but in all of Georgia only Atlanta and Savannah showed UNIA branches. Apparently the Association existed in deepest Dixie only where it was lucky enough to escape the notice of whites, or where it could arrange a détente by assuring whites that Garveyites opposed social integration and miscenegation.

The southern divisions also faced serious opposition from the local black bourgeoisie. The National Negro Business League and the fraternities, sororities, and associations of Negro colleges and finishing schools were the dominant organizations of middle-class blacks in the South. The leading lights in Negro Greek-letter societies and other middle-class social clubs epitomized the shallow, escapist way of life depicted by E. Franklin Frazier in *Black Bourgeoisie.* The Negro press in the South was so firmly tied to these groups that some papers, such as the Columbia, South Carolina, *Southern Indicator,* reported their activities exclusively, apparently fearing to mention the NAACP, much less the UNIA. The more daring Atlanta *Independent* and Savannah *Tribune* printed news of the NAACP but ignored Garveyites—except for the most damning slanders: the *Tribune* published a fantastic account linking Garvey with the mailing of a human hand to A. Philip Randolph.[5]

With the ever-present threat of lynching on the one hand, and a black "leadership" which had abdicated its responsibilities on the other, the UNIA worked in two ways. Garveyites avoided the lynch mob by emphasizing their distaste for race mixing, and they sought members from among the black masses who were disenchanted with the aloof race leaders. A statement from the New Orleans division combined these two approaches: "We like your Jim Crow laws in that they defend the purity of races. . . . We are not members of the Negro four hundred of New Orleans, which is composed of that class who are spending their time imitating the rich whites, with card parties, eating parties, studying Spanish . . . to be able to pass for anything but a Negro. . . . We are not ashamed of the race to which we belong."[6] One Florida UNIA official claimed, "The Klan has helped us a great deal by driving the Negro to thoughts of Africa as their only hope." Garvey himself showed a sensitivity to the special qualities of the South and tended to adopt a more conservative line there. In 1922 Garvey told a North Carolina crowd that Southern whites should be thanked for having "lynched race pride into the Negro." On another occasion, New Orleans police held Garvey at the door to the hall to prevent him from speaking. Garvey eventually convinced them that his advocacy of race awareness and race pride was not antagonistic to Southern white ways, and he was allowed to give his speech—with police as front-row guests.[7] In the American South, separatism became equated with a reluctance to fight racism. Although the UNIA could not have existed in the South without some concessions to whites, the southern Garveyites' strong separatist position aided those critics who were trying to discredit the whole movement.

In the Far West, powerful UNIA divisions developed in Los Angeles, Oakland and Seattle, with smaller branches in Portland, San Francisco, throughout California's San Joaquin Valley, and in Watts, San Bernadino and San Diego. Divisions in the Far West remained strong into the late twenties when the movement elsewhere was in decline. The movement's international leadership benefited from the services of many West Coast blacks in important positions,* and during the early twenties the Los Angeles UNIA was one of the biggest money-raisers in the Association.

On the West Coast, the schism between Garveyites and conservative middle-class blacks was slow to develop. This was still "the Wild West," where the conventional wisdom was suspect and new ideas were the norm rather than the exception. Moreover, the small size of black communities helped bring together individuals of all classes—building a church or club, for example, required cooperation between well-to-do and poor blacks. In Los Angeles and Oakland, newspapers run by local NAACP officials willingly carried UNIA advertisements and published news items favorable to the Association.[8] This rarely happened in the East and was unknown in the Deep South. In Los Angeles, the UNIA and NAACP used the same church for meetings, and early in 1921 the two associations joined to host Louis B. Anderson, a black alderman from Chicago, where the UNIA and NAACP were already bitter enemies.[9] In Los Angeles, the Urban League also cooperated with the UNIA, though the League's national president ardently opposed the Garveyites. In fact, Los Angeles UNIA co-president Noah Thompson was also

---

* Minister of Legions E. L. Gaines from Pasadena, Assistant President General J. D. Gordon from Los Angeles, and Minister of Industries John W. Fowler from the Oakland Division. James A. Hassell and Arthur S. Gray from Seattle and Oakland would play important roles in the International during the late 1920s.

president—and founder—of the Urban League chapter in that city. Garveyites on the West Coast also avoided much of the tension which developed between black socialists and the UNIA elsewhere. The co-president of the Los Angeles division in its first years, Mrs. Charlotta Bass, was a close friend of A. Philip Randolph and Chandler Owen. In California, she was considered the "black woman second in stature only to Mrs. Garvey."[10] As co-editor of the *California Eagle,* widely circulated on the West Coast, she attempted to keep the divisive struggles of the East out of the area. When a national NAACP official denounced the UNIA early in 1921, Mrs. Bass called this "holier-than-thou creature" to task for his attempt to spread disunity at a time when "the leaders of the two great organizations of the NAACP and the UNIA have very diplomatically and adroitly allowed such differences of opinion which they have entertained to lay dormant for the good of all concerned." And as the disunity became more pronounced later that year, Mrs. Bass wrote, "It is our plea that the Negroes of the West . . . will not suffer themselves to become victims of the dread disease of prejudice one against the other."[11]

Late in 1920, Los Angeles presidents Thompson and Bass involved their division in the movement demanding parole for the ailing imprisoned Socialist leader Eugene Debs. Mrs. Bass ran a series of editorials urging Garveyites to send telegrams demanding Debs's release. Thompson printed handbills calling for support of Debs and instructed UNIA members to distribute them throughout the black community.[12] Such moves would have been impossible in the "sophisticated" centers of the East. Though the ideological schism eventually did infect the black community in the Far West, the free-thinking spirit proved hard to subdue: in 1931, despite Association and party orthodoxy, Arthur Gray, head of the California UNIA, endorsed Communist congressional candidates as fellow militants. The Communist Party in the East rejected his endorsement because he was unwilling to couple it with a rejection of Garvey, and fellow Garveyites angrily derided Gray for siding with the white man.[13]

The vibrancy of Garveyism in California may have been attributable in part to the fact that most black ghettoes in the state were adjacent to Mexican-American ghettoes. Mexican-American communities in the early 1920s exhibited strong undercurrents of nationalist pride stemming from the Mexican revolution. Large Japanese and Chinese communities may also have helped make ethnic nationalism respectable. For whatever reasons, Garveyism in the Far West made the most of the few black residents—in Honolulu, for example, a visiting sailor carrying copies of the *Negro World* started a UNIA division which even received contributions from a number of Japanese and Chinese.[14]

* * *

In Latin America and the Caribbean, Garveyism proved strongest in Jamaica, Panama, Cuba, Costa Rica, and British Honduras. The movement was slightly less powerful in Guatemala, Honduras, Mexico, and Colombia. It is difficult to evaluate its following in the Lesser Antilles, Haiti, Santo Domingo, and in Trinidad and British Guiana, where the UNIA faced severe government restriction.[15] The November 1921 *Crusader* reported that the Garveyites' reluctance to use underground tactics had cost them dearly in Santo Domingo, "where they have been suppressed and their leaders arrested by U.S. Marines."* [16]

The strongest UNIA outside the United States was in Jamaica, which had half a dozen divisions and numerous sub-divisions by 1919. Garveyites built support among the island's laboring masses through their involvement in the trade union struggle and by campaigning for broader political suffrage and an end to appointive seats in the colonial legislature (a body in which the British chose a majority of members). Before leaving for the United States, Garvey had made several friends within the ruling circles, including influential members of the religious community, educators, and an ex-mayor of Kingston.[17] These individuals gave the UNIA an air of respectability, which waned as the Garveyites picked up a mass following through militant championing of social betterment—but never waned enough for the British to crush the movement openly.

When Garvey returned to Jamaica in March 1921, however, the British were sufficiently apprehensive to station two battleships in

---

* Ostensibly, the marines were in Santo Domingo—and Haiti, Nicaragua, and other Caribbean countries—to protect American lives and prevent economic chaos. Actually, they provided military control for puppet governments which had agreed to protect huge American agricultural combines like the United Fruit Company.

Kingston Harbor.[18] They had reason: Garvey could have become a "clear and present danger" to colonial tranquility. A high percentage of Jamaicans were out of work, and those with jobs worked under abominable conditions. In addition, an especially volatile election campaign was taking place. Despite the overwhelming support of the people in his district, A. Bain Alves, leader of the Jamaican Federation of Labor and a prominent Garveyite, had no chance of winning a seat in the colonial legislature because only one Jamaican in five was eligible to vote.[19]

Garvey was neither more nor less radical than usual in his speeches, but in the Jamaican context his words directly threatened established authority. In an address delivered at the Ward Theatre in Kingston (the island's largest auditorium), he noted: "The world is reorganizing itself politically, and men and races and nations everywhere are clamoring for and demanding their rights. . . . What was the matter with Jamaica? The whole world was organizing itself. I have been made to understand that Jamaica is made up of cowards. Fellows are afraid to talk because they are afraid to die! Were you afraid to die in France and Flanders? Talk wherever you are! Talk for your constitutional rights! I understand there is a trembling fear in Jamaica. Trembling for what? God Almighty created you as men; as men you live, as men you shall die. . . . Are you afraid of men? I would like to see a man who dared make me afraid. You men of Jamaica, you want backbone! Take out the weak bones you have and put in backbone. Don't let anybody cow you. You have your constitutional rights. Demand them! Englishmen in England demand their constitutional rights; Irishmen in Ireland demand their constitutional rights; throughout the whole Empire men speak up for their rights! You lazy good-for-nothing Jamaicans, wake up!" Garvey concluded by claiming that he was not in Jamaica to preach disloyalty to any government.[20] During this 1921 tour, Garvey addressed crowds in the Ward Theatre many times, and also spoke at Montego Bay, St. Ann's Bay, Port Antonio (in a clearing on a nearby sugar plantation), and Spanish Town.

The program of the Jamaican UNIA sheds light on the regional problems facing Garveyism. In the United States, critics labeled the UNIA "conservative" because it would not work with liberals and trade unionists. But Garveyites adopted this policy because blacks were in a minority. Where blacks formed the majority, as in Jamaica and Trinidad, class struggle was considered a very important part of the fight, and Garvey encouraged building trade unions and economic cooperatives, as well as fighting for more adequate political representation.[21]

In 1929 Garvey produced a program for Jamaica calling for minimum wages, guaranteed employment, social security, workmen's compensation, and expropriation of private lands for public use without remuneration.[22] This was certainly a progressive program, not a conservative one.

 In Jamaica, unions were likely to be run by blacks for a black membership. In the United States those who urged blacks to join labor unions were asking them to beg their way into minority status within organizations run by bigots for memberships composed largely of bigots—the handful of "enlightened" or "revolutionary Marxist" unions notwithstanding. In Jamaica the fight for broader participation in government had national liberation as its goal, but such a goal was difficult to argue in the United States, where the overall political majority was sure to be white. In the United States black voters were pressed to favor every one of the minuscule number of black candidates; but where nearly all candidates were black, as in Jamaica, voters could evaluate the programs and opinions of black office-seekers with some objectivity.

While Jamaican Garveyites could legitimately involve themselves in traditional methods of political and social struggle, they faced the harsh handicap of British imperial rule. They might support trade unionism without hesitation, but virtually all workers on the island labored under plantation conditions with no more freedom to organize than feudal serfs. Still, the UNIA in Jamaica could work openly, unlike other divisions in colonial areas.

The UNIA in Trinidad, for example, had been particularly militant—and was repressed with extreme harshness. At the war's end, Trinidad was seething with discontent: foreign oil companies were just beginning to exploit the island and, with the collusion of the colonial government, small landholders were pressured to sell their property to oil companies. Those who refused watched drilling of their oil begin on adjacent property—and received no remuneration. Discontent among laborers erupted in a longshoremen's strike late in 1919, which grew violent when strike leaders were improperly arrested and detained. Garveyites took a leading role in the strike, and the government responded by prohibiting the importation or sale of the *Negro World* in Trinidad and Tobago, and by barring known UNIA members from employment.[23] Many of those driven from Trinidad later became leaders in the UNIA in the United States. Though delegations of high UNIA officials were periodically sent to the West Indies, none entered Trinidad until Garvey himself went there in 1928, when he was reportedly well received by the populace.

Garveyism flourished in some of the nominally independent countries of the Caribbean, but in a peculiar fashion. In Cuba, Haiti, and Mexico, the UNIA membership consisted largely of immigrant laborers from the British West Indies; they built some of the stronger Garveyite divisions. A number of branches remained active in Panama, Costa Rica and Cuba into the 1930s. In these areas, the UNIA was a protective association, advising newcomers of their rights and helping them avoid exploitation. In Cuba, for instance, the UNIA warned incoming Jamaicans to shun the "men-catchers," who would drag Jamaican immigrants into hotels for "free" drinks and lodging, then pack them away the next day to work off the bill at a labor camp.[24] These black immigrants were sorely in need of help: as immigrants, they had few rights, and the local British consul—supposedly their protector—usually acted as an overseer for the labor contractors.

Not surprisingly, the Back-to-Africa plan had great appeal in these areas, and in 1921 Garvey promised his Costa Rican followers that "at least one of the largest ships" of the Black Star Line would soon come for them. He also told Panamanians "to prepare for the pilgrimage to Africa." [25] There is no record of Garvey having made similar direct promises in the United States. This seems fitting: if any group deserved priority on the return to Africa, it would be immigrant laborers in places like Costa Rica and Panama who had almost no hope for material or political betterment. Blacks in the United States were better off materially, and—though conditions were bad in Jamaica, Trinidad and Barbados—black citizens could at least look forward to eventual control of their own countries.

While the Back-to-Africa plan had great appeal, it was not the UNIA's only attraction in the Caribbean. The organization continued to draw allegiance long after the demise of the Black Star Line. Nor could the UNIA's talents at political agitation have had much appeal, as this was forcibly prohibited in most places where immigrants lived. In Haiti, for example, the three most prominent Garveyites—Eli Garcia, Napoleon Francis and Theodore Stephens—were driven into exile, and in Santo Domingo UNIA leaders were arrested and membership lists confiscated.[26] Beyond this, few people, immigrant or otherwise, had political rights in the banana republics of Central America. Yet despite all political restrictions, the UNIA flourished among the most oppressed group in the Caribbean, the migrant laborers. If any single factor held them to Garveyism, it must have been the sense of identity with a world-wide movement. Thus Garvey, speaking to rural sugar plantation workers in Jamaica, drew prolonged applause when he described the UNIA as "a gigantic world-wide movement of Negroes endeavoring to draw into one mighty whole the four hundred million Negroes scattered all over the world, to link up the Negroes of the West Indies, South and Central America, and Negroes everywhere for the purpose of establishing a Government to be owned, controlled and dominated by Negroes."[27]

The UNIA's internationalism was probably its most appealing quality in British Honduras as well. Editorials written there and reprinted in the *Negro World* show that the UNIA in British Honduras built its following on cultural issues and the promotion of solidarity between black people in the Americas and Africa.[28] In that multi-racial country—with Indians, blacks, a scattering of whites and Chinese, and many people with mixed heritage—the Association earned a respectability unmatched in any other colonized country during the 1920s, and at least two divisions remained active into the 1930s. Elsewhere in the Caribbean, the press covered the Garvey movement only reluctantly, but the weekly Belize *Independent* had a regular columnist who called himself "The Garvey Eye." British Honduras was the only colony in which the UNIA received the government designation "friendly society," a name given to acceptable fraternal and social betterment organizations.[29] The reasons for this tolerance are not clear. Perhaps the 1919 Belize insurrection taught the British that trying to suppress the UNIA was too costly, perhaps the multi-racial population made the Garveyites less of a threat: in a highly mixed society, a UNIA fight for a black nation would be unsuccessful.

Clearly, a successful future for the UNIA's international program depended on success in Africa, where Garveyites hoped to establish their "central nation" from which to lead further battles for the liberation of the race.

In 1920, all of Africa except Ethiopia and Liberia was in the hands of European imperialists. In the French colonies, the authorities believed the UNIA had been involved in a number of violent demonstrations by black soldiers in 1919 and 1920. Consequently they declared the Association illegal—in some colonies the punishment for having copies of the *Negro World* was five years at hard labor; in Dahomey it was life imprisonment. Yet Garveyite groups were active in Senegal, Dahomey, French Togo, and the Cameroons. In Dakar, Senegal, a UNIA division organized late in 1920 (by a delegate from the United States using the name of John Kamara) was apparently destroyed the following year when colonial police raided its offices, confiscated its records and deported four recruiters from neighboring Sierra Leone.[30]

The UNIA was involved in the struggles to free Africa through leaders who worked primarily within other organizations. A leader of independence struggles in French Equatorial Africa, Felix Eboué, was Garvey's close associate for many years, and Caribbean UNIA groups served as his hosts on a tour there just before World War II.*[31] In the early 1920s Garvey was in touch with labor leaders in Kenya and with Abd-el-Krim, the rebel leader in Spanish Morocco.[32] Casely Hayford, the Ghanaian barrister and UNIA delegate, tried to bridge the gap between the Garveyites and DuBois's Pan-African Congress movement, in which he was also involved. (As early as 1918, Hayford had organized a West African National Congress which drew together professional and middle-class elements in British West Africa.)[33] Prince Kojo Tavalou of French West Africa became the leading African in the UNIA after he was elected potentate in 1924, and the Garveyites were formally or informally connected with the West African Student Union and the Paris-based Comité de Défense de la Race Nègre.[34] In British West Africa there was a sizable UNIA contingent in Sierra Leone, with other divisions

---

* Born in the French West Indies, Eboué had been sent to central Africa in the 1920s as a colonial official. It was French policy to declare all colonial subjects citizens of France, and to select a few natives for responsible positions in the lower ranks of colonial administration. This lent an appearance of substance to the largely mythical equality of overseas and continental French citizenship.

in Gambia, the Gold Coast and Nigeria. Although the British authorities suppressed the *Negro World,* the UNIA received favorable
coverage in the Gold Coast and Nigeria through the Gold Coast
Times, the Gold Coast *Leader* and the Lagos *Weekly Record.*[35] In
the Union of South Africa there were UNIA divisions in Cape Town,
Natal, and Johannesburg, and UNIA members worked within the
African National Congress of South Africa, the most representative
black organization in that country.[36] An active UNIA in London
enabled Africans visiting England to learn of the Association and its
goals.

The work of Garveyites in colonial Africa was hampered not only
by government repression but also because the movement did not
have wide enough appeal. The UNIA was simply too radical for
most middle-class Africans. There were exceptions—Hayford,
Tavalou, George O. Marke, and W. A. Burnham of Sierra Leone, and
Emmanuel Johnson of South Africa[37]—but professionals, civil servants and tribal chiefs generally avoided a movement which talked
loosely of revolution. DuBois's Pan-African Congress movement
fared better with these elements by accenting reform and cooperation with progressive groups in Europe and white America. The
UNIA's philosophy appealed largely to the laboring classes, but
there were few trade unions or other social betterment organizations, and the UNIA was rarely able to work openly. Again, some
exceptions appeared—Bishop McGuire's African Orthodox Church
was important in spreading the idea of independent African
churches as an instrument of African liberation, and the UNIA was
active in the Nigerian Federation of Labor—but the UNIA's immediate effect upon the African masses was minimal.[38] The Garveyites' primary contribution to colonial Africa was the articulation of
their long-range internationalist and Pan-African goals—goals which
became imbedded in the minds of many younger Africans who
would lead mass-based independence movements after World War II.

* * *

In its search for an immediate base in a free African nation, the
UNIA considered Liberia, Ethiopia, or one of the former German
colonies then a trust of the League of Nations, preferably Tanganyika. The UNIA repeatedly petitioned the League of Nations to

grant it custodial status over one of these territories, but without success.

Ethiopia was never considered seriously. The Garveyites doubted that colonial powers would allow emigrants free passage into land-locked Abyssinia, though they did set up a division there. The country was represented at the 1922 UNIA convention, and an Ethiopian nobleman came to address a meeting the next year. Garveyites also supported Ethiopian efforts to obtain a land corridor through French Somaliland, but the country was simply too distant.

Thus Liberia became the best hope for a UNIA base in Africa. At the time of the great convention in 1920, the country was suffering through its worst period since the difficult years following 1817, when Liberia was created by the American Colonization Society as a place for repatriation of black Americans. The descendants of the ten thousand original colonizers had become completely estranged from the indigenous Susu and Ghebo Liberians, who worked as virtual slaves on plantations resembling those from which most of the colonizers had come. The colonizers had even built white-columned mansions after the model favored by their former owners, and cultivated a dialect startlingly similar to that of southern whites. As the imperialist nations of Europe overran Africa in the late nineteenth century, Liberia lost much of its backlands to the French and English. By the end of World War I, the government was nearly bankrupt, with large loans from European and American banking houses coming due.

Liberia was nominally a democracy, but leadership had been handed down for generations from father to son among a few families, and political life was stagnant. But between 1910 and 1920, a healthy factionalism had developed within these leading families, especially after the emergence of a few new political spokesmen for native Liberian peoples. The UNIA gained the favor of this sizable opposition (generally known as the "southern group" despite the presence of northerners in its ranks). One leader of this group, Gabriel Johnson, the mayor of Monrovia (who had first become interested in black liberation through the work of Duse Moham-med) [39] was among those who answered the UNIA call for delegates to the 1920 convention, where he was chosen supreme potentate.

An impressive UNIA was built in Liberia under the little-known Milton J. Marshall. The Liberian organization included many important opponents of the ruling party: among them were Arthur Barclay and D. E. Howard—both former Liberian presidents, Supreme Court Chief Justice James J. Dossen, and Chaplain of the Legislature R. Van Richards, all from the Americo-Liberian group; and H. Too Wesley and D. C. Caranda, two of the more notable Liberians of native African extraction. Justice Dossen had incurred the wrath of conservative Liberians for two court decisions striking down peonage laws; Van Richards was also active in the fight against peonage. Wesley was well regarded in the country for his efforts to better the conditions of his Ghebo people and to improve understanding between them and the colonizers.[40] The stronghold of Garveyism was in the Ghebo country of the south coast, Maryland County.

The first UNIA International expedition to Liberia set out from New York in 1920. Due to problems with steamship accommodations, only one of three men chosen could make the trip—Eli Garcia, auditor general of the UNIA. In his report Garcia waxed optimistic about the potential for commercial and agricultural development in Liberia: "The possibilities along those lines are so broad that they can hardly be enumerated." His views of Liberian society, however, were anything but encouraging: "Liberia, although a very rich country in natural resources, is the poorest place on the face of the earth and actually the people are facing starvation."

Garcia saw "class distinctions" as a "great hindrance to the development of Liberia" and called the Americo-Liberians "although the educated [class], the most despicable element in Liberia." He said the Americo-Liberians cherished the leisure afforded by their position and were "absolutely hostile to immigration by American or West Indian Negroes, that is, if said Negroes show any tendency to take part in the political life of the Republic." The Garcia report warned any future UNIA delegations that the power-hungry rulers would not tolerate any involvement in Liberian politics. It cautioned Garveyites that their interest in uplifting the living standards of African natives "must be kept quiet for a while." To illustrate the manner in which every possible class distinction was coveted, Garcia related this incident: "While in Monrovia I went to a store and bought seven yards of khaki to have two pairs of trousers made. The merchant wrapped the khaki and gave it to me. As I was stepping out of the store my companion (an Americo-Liberian) said to me: 'Why, I don't suppose you are going to carry this bundle yourself?'

'Why not?' said I, 'It is a very small parcel.' He answered that it was not the custom in Liberia for any gentleman to carry parcels, therefore the usefulness of having slaves." [41]

Fortunately for the UNIA, not all Americo-Liberians were so rigid, for it was with this class that the Garvey movement would have to deal. The Garcia report, dated August 1920, was held in confidence by the Association leadership. Delegates to the convention that year heard only Mayor Johnson's glowing reports of the wealth awaiting development and a heartening communiqué from Edwin Barclay, the Liberian secretary of state, promising that his government would "afford the Association every facility legally possible in effectuating in Liberia its industrial, agricultural and business projects." [42]

By adroitly emphasizing economic aid while promising not to interfere with internal politics, the UNIA managed to maintain the Liberian government's good will from 1920 until 1924. But the friendship was always a fragile one. Tensions developed soon after Gabriel Johnson's return from the 1920 convention. At a state banquet in his honor, Johnson appeared in the stately robes of the supreme potentate of the UNIA, titular head of *all* the black people in the world. Much impressed, Mr. Cassell, head of the College of Liberia, proposed a toast to the foremost Negro in the world. C. B. D. King, the Liberian president, interpreted this as a slur on the stature of his own office, and lifting his glass he responded, "I drink to the health of the Mayor of Monrovia." Relations between Johnson and King were cold from that time forward. [43]

Early in 1921 a second mission reached Liberia, including a technical team led by the American-trained agricultural expert Cyril Henry. With Henry came deputy potentate George Marke and Cyril Crichlow, a native of Trinidad chosen to be resident secretary of the UNIA legation to Liberia—in effect, the first ambassador of the world-wide UNIA state. On March 22, 1921, Gabriel Johnson, Marke and Crichlow conferred with acting president Edwin Barclay and the Liberian cabinet about sites for a future UNIA colony. Barclay told UNIA delegates his government would "be glad to have your Association occupy . . . certain settlements already laid out," but cautioned against too much publicity for the project. He noted that "the British and French have enquired from our representatives in America about it and have asked definite questions on the attitude of the Liberian Government towards the Universal Negro Improvement Association." The debt-ridden Liberian government was in a delicate position vis-à-vis the European powers, and Barclay suggested that even the negotiations be kept quiet: "It is not always advisable nor politic to openly expose our secret thoughts. . . . We don't tell them what we think; we only tell them what we like them to hear—what, in fact, they like to hear. . . . The Government has felt that the soft pedal should be placed on this side."[44] Barclay's skill in subterfuge would later be turned to undermine the UNIA in Liberia.

Cyril Henry and his team had been instructed to "start work immediately—putting up new buildings and starting farms, etc.," but within two months they stopped work due to lack of funds. The delegation received sporadic payments from the UNIA in America during the summer, but its accomplishments were so minimal that Henry wrote to New York in July lamenting, "I frankly could not advise our people coming out here under present conditions."[45]

Members of the opposition in the Liberian government doubtless saw the UNIA as an agent of modernization and, probably, as a way to change the caste system. At the same time, they may have intended to use the new immigrants as a buffer between the Americo-Liberians and the natives, thus perpetuating their division. The southern group was, after all, the loyal opposition in an aristocratic and reactionary government. Yet their work as reformers is well documented. Long after the UNIA collapsed in Liberia, Dongba Caranda, Van Richards, and D. E. Howard continued to fight government attempts to bring back "forced labor slavery." Chief Justice Dossen, in addition to his court decisions against peonage, also helped modernize the Liberian legal system through his voluminous codifications of national law. Dossen had also served as president of Liberia College, where he reportedly "made many contributions to the advancement" of the institution.[46] Whatever their intentions, the southern group would present a clear danger to the leadership in Monrovia if they were allowed to sponsor a sizable UNIA migration. Settlers brought in by the opposition could not be expected to remain neutral in national politics.

Nevertheless, an area of some five hundred square miles on the banks of the Cavalla River along Liberia's southern border was selected as the site of the first Garveyite immigrant settlement. In

February 1924, representatives of the local UNIA and three delegates of the third international mission to Liberia (Robert L. Poston, Henrietta Vinton Davis, and attorney Milton Van Lowe) agreed on regulations governing the immigration. The first contingent of five hundred settlers was to arrive late that year. The regulations stipulated that "every emigrant before leaving America shall subscribe to an oath that they will respect the established authority of the Liberian government ... that all emigrants shall possess at least $1,500 cash to each family and every single person not connected with a family $500 ... that preference also be given to agriculturists and men of industry." Finally, the pioneers were to be young and "of strong physique and a fixed determination to become citizens of Liberia and remain in Liberia." The Liberians were assured that technical experts would precede the immigrants to survey the land, begin building shelters, and find facilities for medical personnel who would come to serve both settlers and native Liberians.[47] When the three delegates sailed back to New York, the only unfinished business was the official signing of papers on both sides. Then the Back-to-Africa plan would become a reality.

* * *

In the first of a series of tragedies which befell the entire Garvey movement, Robert Lincoln Poston, assistant president general and one of Garvey's closest advisors, died of pneumonia aboard ship on the return from Liberia. Word of his death reached New York the evening of March 17. When the news was read to a massive meeting at Liberty Hall, then discussing the prospects of emigration, there was much weeping over the loss of the "toastmaster general."[48]

Poston's death was followed soon after by two mysterious deaths in Liberia. Justice Dossen, a diabetic, died from lack of vital medicine.[49] It was rumored that enemies of the Association had purposely misplaced the drugs. These rumors gathered force when Milton J. Marshall, head of the Liberian UNIA, was shot to death by an unknown assailant.[50] Even earlier—a month before the Poston mission arrived—Gabriel Johnson had resigned both as potentate and as mayor of Monrovia to accept President King's offer of an ambassadorship to the Spanish colony of Fernando Po. In a lengthy resignation, mailed from Fernando Po on May 7, 1924, Johnson listed a series of disappointments over promised funds for Liberian development which were never received. He concluded, "Up to the day of my resignation having served the Association faithfully for twenty-six-and-a-half months, I had only received one year's salary . . . despite all the risks I took of my life, traveling on alien ships and crossing the ocean every year to meet the conventions and trying to stimulate the divisions with my presence, advice and counsels." [51] Garveyites wondered why Johnson had resigned just when his labor was about to bear fruit, and many assumed he had been pressured to leave the UNIA and his country.

The biggest obstacle to the establishment of a base in Africa proved to be the Liberian government itself. By 1924, foreign creditors were demanding their money, control of the state, or both. Of course, drastic cuts in the luxurious style of government officials, coupled with stringent efforts to break down the caste system and raise productivity, would have provided an answer—and an influx of productive, skilled immigrants would also have helped. Instead, President King sold his country to the highest bidder: the Firestone Rubber Company of Akron, Ohio (and thus continued an infamous family tradition: his father had fought as a mercenary for the British in their wars against the Ashanti, Zulu, and Basuto). King had misled Garvey completely—consenting to negotiate with the Poston mission, even helping select the Liberian negotiators, at approximately the same time he was being approached by Firestone. Garveyites would later insist that Firestone had first learned of the Liberian rubber potential through reports published by the UNIA! [52]

In June of 1924, the UNIA—still unaware of King's agreement with Firestone—sent its team of experts to prepare for the first five hundred colonists. When the technicians arrived in Monrovia harbor they were not permitted to land, and their leader, the Jamaican educator James O'Meally, was forced to sail for Nigeria rather than return to America. Two months later, the contract between Fire-Stone Rubber and the Liberian government was made public. Ironically, the first land developed by Firestone comprised almost the exact acreage slated for UNIA settlement. Word of the deal came in the midst of the fourth international UNIA convention in New York. An enraged delegate from Chicago, Dr. J. J. Peters, shouted from the Liberty Hall podium: "The day is not far distant when every damn white man is going to pay for every oppression he is giving the Negro." The delegates were ready for war, and Garvey tried to calm them by pointing out that rash action could easily ruin the movement.[53] It was not hard to sympathize with the Garveyites. The white editor of the New York *Evening Bulletin* commented, "The gang now controlling Liberia oppose Garvey's entrance and they want no one in his organization, fearing, of course, that their own game will be spiked. Here are a few facts ... to consider. Liberia grants Harvey Firestone a concession, which gives him absolute control of 1,000,000 acres of land where crude rubber is procurable. This land is the most valuable rubber-growing territory available in the world; the British Empire controls practically all the rest. . . . When Garvey says there is something rotten in the state of Liberia you should not dismiss his allegations. Perhaps he knows what he is talking about. He thinks Liberia's rubber supply should belong to his race, not to Firestone. Is there anything dangerous or menacing in that belief?" [54]

The Liberian adventure had absorbed the Garvey movement's major energies in Africa, and their failure there was a crushing defeat. The UNIA's only other prospect for a base in Africa—one of the former German territories—also seemed hopeless by this time. The UNIA had shown an interest in these colonies as early as 1918, and asked the Versailles Peace Conference in 1919 to consider the Association as a possible trustee for former German East Africa. The Garveyites would gladly have accepted even less than outright trusteeship: when the League gave Tanganyika to Great Britain, the UNIA still offered to send skilled workers to speed the modernization required under the mandate. The UNIA preferred Tanganyika to the other trust territories because it held ample fertile but uncultivated land, and was the largest and most temperate of the territories, with less tropical disease than the other trust areas—the Cameroons, Togo, and South West Africa.[55]

In 1922 the UNIA petitioned the League of Nations directly on this question. Its delegation to Geneva, sent as representatives of the Negroes of the world, included William Sherrill from the United States, George O. Marke from Africa, James O'Meally of Jamaica, and, as translator, the Haitian Jean Joseph Adam. The delegation declared its willingness to accept any or all of the former German territories in whatever fashion the League decided. It also brought a

UNIA document detailing the many grievances of the world's black people, and requesting redress through the League. The Garveyites were not allowed to present their petitions directly, but the Persian delegate proved a willing ally and the League did hear the Garvey requests. Instead of acting upon (or even debating) them, the League became embroiled in a procedural discussion, and eventually decided "that all nationals who had grievances should present them through their respective governments." [56]

In 1923 another delegation was sent to the League, with J. J. Adam instructed to set up an office in Paris and act as the "First Provisional Ambassador of the Negro peoples of the world to France." Over the years, the Garveyites also petitioned the British government and the kings of England and Spain. In 1922 they tried to interest the president and the United States Senate in the Back-to-Africa idea, and once even cabled the pope.[57] This series of futile excursions into polite diplomacy embittered Marcus Garvey, and in later years he turned to more militant means for African liberation.

The failure to obtain a foothold in Africa damaged both the prestige of the UNIA and the morale of its members. Though the Garvey movement in the United States was strong in terms of financial resources and membership, with a black population of only ten per cent in a nation of racists it could not continue to function without some sort of foreign base. Identity with a power beyond the borders of the United States had given American Garveyites the strength to face their predicament squarely and to insist upon power. The resurgence of the idea of black power in the 1960s, as most of Africa became independent, is no coincidence. Renewed pride in an African heritage and the hope of assistance from Africa have been important catalysts in this latter-day movement. This aid from the Third World has been largely psychological, and in the power of Third World public opinion upon America. Garveyites longed for such aid, and from Marcus Garvey's innumerable references to the potential power "of four hundred million Negroes of the world," one might conclude that black internationalism was what Garveyism was all about.

8

DISSENSIONS AND THE DECLINE OF GARVEYISM

THE IMPERIAL POWERS, more than any other single factor, caused the collapse of the Garvey movement. Whites outlawed the movement in their colonies, bought off Liberia, and narrowly circumscribed UNIA activities in the United States. While Garveyism was in some places suppressed by colonial edict, in other areas it was subdued by the more modern techniques of neo-colonialism. The neo-colonialists manipulated various racial and national groups through puppet regimes and encouraged power struggles within oppressed minorities in their own lands. Today there are only a few outright colonies remaining. Thus the most relevant lessons for the present in Garvey's downfall may be discovered by examining the UNIA's black opposition and the debilitating factionalism within the UNIA itself. Not all of this opposition was destructive by design; some of it—including most of the internal turmoil—involved legitimate differences over tactics in the anti-imperialist struggle. But it is the nature of the neo-colonialists to pit one well-intentioned faction of the oppressed against another for the colonialists' own benefit.

* * *

Black opposition and internal factionalism proved most destructive in the United States. The possibility of bribery, through the promise of money or social standing with the ruling whites, was greatest in this country, and the blacks' chances of attaining real power were smallest—freedom of the press, assembly, etc., notwithstanding. Whites ran almost all labor unions, all political parties, farm cooperatives and philanthropic agencies, and many blacks were convinced they could only gain power with white assistance. The Garveyites tried to prove this conviction false by building alternative black institutions, and for a while the black masses were sufficiently excited by Garveyism to silence black critics. But when the UNIA was hit with financial and legal problems, black establishment leaders of every political persuasion began to condemn the Garvey-ite program as "visionary" and asked pointedly what Garvey was doing to stop lynching, discrimination, and race prejudice.

The one event which did more than any other to strengthen this opposition was Garvey's visit to the Ku Klux Klan in June 1922. Southern divisions had complained to UNIA headquarters that the KKK was harassing its members, stopping them in the streets, and coming to their homes to demand information about the UNIA.[1] Klan membership was at an all-time high in the early 1920s. (A massive KKK parade down Pennsylvania Avenue in the nation's capital in 1925 seems, in retrospect, a portent of Hitler's storm troopers.) Members of the black establishment and white liberals or leftists would choose to visit the devil in hell before fraternizing with the Ku Klux Klan. The NAACP's Walter White had become a hero by secretly associating with and reporting on the KKK while passing as a white man.[2] It is not surprising that the black establishment reeled in horror when Marcus Garvey actually went to Atlanta to explain the UNIA to the Klan.

Garvey thought he should be congratulated for bravery. Only one UNIA member accompanied him to Atlanta; his bodyguard, who had been with him constantly since an assassination attempt in 1919, stayed in New York. Garvey had hoped to meet the Grand Wizard, but was met by his assistant instead. No public statement was issued after the meeting, but according to his widow, Garvey told the Klan representative that the UNIA was a separatist organization seeking a home in Africa, that it opposed miscegenation or any social contact between the races, and that it had no desire to take over America.[3] (The two evidently failed to reach any significant agreement, as the assistant testified against Garvey at his mail fraud trial the following year.)

The meeting exposed the sensitive posture of the Dixie UNIA—which, as we have seen, had been forced to take an extreme separatist position, and do little to combat white racism. On his return to New York, Garvey was pressured for a statement of UNIA policy on the Klan—in effect, for a statement of the UNIA position on racism the world over. The New York *Age* quoted Garvey on the Klan:

"The attitude of Negroes should be not to fight it, not to aggravate it, but to think of what it means and say and do nothing. It will not help us to fight it or its program. The Negro numerical disadvantage in this country is too great. . . . The wish of fifteen million Negroes means nothing when ninety million white men don't wish it." As for the problem of the black man, "the only way it can be solved is for the Negro to create a government of his own in Africa."[4]

This response did nothing to quiet those who claimed that Garvey had sold out to the Klan and had done irreparable harm to the freedom struggle. Garvey had committed his most grievous error. As a believer in an international solution for the black American's problems, he should, and could, have explained the special conditions in the South with regard to the UNIA. The position Garvey took on the Klan prior to 1922, and again in later years, was that blacks should fight its abuses, and that the battle against it could best be waged through the UNIA. Garvey's explanation of 1922, however, was disastrous.

The opposition jumped on his statement as well as on the very idea of conferring with the hated KKK. The uncommitted were pressured to take sides. Carter G. Woodson stopped contributing historical articles to the *Negro World* despite pleadings from his friend William Ferris. The NAACP's William Pickens, a personal friend of Garvey, refused to attend the August UNIA convention to receive a title of nobility in the Order of the Nile. Pickens declared, "Wherein I have thought Marcus Garvey to be right I have said so, regardless of the opinions of those opposed to him. Now that I know him to be wrong I say so." And in the same letter to Garvey, Pickens concluded, "I gather from your recent utterances that you are now endorsing the Ku Klux Klan, or at least conceding the justice of its aim to crush and repress Colored Americans and incidentally other racial and religious groups in the United States."[5] Pickens became a leader of the anti-Garvey movement, and many former fence-straddlers and secret opponents of Garvey and his program now saw their chance to come out in the open. DuBois, an open critic of the UNIA since 1920, lashed out in issue after issue of *Crisis.* Randolph and his associates planned a series of "Garvey Must Go" meetings to be held in New York concurrent with the summer UNIA convention. Cyril Briggs, who had turned on the UNIA after the African Blood Brotherhood was expelled in 1921, arranged a number of anti-Garvey street meetings, and Robert Abbott in the *Defender* and Fred Moore in the New York *Age* unleashed withering attacks on the UNIA, while other papers printed anti-Garvey releases from Briggs's *Crusader News Service.*

These battles of 1922 highlight a bleak period in Afro-American history. Randolph and others committed to cooperation with whites had been watching the white radical movement collapse; black professionals and businessmen were witnessing the failure of their hopes for black capitalism. These shared disappointments brought civil rights advocates, socialists, and more conservative blacks together. They now found common cause in blaming Garvey for their troubles; Garvey, in return, labeled them traitors to the race. No one benefited—though most of Garvey's enemies had little to lose. Those seeking a coalition with whites could do little but wait for the re-emergence of a powerful progressive movement in mainstream America. Those who desired black bourgeois respectability might appear to benefit from the collapse of Garveyism—but without freedom, jobs, and honor for the black masses, there could be no security for the bourgeoisie.

Of all Garvey's opponents, the African Blood Brotherhood probably suffered the most from this dissension, since it lost its place as a revolutionary vanguard organization. The ABB tried to retain its radical image by staying at odds with the socialists and refusing to participate in Randolph's anti-Garvey rallies and meetings. Instead, Briggs and the Brotherhood joined forces with the anti-Garvey publisher of the New York *Age,* Fred R. Moore.[6] It would have been hard to find a more stolid black conservative north of the Mason-Dixon line. An early organizer for Booker T. Washington's National Negro Business League, Moore had been Washington's hand-picked assistant to T. Thomas Fortune on the *Age,* and took control of the paper when Fortune went into semi-retirement prior to joining the staff of the *Negro World* in the early 1920s. Moore had opposed every expression of militancy since the war, but in 1922 his newspaper covered ABB activities extensively—in the cause of fighting Garvey. Briggs sponsored street rallies for, and Moore published a pamphlet by the anti-Garveyite African Mokete Manoedi, the son of a chieftain from Basutoland and allegedly a true representative of African opinion. "We are not favorably impressed with the unmitigated presumption of this man Garvey in electing himself provisional president of Africa," said Manoedi. In reply to a Garvey warning that UNIA enemies would soon meet their Waterloo, Manoedi said, "We are bothered less by the water in Waterloo than by the gas in Garvey and the gullibility of his poor dupes." [7] Night after night Manoedi derided the Garveyites. Finally, on August 11, 1922, a street brawl erupted at the corner of 135th Street and Seventh Avenue as Garveyites attacked Manoedi. Police stopped the riot, and allowed the South African to continue.[8]

In a pamphlet published by Moore, the African suggested his people's problems were "first, retaining possession of the land; second, setting up strong, sufficient inducements to foreign white European and American capitalists—as will assure progressive industrial, agricultural and commercial development upon a basis advantageous to both—white capitalists and Africans alike. But the question naturally arises, why white capitalists? The answer is the question: 'What other capitalists are there available for the task?' None. . . . Our only resource is the white European and American capitalist. To Brother Marcus, it is merely a matter of yelling, White man, get out of Africa! and presto! it is all over." Elsewhere in the pamphlet Manoedi states: "That Africans are not the most intelligent people in the world I readily admit. Nor is Mr. Garvey. True, they are not always capable of protecting their interests. Nor are any of the weaker peoples, white or black, yellow or brown." Manoedi wanted Africans to preserve native law and custom and create "an international African Commission whose purpose shall be to hear all grievances of the Africans." [9] Cyril Briggs sponsored Manoedi, not only to fight Garvey, but also in the hope of gaining greater respectability for the African Blood Brotherhood. This, in turn, was part of Briggs's attempt to build a new black federation composed of moderates and liberals, a substitute for the UNIA. Manoedi's presence only emphasized the fact that the black establishment had nothing to offer, and that its position necessitated selling out to whites.

The development of conservative attitudes among leftists opposing the UNIA was displayed in the October 1922 *Messenger,* in which Randolph brought up a law-and-order issue. He quoted from the UNIA Constitution, Article 5, Section 3—which concerned official receptions for dignitaries. "No one shall be received by the Potentate and his consort who has been convicted of crime or felony, except such crime or felony was committed in the interest of the Universal Negro Improvement Association and the African Communities League." Randolph decried this as an open invitation to criminality. He overlooked the distinction this section drew, which is basic to revolutionary movements, that there is a difference between illegal acts taken in the cause of justice, and common anti-social behavior.

The verbal barrages continued through the summer and on into 1923. It was politics of the gutter, especially for the enemies of the UNIA. The critics resorted to name-calling against Garvey: "half-wit Lilliputian" and "monumental monkey." were two choice examples. They found a former UNIA officer, Adrian Johnson, who claimed officials of the International were secretly paid large sums.[10] (Years later Johnson sued the UNIA, claiming he had hardly been paid at all for his year of services.)

In replying to such attacks, Garvey argued that the "Association for the Advancement of Certain People ... was fomenting the trouble between the races in the South by giving the impression that the Negro wants intercourse with the whites. We stand for a clean-cut Negro policy. . . . All we ask is a fair chance in the fields of industry and commerce and we can take care of ourselves. There can be no coming together of the two races, each has a distinct destiny. Our doctrine is to teach the Black man to stick to the Black woman." He added that the UNIA welcomed "any person with one-sixteenth or more Negro blood." In less reasonable moments, Garvey was given to noting that his enemies usually had a high percentage of white blood, and equated their pale complexion with affection for whites, condemning "light-colored Negroes" who deride the idea of nationhood in Africa and "resent the fact that a Black Negro is a leader." [11] The *Negro World* went so far as to report that Cyril Briggs was secretly a white man passing as a Negro. The irate ABB leader brought suit and forced a retraction. This hardly settled the matter: the retraction came in a statement that Briggs was white anyway, even if his physiognomy was partly black.[12] Garvey's *Philosophy and Opinions* lists nine publications and their publishers opposed to the UNIA, including the "*Crusader* and Cyril Briggs: Miscegenationist Light-Colored Communist Monthly Magazine; the *Messenger* and Chandler Owen and Asa P. Randolph: Miscegenationist Red Socialist Monthly Magazine; the

Chicago *Defender* and Robert S. Abbott: Miscegenationist Light-Colored Weekly paper; the New York *Times:* White Capitalist Paper." [13] The UNIA assistant president general William Sherrill expressed his hostility toward the critics in a Baltimore speech in which he declared: "Black folk as well as white who tamper with the Universal Negro Improvement Association are going to die. Black men and black women will be free even though the price of freedom is blood." [14] All things considered, the UNIA opinion of its critics was more respectful than were the accusations of the anti-Garveyites. An article in the August 26, 1922, *Negro World* listed, "in response to numerous queries," the editors' version of the twelve "greatest living Negroes"; included were the NAACP's DuBois, Archibald H. Grimke, and Kelly Miller—all arch-enemies of Garvey.

The UNIA had ridden the wave of post-war radicalism; as that wave subsided, so troubles beset the Garvey organization. Reaction set in throughout the world during the 1920s. In 1922 Mussolini came to power in Italy, and Salazar in Portugal. Later the peasants lost the Mexican revolution and the bureaucrats won in the Soviet Union. In America in 1922 more than one hundred leftists and anarchist radicals were serving jail sentences for "sedition," and hundreds more had been exiled as undesirable aliens. Growing prosperity in middle-class circles led to conservative political outlooks. Though middle-class blacks resented not sharing the prosperity, they did retain their expectations of success and soon included the Garvey movement in their opposition to any form of militancy.

It would be difficult to say whether the organized opposition outside the convention hall was more disastrous for the Garvey movement than the dissatisfied internal factions. Within the UNIA, a strong undercurrent of discontent had been smoldering for over a year. This was partly because the Association's growth had begun to taper off. Money continued to come in, but less regularly than before. Many workers who had contributed savings earned in defense industries no longer had lucrative factory employment, and those who still had money to invest were less than optimistic about the possibility of profits in UNIA industries. The growth of new UNIA divisions had slowed, with a consequent loss of initiation fees. Government repression made recruiting increasingly difficult in the United States, the Caribbean, and Africa. Many Garveyites believed a new approach or new leadership was needed. There was widespread suspicion of fiscal corruption among Black Star Line officers, a charge first aired at the 1921 convention.

Reverend Eason emerged as the leader of a strong opposition to Garvey within the UNIA. He raised objections to Garvey's management of business affairs, and suggested that Garvey had involved the movement in personal controversies, thus damaging its influence and prestige. The Chicago *Defender* reported open criticism within the movement of Garvey's acceptance of the ideals of the KKK, which had "brought him into public ridicule and embarrassed the Association." [15] The New York *World* quoted Eason's statement that Garvey had made an alliance with an "unfriendly organization." Certain members were reported to have announced, "If the movement is to succeed Garvey must follow others who possess saner and wiser policies." [16] As the August convention approached, a showdown appeared certain.

At the opening session of the 1922 convention, Garvey acknowledged the need for change and surprised everyone by announcing that he and four other members of the Supreme Executive Council were resigning. The next few days saw furious behind-the-scenes activity and mounting tension in Liberty Hall. This tension finally erupted into violence when Garvey, speaking before a packed hall, accused Eason of double-dealing and attempting to ruin the "Empire." Eason rushed Garvey and had to be forcibly restrained from punching the leader. Police stationed outside were summoned to quell the ensuing disturbance. The battle had begun when Eason rose to demand a retraction from one of several speakers who had accused American blacks of being unconcerned with politics. The speaker refused. As chairman, Garvey told Eason he had probably misunderstood the statement. Eason demanded a vote, to see what the other delegates thought. The vote was only confusing and Eason came to the podium and started arguing with Garvey. The president general then accused Eason of dragging in "differences between the American Negro and the West Indian Negro" (a recurring problem for the UNIA), and added the accusation of treachery.[17]

On the surface, factions within the UNIA were engaged in a simple power fight, which Garvey won with shrewd parliamentary maneuvering. He allowed the delegates to make him retain his post, and to reorganize the Association leadership so that half the top officers were to be chosen by Garvey as president general, rather than elected by the convention delegates. When the reorganization plan was passed, Garvey announced a slate of approved candidates for the remaining elective offices, omitting the names of a number of incumbents. His candidates won, but the elections were bitterly contested. William Ferris (unapproved) ran for re-election as assistant president general against William Sherrill and won—but without the two-thirds majority required; a run-off election had to be held. Two candidates eliminated in the first balloting threw their support to Sherrill, and he emerged the victor. But the nominations, debate and voting for this one office had occupied an entire evening session, lasting well into the early morning hours.[18]

These battles might have strengthened the Association if serious policy questions had been raised. Instead, both sides became embroiled in procedural problems, in charges and countercharges of corruption, poor work and poor public relations. Garvey failed to approve Ferris on the rather trivial grounds that Ferris's obligations as *Negro World* literary editor diminished his effectiveness as an assistant president general. Ulysses Poston, also defeated and also unapproved, felt that decentralizing leadership was of major importance. He advised Garvey, "In your mad rush to serve your race, in your mad rush to serve humanity, pause long enough to study yourself introspectively. . . . Remember Napoleon was ambitious to serve his people."[19] Behind the power struggle lay a growing awareness of one major shortcoming of the UNIA which Garvey's Atlanta visit had exposed—the lack of a coordinated policy to reconcile regional differences in styles of action.

The Garveyites did try to deal with troublesome local issues, but without much success. The KKK was discussed at length during the 1922 convention. One committee presented an evening of talks by Dixie delegates who had witnessed lynchings, including a comparison of race riots in Houston, Chicago, and Atlanta by a delegate who had watched all three. One man, witness to a lynching in Oklahoma, described the lyncher as temporarily insane and concluded, "There is but one way to stop him, and that is by meeting a destructive force with organized force, by fighting fire with fire." Some delegates suggested the UNIA should support the federal anti-lynch law, but one committee member disagreed: "Laws against lynching will not save you when an infuriated gang of roughs gets after you.

197

The only way to protect yourself is to keep them off by force."
And a Louisianan then told of an incident in his state where blacks
had acted to defend themselves. Many speakers seemed ready to
lynch the lynchers, but others—including Garvey—cautioned against
such action.[20] The committee might have suggested firm resolutions, but it lacked the resolve to reconcile conflicting opinions, and
the discussion degenerated into a fight over personalities.

During the last week of the convention, Eason was tried on
charges of conduct unbecoming a member. As the UNIA's leader of
American Negros, Eason had traveled constantly. On occasions, it
was charged, he had been too inebriated to read his prepared speech.
In Pittsburgh he had tried to engage in a little romance with two of
the UNIA singers accompanying him, allegedly while under the influence of alcohol.[21] Eason's drinking was exaggerated to obscure
the issue of his policy differences with the UNIA leadership. His job
was a most difficult one: in the preceding year, he had dealt, quite
successfully, with disgruntled Garveyites in a number of divisions.
The Los Angeles division, for example, had been up in arms over
reports of Black Star Line corruption. The International had first
sent Minister of Legions E. L. Gaines to quiet things down, but he
had only antagonized the local leadership further. Noah Thompson
and Charlotta Bass broke away and formed their own Pacific Coast
Negro Improvement Association, taking four-fifths of the membership with them.[22] Eason was then dispatched to Los Angeles, where
he heard complaints not only of Black Star Line corruption, but
concerning UNIA neglect of local issues and problems, as well. At
one public meeting, Thompson told Eason, "Do something here on
the Pacific Coast and you will do more, yea ten thousand times
more, to redeem Africa than you could by buying shares in Garvey
ships, which very truly are ships that pass in the mist."[23] Eason was
apparently sober enough to be quite effective with Thompson: the
Pacific Coast Association was disbanded, and Thompson and Mrs.
Bass returned to the UNIA—revitalizing, for a time, one of the big
money-making divisions.[24] Eason's West Coast experience doubtless
helped him decide to challenge the International in 1922. At his
trial he was defended by Assistant Counsel General J. Austin Norris,
who argued that Eason was loyal to the movement, but his pleas
were unsuccessful—Eason was expelled. Norris was soon afterward
severely censured for making anti-UNIA statements during the

trial, and he subsequently resigned from the organization.[25]

In addition to fights over personnel, the 1922 convention worked on colonization plans for Liberia and drew up a policy for the delegation to the League of Nations. Other than that, the delegates took little substantive action. The next convention, in 1924, would devote considerable attention to domestic issues, but by then the policy of neglect had taken its toll.

Meanwhile, external opposition was growing. Soon after the 1922 convention, Randolph, Owen, and Pickens made a nationwide tour to speak against Garvey. During the first weekend in September, New York saw at least four separate meetings denouncing the UNIA, including one chaired by Rev. Eason, who had joined Norris to form a new Negro Improvement Association. Eason announced this organization would be interested only in domestic issues, because pressing problems in the United States "leave no time for activity abroad."[26] The new group's only known reference to African problems was a strained argument from Norris charging that Garvey's activities in Africa kept the British from granting passports to qualified African youths who wished to study in American colleges. The Baltimore *Afro-American* reported that Eason was not only uninterested in the problems of West Indians, but actually resented them on the grounds that they were prone to slander black Americans.*[27]

Eason's attacks were especially damaging to the Garveyites. Enraged at his expulsion, he broadcast anything unfavorable he could remember about his three years with the movement. The New York *Age* printed a story from Eason telling how the power-mad Garvey had secretly paid a New York white newspaper $250 to announce that the "Honorable Marcus Garvey, the greatest Negro orator the Negro race ever produced, will speak. . . ." Eason neglected to mention that such payment was common practice, or that this particular announcement was to recruit for the 1920 Madison Square Garden meeting—the success of which was well worth $250.[28]

His attacks on Garvey eventually made Eason a target of violence. After his break with the UNIA he returned to Philadelphia to seek support for his new organization in the city where he had once

---

* Of the major black weeklies, the *Afro-American* gave the most objective and balanced reporting on the UNIA and its related organizations.

been a prominent minister. Local Garveyites stopped his supporters in the streets and often manhandled them. In Chicago that November, a Garveyite shot and seriously wounded a policeman while trying to kill Eason.[29] In December, Eason went to New Orleans, hoping to benefit from the widespread unrest within the Garvey movement there. On New Year's Day Eason held one last meeting before leaving to confer with government officials about testimony he was to give against Garvey in his coming trial. Eason was returning to his place of residence when two men stepped from an alleyway, called his name, and shot him down. Before he died, Eason identified the assassins as members of the New Orleans UNIA police force. The two were arrested two weeks later. Though they stated openly that Eason had it coming,[30] both pleaded innocent and they were never convicted.

Shortly after Eason's murder, eight leading black opponents of Garvey sent a letter to the U.S. attorney general, demanding speedy prosecution of Garvey for mail fraud and adding a long list of illegalities allegedly committed by Garvey or the UNIA. They asked that the attorney general "use his full influence completely to disband and extirpate this vicious movement. . . ." * [31]

The *Negro World* published the letter to show the treachery of Garvey's opponents. Garvey called the eight signers "good old darkies" who had "written their names down everlastingly as enemies of their own race." He said they were "nearly all octoroons and quadroons" or "married to octoroons," which he interpreted as indicative of their solution to the race problem. One was a "race defamer" whose newspaper published "week after week the grossest scandals against the race." Another was a "real estate shark who delighted under the guise of race patriotism to raise the rent of poor colored people even beyond that of white landlords"; a third was a "hair straightener and face bleacher" whose self-conceived duty to the race was "to get the race to be dissatisfied with itself." [32]

The mail fraud trial began in mid-May 1923. Charged with Garvey were three officers of the Black Star Line: Eli Garcia, George Tobias and Orlando Thompson. Although technically it was the Black Star Line and its officials who were on trial, Garvey saw

---

* The signers included businessmen Harry Pace and John E. Nail, William Pickens and Robert W. Bagnall of the NAACP, newspaper publishers Robert S. Abbott and George W. Harris, and Dr. Julia P. Coleman and Chandler Owen.

the action as a political attack on his entire movement. The initial prosecution statement could only have reinforced this opinion. It read, in part, "While there center around Garvey other associations or corporations having for their object the uplift and advancement of the Negro race, the entire scheme of uplift was used to persuade Negroes for the most part to buy shares of stock in the Black Star Line . . . when the defendants well knew . . . that said shares were not and in all human probability never could be worth $5 each or any other sum of money." [33]

Further proof of the government's intentions had been provided by actions taken in the months immediately prior to the mail fraud trial:

(1) a raid on the New Orleans UNIA office, in which government agents, supposedly in search of evidence on the Eason murder, seized files and membership lists and arrested fifteen local UNIA members; [34]

(2) a raid on a New York meeting, with the arrest of eight UNIA members, including the minister of industries and head of the Negro Factories Corporation, Thomas Anderson, on the charge of inciting to riot; [35]

(3) the arrest in Ohio of Arden A. Bryan, the head of American UNIA membership recruiting, on the charge of selling Black Star Line stock illegally; [36]

(4) the seizure of all files in the UNIA's New York offices (allegedly to obtain necessary information for the trial), including all transcripts of convention proceedings; complete financial records of the International and all associated businesses; correspondence, membership lists, and mailing lists for the *Negro World* and the new daily *Negro Times*. None of these records was ever returned to the UNIA except the newspaper mailing lists—and these only after court action. [37]

The trial lasted nearly a month. It began with a shouting match between federal judge Julian Mack and defense attorneys who demanded that Mack disqualify himself because he was a member of the NAACP. After two days of proceedings, Garvey's lawyer, UNIA Counsel General William C. Matthews, advised Garvey to plead guilty on a technical charge and work out a deal in closed chambers. An angered Garvey fired Matthews, telling him he did not seem to understand the political motive behind the prosecution. [38] Garvey then took over his own defense—unprepared, and with little knowledge of the law—though his co-defendants retained their lawyers. In the weeks that followed, Garvey made innumerable errors in procedure, sometimes bringing laughter from the jury and spectators, particularly after condescending correction from Judge Mack. As the trial progressed, it became clear that neither defense nor prosecution was concerned with the legal question. The government produced an assortment of ex-Garveyites who testified to all sorts of slipshod financial practices among the defendants (including the fact that Garvey bet on the horses while visiting Jamaica in 1921). The defense produced a stream of loyal Garveyites who testified to the value of the movement. Garvey was out to prove that the UNIA was "more intent on the ultimate uplifting and salvation that was promised to the Negro race of America than in the paltry profits that might be realized from the stock investment." As one lawyer for Garvey's co-defendants put it, "If every Negro could have put every dime, every penny into the sea, and if he might get in exchange the knowledge that he was somebody, that he meant something in the world, he would gladly do it. . . . The Black Star Line was a loss in money but it was a gain in soul." [39]

Actual evidence to support the government's charge that the Black Star Line had used the U.S. mail to defraud the public was scant indeed. The prosecution had lined up a number of alleged victims—but all but one had either purchased stock without using the mail, or had not purchased any stock at all. The prosecution's most important witness, Benny Dancy, produced an envelope which the Black Star Line had mailed to him, but could not produce the contents of the envelope. The historian David Cronon called his testimony "halting, uncertain, and riddled with inconsistencies and frightened confusion." [40] Yet Dancy's claim of being defrauded was the evidence upon which Garcia, Tobias and Thompson were found innocent and Garvey was found guilty. Why the split verdict? Most likely because Garvey had identified himself with the UNIA throughout the trial, while the others had remained individuals. In the courtroom, obvious tension developed between Garvey and his co-defendants, who he thought were more interested in saving themselves from jail than in saving the Universal Negro Improvement Association.[41] The prosecution's ability to prejudice the jury against the UNIA in general no doubt helped the jurors to overlook the lack of concrete evidence of fraud. Garvey and the lawyers for his co-defendants had shown quite clearly that the government had invented testimony for its witnesses to recite in court—which should have been sufficient grounds for a mistrial. For instance, one Schuyler Cargill testified that he had worked in the Black Star Line offices in 1919 under a Mr. Prentice as a mail clerk. But when Garvey showed that Prentice was not employed by the BSL at that time, the mail clerk admitted that prosecutor Mattuck had schooled him as to dates. Cargill stated emphatically that part of his job was the delivery of mail to the College Station post office, but under Garvey's cross-examination Cargill was unable to state the location of this post office, and—with further probing from Garvey— admitted having been provided the name of the post office by a police inspector.[42]

Garvey received the maximum five-year penalty—though, as the brief prepared for Garvey's appeal demonstrated, sentences for mail fraud usually ran from probation alone to one year in jail. Immediately after the sentencing, Garvey was taken to the Tombs prison in New York and held for three months without bail, although bail was a right due to him while his case was on appeal.[43]

UNIA members, already familiar with government repression of their organization in Africa and in Latin America, now saw it begin in the United States. The government's refusal to return the records seized in New York created havoc. Large sums had been raised through loans from members, paid officials and workers in the Garvey businesses. These loans (usually in the form of wages not paid) were recorded in small books, with duplicate records kept at the International's office. Without such records, renegades could forge additions in their loan books and enter claims for back pay UNIA businesses were not prospering, and the loss of records proved fatal for some. A Baltimore *Afro-American* correspondent who visited UNIA headquarters early in September reported: "When I arrived the place had taken on a beehive appearance. . . . Literally hundreds of men and women were crowding in and out of the building." He heard many animated discussions of the "financial disaster" which followed the indictment and trial. At the printing plant, this reporter found that "the linotype and stereotyping machinery purchased to print the UNIA publications was idle and covered with canvas." He was told that the *Negro World* was being printed elsewhere, and that the Association was about to lose this machinery to its creditors.[44]

In the year between Garvey's trial and the 1924 convention, the movement lost a number of important men. Some resigned with bitterness, including Garvey's lawyer, his co-defendants, and their lawyers—a group which comprised most of the UNIA legal staff and the auditor general. The lawyers felt their services were not appreciated, and the other defendants had been personally offended by Garvey's post-trial remarks accusing unnamed subordinates of betrayal and dishonesty. External pressures and internal frustration led Potentate Gabriel Johnson to send his letter of resignation from Liberia, and LeRoy Bundy, assistant president general and leader of the Cleveland division, resigned after that chapter split into violent factions, one of which wanted to sell the division's Liberty Hall to pay bills for health and death benefits and other obligations to members. Reverend Francis Ellegor resigned as high commissioner but remained active in the movement, as did former secretary general J. B. Yearwood, who had stayed on for one year, at Garvey's request, despite sickness and financial difficulties in his family.[45] Death, too, hurt the Garveyites severely in the year after the trial, with the loss of Chaplain General J. R. L. Diggs, Assistant President General Robert Poston, *Negro World* columnist John "Grit" Bruce, Liberian leaders James Dossen and Milton Marshall, and one of the movement's biggest financial contributors, Isaiah Morter of British Honduras.

* * *

Had the UNIA not been deeply rooted in black society, these setbacks would have destroyed it. But the Garveyites managed a show of strength at the 1924 convention and, though torn with factionalism, the movement continued to broaden its activities in the late 1920s. After the Eason episode, Garvey and his remaining supporters realized that the organization could no longer risk the charge of neglecting local problems, and advertisements for the 1924 convention promised more involvement in local affairs.[46]

The Fourth International Convention, held in New York in August of 1924, with Garvey out of jail pending his appeal, was in number of delegates close to the size of earlier ones. The convention's primary emphasis was still on the ill-fated plans for colonization in Liberia;* however, a major topic was the launching of a Negro Political Union—a world-wide effort to bring UNIA support to local political struggles. Its initial prospectus stated: "The political union shall represent the political hopes and aspirations of the fifteen million Negroes of the United States of America on American questions, domestic to America, and shall represent the interest of the millions of Negroes of the West Indies in their different and respective islands, affecting their domestic political questions, and so also in the scattered communities of Africa. . . . Each country or community will have its own domestic program for the betterment of the race in that country or community. But the strength of the Union shall be given to any community or country to politically assist it in putting over its political program. As for instance, if the Negroes of America were politically agitating and working for the passage of any special measure for the benefit of the race, the entire strength of the Union would be placed at the disposal of the American section. If the Negroes of Trinidad desired to carry out any political measure for the benefit of that community, the Union would give its strength in assisting them, and so with any community where the Negroes live throughout the world. No longer, therefore, will individual politicians represent the interest of the Negroes but the Negroes will unitedly be represented by the Negro Political Union."⁴⁷

In the United States, much of the Union's activity took the form of involvement in electoral politics. Before this, UNIA political activity had been largely unofficial and often confusing. Through the Political Union the Garvey movement endorsed and campaigned for a wide range of electoral candidates; the Union also took—and explained—stands on key political issues. The question of the Ku Klux Klan came up again in 1924 and the UNIA convention adopted two resolutions drafted by Bishop McGuire and Garvey: "I. Resolved, that the Fourth International Convention of the Negro peoples of the world regards the alleged attitude of the Ku Klux Klan to the Negro as fairly representative of the feelings of the majority of the white race toward us, and places on record its

* The announcement of the Firestone deal was made toward the end of the convention.

conviction that the only solution of this critical situation is that of the UNIA, namely, the securing for ourselves as speedily as possible a government of our own on African soil. II. Moved, that it shall be the policy of the UNIA to protect against the brutalities and atrocities alleged to be perpetrated upon the members of the Negro race by the Ku Klux Klan or any other organization."[48] This was a far cry from the indecision shown at the 1922 convention—even though the resolutions were, as intended, open to differing interpretations for different geographic areas.[49]

At the 1924 convention there was renewed optimism about the Black Star Line. It had been rechartered as the Black Star Steamship Company with a new stock issue, and a new flagship had been purchased shortly before the convention. This was the *General G. W. Goethals,* the ship obtained at a reasonable price through the efforts of Cyril Briggs, who passed as a white man to do the buying. (This was part of Briggs's attempt to get back on good terms with the UNIA.) The *General Goethals* was the largest and most seaworthy vessel ever purchased by the Garveyites.

International officers also inspired confidence in the delegates. The leadership was bolstered by a number of new officeholders with a broad range of political experience and professional activities.* But the renewed optimism of the 1924 convention was based largely on continued faith in the Liberian plan. Had the Garveyites won their base in Liberia, all UNIA operations—conventions, businesses, the Negro Political Union—would have been managed from the (at least nominally) independent Third World.

The hopes of 1924 were never realized. Garvey was eventually forced to base his operations in Jamaica—an inadequate substitute. The island was still a colony, and the move accentuated long-simmering antagonisms between West Indian and American blacks.

On the heels of the loss of Liberia, Garvey lost his court appeal. He was jailed without even one day to arrange for the UNIA's future. On returning to New York from Detroit, he was hauled off

---

* Including James O'Meally, headmaster of a college in Jamaica; Madame M. L. T. DeMena, later an important figure in the Jamaican independence movement; West Indian educator J. C. St. Clair Drake; R. Van Richards, chaplain of the Liberian legislature; Prince Kojo Tavalou of Dahomey; and the Indian journalist H. G. Mugdal. Leadership positions were also taken by some long-standing heads of local divisions—William A. Wallace of Chicago, J. A. Craigen of Detroit, Samuel Haynes of Pittsburgh, and George Weston of New York.

the train by heavily armed federal agents who conducted him to the Tombs prison, from which he was taken to Atlanta Federal Penitentiary in February 1925.[50] His incarceration was an especially hard blow to the UNIA, and during his two-and-a-half years of imprisonment, the UNIA became a shambles.

As Garvey entered Atlanta prison, the *General Goethals*, on its maiden voyage for the Black Star Steamship Company, was idled in Kingston Harbor with a broken boiler—which broke again a few miles out to sea. Published reports of the voyage reaching the United States told of dissension and lack of discipline among the ship's crew. Years later, one member of this crew could recall no unusual discipline problem, but he remembered the sailors were convinced the white captain and his chief mate were bent on ruining the trip for the UNIA, and also thought the second boiler breakdown was the result of sabotage at the Kingston repair company. The *General Goethals* eventually made it to Colón, Panama, where ownership was transferred to another company to meet repair payments. Thus the Black Star Steamship Company was finished, and this, along with the Liberian defeat, marked the end of any hopes of the UNIA ever becoming a world power.[51]

By the summer of 1926 the Association was no longer a coordinated unit, even though it still had hundreds of thousands of followers, perhaps a million. The official Universal Negro Improvement Association was still there, and there was one last gigantic international convention in 1929, but the organization was no longer what it had been before Garvey entered prison.

Given the strength of imperialism in this period, it seems unlikely the Garvey movement could have made significant progress toward its goals until World War II. Garvey's vision was larger than that of most men, and so was his patience (notwithstanding his recurrent irritation with subordinates). In a way, Garvey had been awaiting the Second World War from the beginning. As he predicted on many occasions, war did ruin the Western European powers and permit a successful anti-colonialist struggle. Although Garvey himself died in 1940, his organization might have survived to play a more prominent role in the post-war years. It failed to survive because it was unable to resolve questions which still trouble black militants: Under what conditions must a movement risk confrontation with the white establishment to maintain mass following? Can militant confrontation precede the building of a solid base of operations, or can the two be carried on simultaneously? How far can the policy of separatism be carried without becoming a policy of avoiding struggle?

The UNIA produced no *Das Kapital* of color, and the only practical substitute for an ideological blueprint was to win a base in Africa so ideology could grow with practice. In his oratory and his writings, Marcus Garvey sketched an outline of a new humanist philosophy to which black people could relate. The UNIA—with its lively press, open conventions, and broad international representation—might have developed into a workable implementer of this ideology, but no such development was possible when the organization was widely suppressed, its leader jailed, its records confiscated, and its costly business ventures bankrupt.

Real internal differences also contributed to the demise of the UNIA. UNIA internationalists thought in terms of the future; they were building a movement which hinged on a non-existent international situation. Regionalists, on the other hand, emphasized the real and immediate problems of black oppression. The many splits from the UNIA reveal the seriousness of the conflict over this question. The short-lived rival UNIA established in New York in 1918 to protect West Indian immigrants, the Pacific Coast Negro Improvement Association, and Eason's short-lived organization were all attempts to deal with regional issues. A major split occurred in 1926, when one group formed a separate UNIA geared to problems of blacks in the United States, and in 1929 a second contingent broke away to join them. Nor was such conflict peculiar to the United States: a split in the Central American UNIA in 1929 led to the formation of a separate organization designed specifically to help local black immigrants from the British West Indies, who constituted the majority of UNIA members in Central America. During the early 1930s a number of prospective Garveyites were attracted to the Communist party, which claimed to have a black nationalist program. Other internationalist defections came in the form of escape to otherworldly movements: Noble Drew Ali's Moorish American Science Temple, Elijah Muhammad's Nation of Islam, the social movements of Father Divine and Daddy Grace, and in Jamaica, the RastafarI.

Garvey always looked toward the day when black militants, operating from a free Africa, could strike fear into the hearts of white colonialists, as Robert Williams, Eldridge Cleaver and Stokely Carmichael have done in recent years. The vast majority of the Garveyite rank and file were internationalists—rejecting the America around them to construct an identity of their own in a world of their own. This position is today basic to black power, but in Garvey's time it often appeared escapist and conservative. The internationalists in the American UNIA were strong separatists: they wanted to avoid direct struggle with whites, and excused this lack of militancy on the grounds of saving the movement for the struggle abroad. Regionalists sought to engage in civil rights, labor, and political battles at home. One of Garvey's objections to socialism was that socialists within his organization were constantly demanding involvement in local battles. They appeared more eager to fight for the Red International of the proletariat than the Black International of the UNIA.

This dichotomy within the movement had been apparent even in the midst of the optimism of the 1924 convention. The split was most visible in debate about the McGuire-Garvey resolutions on the Ku Klux Klan. Members of the African Blood Brotherhood (who had been allowed into open convention sessions, perhaps as a reward for Briggs's help in purchasing the *General Goethals*) demanded a virtual declaration of war on the Klan, an expression of regionalism. At sessions open only to official delegates, one faction asked for such a declaration, while others urged no action at all; the McGuire-Garvey resolutions were offered as a compromise. Freeman L. Martin of the St. Louis division denounced the compromise resolutions as weak because they referred only to "alleged" attitudes of the Klan. Heated debate followed: "Keep your mouth shut about the Klan," said one delegate from Seattle; another, from Mobile, Alabama, claimed, "The Klan is a help to this movement by increasing the membership, by making the black man think of Africa." J. J. Peters of Chicago questioned the need for any resolutions, and reminded delegates of the black liberals' futile fight for a federal anti-lynch law, and of the NAACP's failure to get even La Follette's Progressive Party to come out against the Klan. "When the other fellow holds the marbles and has control," said Peters, "the best thing to do is to get into friendly relations with him if you can. I don't mean to condone the Klan for the wrong things it has done.

But after a while when we have got our own country and our own battleships we can tell them to go to hell." D. M. Brown of Florida, claiming to speak for many Southern delegates, said, "I can't afford to be against an organization of that kind, especially considering the place where I am living. . . . I don't say we ought to endorse an organization that is oppressing us, but I do say we ought to remain neutral." Supporting a strong resolution was Assistant President General William Sherrill, who noted that the Klan was no friend of the Negro "and to state otherwise would be both untrue and cowardly." [52]

Debates such as these did not stem from clearly defined factions. Some formally recognized division of opinion could have helped reconcile the two versions of black nationalism, which were really only differences in emphasis. For example, Dr. Peters, who argued against the Klan resolutions, was quite eager to have the UNIA involved in other domestic matters. In fact, he led a splinter group away from the Association in 1929 because it appeared to be neglecting local problems. Peters was enthusiastic about the Negro Political Union, and even suggested the UNIA might find itself endorsing a white against a black in some situations where the white candidate had a better reform program.[53] It was Peters who had threatened, "The day is not far distant when every damn white man is going to pay for every oppression he is giving the Negro," prompting Garvey to tell the press that Peters spoke for himself and not the Association.[54] Peters was definitely willing to risk confrontation with whites, and his argument against the Klan resolutions was in reality an argument for an attack from a different direction. It was not understood that way, and added to the UNIA's reputation as an evasive organization run by "unrealistic visionaries." As the Communist *Daily Worker* put it, "Garvey Movement Bows to Ku Klux Klan." [55] The Klan debates helped convince Briggs to drop the Garveyites for good.

In these important debates, members turned to Garvey for leadership—but he too often responded with diplomacy. When the ABB representatives raised the Klan issue, Bishop McGuire said to Garvey, "You are our leader, sir, in this respect as well as others. We feel that you have an advantage over us through the knowledge that you gained in an interview [with the Klan]. We want to know what is your attitude." Garvey replied, "My attitude is that of the majority of the convention. This Ku Klux Klan question is an extremely important one. And I don't want to influence the convention. I want to hear what the discussion brings out." [56] Later Garvey defended his resolutions on the grounds that they were an effective compromise which gave the Klan no excuse for a reign of terror against the one hundred UNIA divisions in the South.[57]

The McGuire-Garvey resolutions may have been internally statesmanlike, but from the outside they appeared meaningless. For Randolph, Abbott, Fred Moore, and those around them, forthright opposition to the Klan was a test of loyalty to the race. Moreover, the attempt to turn white people away from the Klan was probably their single most important concern. Fighting the Klan by building independent black power was inconceivable to them. Thus Garvey's statement that the Klan's attitude was "fairly representative of the feelings of the majority of the white race towards us" was, in the opinion of these men, an insult—both to fair-minded whites and to those blacks struggling to win white support against the Klan.

The Communists, always interested in mass movements of the dispossessed, were trying to understand Garveyism, and the *Daily Worker*'s accounts of the 1924 convention proceedings were the most thorough ever presented in a white newspaper. *Worker* reporters could understand generalized outbursts of militancy, and wrote of "the hall ringing with belligerent speeches implying a determination to form a world wide organization for stirring up all the colonial peoples of the world to revolt against all imperialist governments." They reported the wild reception which greeted Garvey's announcement that Turkish armies had roundly defeated a British expeditionary force in the Near East, as well as Garvey's "scathing attack" on "the capitalist class of Negroes whose only concern is to rob and exploit the unfortunate of their own race." [58] But the *Daily Worker* reporters could not fathom black nationalist thinking. They concluded that the resolutions on the Klan left "hardly any room for doubt that Marcus Garvey, president of the Negro organization, two and a half years ago . . . entered into an agreement with the Klan." [59]

The trouble over an official position toward the Klan was only one example of the difficulties with the UNIA's leadership. As president general, Garvey had to mediate ideological disputes, direct the use of Association funds, and perform a host of similar tasks.

Dealing with subordinates proved most difficult for him. Either they avoided responsibilities or he was reluctant to grant them. Some of this difficulty was built in: the UNIA Constitution delegated authority through the conventions to the supreme council, which had little authority to coordinate the activity of local branches. The UNIA's goals were, at least in part, quite revolutionary, and revolutions are not won without coordination. Garvey bewildered many of his followers by acting as a democrat one moment and a revolutionary dictator the next. When subordinates questioned or failed to understand his actions, he reacted intemperately, often questioning their intelligence or their loyalty.

Few Garveyites were able to advise Garvey. Amy Jacques could, because she showed him respect and was tough enough to talk back to him. James B. Yearwood found he could get Garvey's attention by first announcing he was going to resign if such and such was not done.[60] Garvey's short temper turned often to suspicion, especially after one-time allies began to leave the movement—as had his boyhood friend Domingo, and Pickens, to whom Garvey had once lent money and provided lodging. Former followers who testified against him at his trial added to Garvey's bitterness, which he nurtured while in prison. Garvey warned one visitor to the Tombs, "Watch that man Plummer, I've been watching him and I know what he is up to," referring to an alleged plot by the Association's publicity director to form an anti-Garvey group within the UNIA. Plummer, long a close associate of Garvey, did leave the movement soon after.[61]

Garvey's suspicions were echoed by the distrust which swept the movement during his imprisonment. The government seizure of UNIA records contributed to this. When fifteen former leading Garveyites sued the Association for back pay, it looked like an indictment of the entire movement and everything it stood for. Yet many of those who defected had not lost faith in the philosophy of black nationalism. Most UNIA leaders who left the movement did so because of disputes over tactics within a black nationalist context— principally over the question of internationalism versus regionalism. Some were disturbed over prejudice between blacks of different ethnic backgrounds, a vital problem for the Association. West Indian blacks felt superior to American blacks; Jamaicans looked down on Panamanians; Trinidadians and Barbadians derided Jamaicans for being more English than the English. Anti-Garveyite blacks in the United States played up the differences between natives and immigrants. "Garvey and his followers constitute a group of aliens, who lose no opportunity to show their lack of respect for American institutions as well as for Americans of their own race," said Fred Moore in the *Age,* adding, "They steadfastly refuse to become naturalized citizens and profess great respect for the protection of the British flag." [62] (Moore was raising a specious issue. Even though it was true that many Garveyites retained foreign citizenship, this was not necessarily a sign of disrespect for American institutions.) Moore's statement was typical American parochialism. Similarly, another critic declared, "How dare Marcus Garvey, a West Indian Negro, come here from Jamaica trying to tell us American Negroes how to lead our people! We are the real Americans, we will redeem the race!" [63]

Garveyites were well aware of the danger to the movement in these prejudices and attempted to play them down. But their approach to the problem often aggravated it further. Assistant President General William Sherrill addressed this matter in a lengthy speech before the 1924 convention. "I am an American Negro," began Sherrill, "born and raised under the Southern psychology. I know what that psychology is—its peculiar oppressive effect. And I tell you . . . that if the Negro was ever to have a real, energetic, courageous Negro leader, able to tell his people to be men and to look the world straight in the face—that if our people were ever to have such a leader . . . he would have to come from somewhere else than in the United States of America. The Negro of America raised under such conditions finds it difficult to develop the qualities of leadership. The fine material that is fit to lead the race is killed in the American environment. Here the Negro from childhood is jim-crowed, lynched, kicked about, cursed and made to conduct himself as an inferior until he has not grit enough left to be a leader. The West Indian Negro, on the other hand, from the cradle up develops a certain independence and self-reliance that the American Negro never has the courage to exercise. The British government is bound to allow the development of some initiative among individual Negroes, for her position in Jamaica is such that she has to use certain types of Negroes to exercise authority over the others. Of course, those who arc used that way are betraying their own people

. . . but even at that, in Jamaica there is a different psychology that permits some men of independent spirit and self-reliance to develop."[64] Sherrill's analysis was unquestionably poor politics—almost denying his own worth, and that of other Afro-Americans who did have "grit enough" to become leaders.

Parochial social prejudices had been present throughout the Garvey years; they became a real danger to the movement when added to outside political, legal, and financial pressures in the late twenties. These prejudices helped to destroy the dynamic worldwide context of the Universal Negro Improvement Association, and yet, ironically, they fostered the growth of local black nationalism. During the past three decades, Garveyites and ex-Garveyites have been prominent in the independence struggles of Caribbean colonies and have been notable to a lesser extent in Africa. Garvey himself shifted his views while in prison, deciding that for the time being emphasis on local independence struggles would have to take precedence over considerations of international unity, if possible without destroying the unity of the UNIA. In this vein, the *Negro World* of the late 1920s produced elaborate analyses of the weakness of white political structures as they affected blacks. The Garveyites also injected an international perspective into national politics by backing Democrat Alfred E. Smith in the 1928 presidential election. Declaring "Smith Better Than Hoover," the *Negro World* emphasized Hoover's role in securing the Firestone Rubber contract for Liberia.[65]

Unfortunately, this new sophistication came too late to save the troubled UNIA.

9

TWILIGHT ACHIEVEMENTS

DURING HIS LAST YEAR in the Atlanta penitentiary, Marcus Garvey made a decision which fundamentally altered the direction of the UNIA Visiting Garveyites who brought news of declining membership and difficulties in maintaining various branches were told to keep the Association alive by working within other organizations, if necessary. Garvey's public statements revealed little of this new approach—which was, in essence, a contingency plan in case the UNIA could not reverse its gradual decline. Even though the UNIA membership was still large, this was a necessary step and a recognition that the Association no longer had the strength to launch broad programs on its own.[1]

The plan may also have been a response to the 1926 international convention—the only one Garvey did not attend—at which a dissident faction had elected a new international hierarchy excluding Garvey. This splinter group was a product of the confusion and distrust which abounded during Garvey's absence. At first William Sherrill led the rebels, declaring at a midwestern UNIA conference in October of 1925 that Garvey should relinquish some of his authority because the organization could not be managed from prison. Sherrill then discovered his allies were intent on ousting Garvey entirely. This Sherrill could not agree to, and finding himself in disfavor with all sides, he temporarily dropped out of the organization. A much more hostile group then took over, led by George A. Weston, a native of Antigua who had organized the Pittsburgh division and later moved to become president of the huge New York UNIA. Weston accused Garvey of padding the salaries of favored officials, of being a "reckless squanderer of funds and promoter of disruption," and declared Garvey "and his unscrupulous henchmen have driven away and prohibited from participation in the activities of the Association, various individuals, whose experience, integrity, educational attainments and high influential positions especially fitted them for useful service." [2]

Using his New York position, Weston gained control of the planning committee for the 1926 convention, and succeeded in winning over a majority of the delegates. The convention's opening parade was marred by fistfights between dissidents and those loyal to the jailed leader. The following day loyalist delegates marched out of Liberty Hall, declaring the proceedings a sham, and opened their own convention in the Commonwealth Casino. Here Fred Toote declared, "Garvey is the Negro leader and against him is the reactionary Uncle Tom group." The loyalists maintained control of the *Negro World* and UNIA office buildings; one contingent managed to get into Liberty Hall early one morning with the intention of nailing the doors shut, but they were driven off by a rebel group of Black Cross nurses. The rebels argued they were a legitimate majority with "true UNIA status," and elected Weston the new president general, with George O. Marke as potentate.[3] In subsequent court action the rebels won the right to the title UNIA Incorporated, making Garvey the leader of UNIA Unincorporated. The rebels' organization became something of a catch-all for disaffected Garveyites who were still believers in the general ideas of the movement.

Garvey expected on his release from jail to unite the masses through personal contact. But this was not to be: in December 1927 Garvey was taken from his cell to New Orleans and put aboard a ship headed for Panama. He had been pardoned by President Coolidge—perhaps because the Negro Political Union had campaigned for Coolidge. The president had issued an unconditional pardon, but U.S. immigration authorities managed to effect Garvey's deportation, with debatable legality. The government used a law which stipulated that an alien convicted of a felony within five years of his arrival in the United States could be deported. As Garvey's lawyers pointed out to no avail, he had been in this country more than six years prior to his conviction.[4]

In New Orleans hundreds of Garveyites came to witness Garvey's forced departure, and many were moved to tears. From the deck of the ship, Garvey thanked his followers for their confidence in his leadership and promised that the movement's best and most productive years lay ahead. "To the millions of members of the Universal Negro Improvement Association throughout the world," he declared firmly, "I can only say: Cheer up, for the good work is just getting under way. Be firm and steadfast in holding to the principles of the organization. The greatest work is yet to be done. I shall with God's help do it." [5] He never returned to the United States.

During the next year Garvey traveled constantly: first through the West Indies, trying to patch together what remained of the UNIA in that area, then on to London, and finally to Canada—where he was immediately arrested. As a British subject, he had every right to visit Canada, and Garveyites saw the hand of the United States government behind this new incarceration. The UNIA was actively supporting Al Smith in the upcoming election, and the Republican administration apparently feared Garvey's influence if he came close enough to make his word known to black voters. Whatever the cause, he was quickly released. In ensuing years he found himself prohibited entry to all North and South American countries outside the British realm.

With their leadership torn and changing rapidly, Garveyites were thrown upon their own resources. Many turned toward cooperation with other organizations. This new approach enabled regionalists to involve the movement, more than ever before, in the struggles for political rights, employment, housing, and other immediate issues. Internationalists, too, gradually came to work through other organizations, where they produced a much more radical separatism than the UNIA had shown. The change in mode of operations was reflected in a 1932 convention of U.S. Garvey groups which was publicized as representing eighteen different organizations under Garveyite leadership.[6]

As Garveyites representing the two poles of black nationalism went their separate ways, the UNIA was gradually split apart. During the worst years of the Depression, Garveyites transferred to new nationalist and religious separatist groups by the thousands, and in the summer of 1933 the *Negro World* ceased publication. The UNIA as an all-encompassing vehicle for black nationalist activity died with it. But outside the big cities Garveyism itself was very much alive. Garveyites had come close to building a separate world in rural communities, even though they lacked Liberty Halls, businesses, and other tangible achievements. The UNIA had become the lodge, the socializing agency—in a sense, the political and religious center—in a great many small towns. In Southern hamlets, restrictions on voting, social and legal discrimination, and other inequities, left no alternative but autonomous development, and blacks in these areas continued to express their needs for self-determination through the UNIA. The *Negro World,* and later a new monthly magazine, *Black Man,* reported more than two hundred of these rural divisions well into the 1930s.[7]

Garveyism also persisted in the minds of many who helped build the Association. They had fared poorly as coordinators of the massive UNIA, and often fought among themselves, but most remained loyal to the Association long after its organizational structure had collapsed. In all, forty-three of the sixty leading Garveyites who served as International officials and presidents of the larger divisions during the formative years remained loyal to the movement throughout their lives, or at least into the late 1930s.[8] This continued support is the more impressive when one recalls that many of these men and women had been involved in bitter power struggles.* Only twelve of the sixty severed all ties with the UNIA, most for obviously personal reasons. Assistant President General LeRoy Bundy and Surgeon General J. D. Gibson were forced out of the movement because of suspected misappropriation of funds; a number of African leaders left under strong pressure from government authorities. Despite their dissension over the mail fraud trial, one of the lawyers who dropped out of the Association, Vernal Williams, later cooperated with Garveyites in New York in raising money for the Jamaican independence movement,[9] as did High Commissioner James O'Meally—one of those who sued for back pay during Garvey's imprisonment.[10] (O'Meally had certainly paid a high price for his work with the UNIA: he had given up his post as headmaster of Calabar College in Kingston for a job with the UNIA International, and led the ill-fated delegation to Liberia in 1924, where he was not allowed to land; he was transferred forcibly to Nigeria and much later to London, then sent back to Jamaica without being permitted to come to America.) Some leaders did

---

* There are no reports on the activities or opinions of six former leaders of the Association; the loyalty of others can be seen from their correspondence with Garvey (and later his widow), in newspaper and magazine articles they wrote, and in their attendance at periodic UNIA meetings and conferences.

quit (or were expelled) for ideological reasons: Reverend Eason and J. Austin Norris, who formed their own black nationalist organization; and socialists Hubert Harrison and W. A. Domingo. However, Harrison remained on favorable terms with the Garveyites and in the late 1930s Mrs. Garvey coaxed Domingo into working with other Garveyites in the Peoples National Party of Jamaica.[11]

David Cronon's *Black Moses* gives the impression of large-scale disloyalty on the part of UNIA leaders. Cronon deals with the later years only lightly, and he may have been unduly influenced by a lengthy section in volume two of *Philosophy and Opinions of Marcus Garvey,* published in the troubled year 1926, which takes note of the fifteen ex-leaders who sued for back pay. In the confusion following the confiscation of financial records, a few of these suits might have been justified—but four of those involved later returned to the movement, and a fifth, Ulysses Poston, wrote favorably of the Association in the New York *Contender, Inter-State Tattler* and Pittsburgh *Courier.*[12] The four who returned were Rudolph Smith, International leader of the West Indies, who again became a leading figure in the late 1930s; William Ferris, who joined the anti-Garvey faction in 1926, but later returned to the parent organization; Assistant President General J. D. Gordon, who returned to become president of the Los Angeles division; and Adrian Johnson, who had broken down and cried, pleading futilely for reconsideration when he was voted out as convention chairman in 1921. Johnson became an outspoken critic of Garvey but later returned to the movement and was still active in the 1940s.[13] Of the others who sued, three had left the movement in 1921. Among the five dozen leading Garveyites, outright treachery—that is, conscious attempts to sabotage the UNIA—was rare.

* * *

Among the hundreds of thousands, perhaps millions, of black people who had joined the Garvey movement, few were willing to reject the movement's philosophical, political, and cultural outlook. When the UNIA could no longer coordinate this sentiment, its members moved to build new organizations based upon what they considered important in their Garveyite experience. Columnist Samuel Haynes condemned these deserters bitterly in the *Negro World.* "Former Garveyites are now enrolled in the Moorish

American Society, in the various Africa movements, most of them founded by ex-Garveyites themselves," wrote Haynes, who also saw a move of "thousands" to "new religious movements claiming to be associated with Garveyism. Former Garveyites see in Father Divine, evangelist George Wilson, Bishop Grace and others the incarnation of Marcus Garvey." [14]

Perhaps as many as half of the rank and file Garveyites did go into religious separatist organizations, including some which had been part of the UNIA. Bishop George Alexander McGuire, for example, gradually loosened his ties to the UNIA, devoting more time to the spread of his African Orthodox Church. (McGuire had lost his position as chaplain general at the 1922 convention but returned to the leadership in 1924.) In 1932, he joined the UNIA Incorporated faction in New York; later he returned to the parent organization. Through all this his African Orthodox Church came to stand on its own, developing its own social world and living arrangements—in short, a substitute for the communal life of the UNIA. In the late 1960s the AOC still had a number of active congregations. [15]

Most of the six hundred black Jews who had come into the UNIA with Rabbi J. Arnold Ford were no longer connected with the UNIA by the late twenties. Ford himself was still UNIA musical director in 1926, and tried to mediate between the factions that year. Unsuccessful, he took his family to Ethiopia to practice Judaism among the native black Jews. He corresponded periodically with Garvey, but his main interest was now with his religion. [16]

By far the most important of these re-alliances was that of Elijah Poole. Poole, a corporal in the Chicago division, was one of many Garveyites attracted to Prophet Wallace Fard and his "Nation of Islam." [17] Poole replaced Fard as the leader of the movement in 1934 and, under the name Elijah Muhammad, had some ten thousand Black Muslim followers by 1940. Fard's group was an offshoot of the Moorish American Science Temple of Noble Drew Ali, formed in 1913; it remained an insignificant sect until large numbers of Garveyites joined in the late 1920s. At its height, in 1929, the group had ten thousand members in its Chicago temple, and smaller congregations in Pittsburgh and Detroit. [18] Muhammad acknowledged these connections in recruiting for the Muslims: "I have always had a very high opinion of both the late Noble Drew Ali and

Marcus Garvey and admired their courage in helping our people (the so-called Negroes) and appreciated their work. Both of these men were fine Muslims. The followers of Noble Drew Ali and Marcus Garvey should now follow me and cooperate with us in our work because we are only trying to finish up what those before us started." [19]

Noble Drew Ali taught his followers that they were descendants of the once-proud Moorish Empire of North Africa, an Islamic state, and gave them Moorish names to replace the slave names given by the white man. Like Garvey, he insisted the black American must have a nation, but Ali held that North America was but an extension of the true African homeland, Morocco, and that a Moorish nation should be built in America. As his movement grew, a contest for leadership developed, and on March 15, 1929, Noble Drew Ali's chief rival was shot and stabbed in the organization's offices. Ali was arrested and charged with murder but released on bond. A few weeks later he died mysteriously—some claimed he died of injuries inflicted by police, others that he had been killed by partisans of the slain contender.[20] Shortly thereafter Fard founded his new organization.

Under Fard (and later Muhammad), the Black Muslims carried separatism to its logical extreme. In the long run, the Muslims hoped the government would grant them a separate state somewhere within the territorial United States; in the meantime, Muslims would avoid all social, political or spiritual contact with whites. During the Depression, Muslims refused relief checks, WPA or other government-sponsored employment, and even social security numbers. In 1942 Elijah Muhammad went to jail for five years because he refused to acknowledge the draft.[21]

The Muslims' withdrawal was motivated by very much the same force which had moved the Garveyites to create their separate world: the need to escape the oppressor in order to find individual and group identity, and to discuss common problems and aspirations with their brothers. The Muslim approach was more shocking because it lacked the humanism which attracted great masses to Garveyism. In seeking to build a coalition of all black groups fighting for self-determination, the UNIA couched its arguments in broad phrases to attract those who expressed bitter hostility toward whites, as well as those advocating mutual respect. The Nation of

Islam worked on the principle that blacks had already expended too much respect on the white man. Elijah Muhammad, the late Malcolm X, and other Muslim spokesmen prided themselves on holding to the truth even if it meant their organization remained small. And the truth was that whites were "devils." Muslims delved into the objective history of slavery to prove their point, and even added some prehistory of their own, arguing that whites were created six thousand years ago by the evil science of a sinful black, blacks having been the original and only true humans. Muhammad has consistently told his followers to seek "freedom, equality and justice," adding that they "are not going to get that from the enemy of freedom, equality and justice," the "white devils." [22]

The Nation of Islam included many features which were present in the UNIA. The Muslim defense corps, the Fruit of Islam, is analogous to the UNIA's African Legions and police force. More significantly, part of the Muslim way of life entails what Muhammad has described as "communalism" in economics: the second of his three commandments is "Thou shalt pursue wealth only for the common good." [23] In practice, the Muslims' heavy accent on respectability and propriety has led them into a rather bourgeois approach to money. But even though they shower status and prestige upon members who find success in business, individuals are still expected to share their profits with the group. Working-class members participate in cooperatively owned business enterprises, with all profits going to the group (since 1958, to pay health and death benefits for members). [24]

The spirit of withdrawal into a separate world found a less belligerent form in Father Divine's communitarian Heavens, which attracted thousands of ex-Garveyites during the Depression decade.* Where the Muslims preached worship of the true God, Allah, Divine simply intoned that he, in fact, was God. Where the Muslims foresaw a long struggle to achieve a new world, Father Divine announced that the new world was here, with him. Muhammad announced that this was the time for the "end of the wicked," but Divine proclaimed, "Peace, Good Health, Good Appetite, Good Will and a heart full of Merriness, with Life, Liberty, Happiness, and

---

*During the late thirties and early forties there was correspondence between Father Divine and Mr. and Mrs. Garvey. [25]

Eternal Life. . . . I give you joy and peace. . . . I am your happiness and I am your joy. . . . Whatever you need, let my spirit do it. . . . I command and demand anything I desire. . . . God in the midst of you is mighty to save. I am here, there and everywhere. Dial in and you shall find me. Aren't you glad?" And his followers responded, "I thank you, Father." [26]

The Father Divine Peace Mission was not ideologically black nationalist, nor even all black—Divine declared he did not distinguish on the basis of skin color, and nearly ten per cent of his followers were white. Yet the Peace Mission had a strong attraction for UNIA members. Whereas *Negro World* columnist Samuel Haynes complained that Garveyites were seeking a "reincarnation of Marcus Garvey" in Father Divine, what they were really seeking was a continuation of the social, psychological, religious, and economic autonomy which had been the goal of the Garvey movement.

In the midst of a world-wide economic depression, Divine constructed the most successful communal movement ever developed in the United States. Between 1931 and 1936, his Peace Mission grew from an insignificant handful into an organization claiming over a million followers. All wages and benefits acquired by members went to support the cause. Some of these earnings were used to purchase apartment houses, which were turned into communal living quarters segregated by sex (even husbands and wives were separated, celibacy being one of Divine's many stringent rules). Followers could find work in Father Divine's restaurants, laundries, or numerous communal farms in New York and New Jersey. The best-remembered aspect of the Peace Missions during their heyday was the ten to fifteen cent meal, with its inspired cooking. All were welcome at the Heavens, and after dinner the visitor could find lodging for minimal rates in Divine Hotels. The devout believer was rewarded with personal communion with God and the benefit of "faith-healing" and "holiness" or sanctification at gala affairs and banquets. In return, members were expected to give total dedication to the Father and the work of the Mission.

The Depression doubtless helped the movement. Thousands of blacks desperately needed food, housing, and employment, and the requirement that all income be given to the Mission was easy to bear when there was no appreciable income earned outside the movement. Even the prohibition on sexual relationships was palatable for the many followers too impoverished to afford the luxury of family life.[27]

Father Divine's ability to provide food, housing, spiritual guidance and jobs prepared the faithful for his conception of society which poet Claude McKay described as: "(1) no sex; (2) no race; (3) no color; (4) no money." These things were irrelevant because the Father had brought Heaven to Earth, and in Heaven such matters did not count. Yet the mundane world was not entirely ignored. The Divine world's relationship to society at large was defined in a fourteen-point Divine Righteous Government Platform. One point opposed trade unions—economically self-contained Heavens had no place for unions, which fought for higher wages, while Divine was striving to abolish money entirely. A secret of Father Divine's success was his ability to undersell competitors; thus his platform also opposed New Deal legislation which "deprives the individual of the right to sell his goods for little or nothing if he chooses." Another plank reflected the belief in economic communalism and suggested nationalization of "all idle plants and machinery." As many of the faithful were former receivers of the dole, Father Divine was particularly aware of the degrading methods of welfare departments, and one of his planks called for the "abolition of regulations requiring Americans to declare themselves destitute and go on relief rolls to obtain WPA jobs." Other planks demanded a federal anti-lynch law and immediate legislation making it a crime to discriminate in any public place against any individual on account of race, creed, or color.[28]   Aside from position statements such as the Divine Righteous Government Platform, the movement was rarely involved in political or social struggles. To display the Father's concern for black people outside his movement, the Divinites did make token appearances in a few rallies and parades in Harlem called by other organizations fighting for better housing and jobs.

Though the Divine Peace Mission's only tie to the UNIA was through its large ex-Garveyite membership, the movement's lifestyle was not unlike that of the UNIA. Whites were present, but the Peace Mission was run by blacks under a black God. Grass-roots followers in both movements found spiritual escape from established Christianity, and sought to build separate economic institutions and overcome white racism primarily by developing independent power bases within black society. Many Garveyites were no doubt reluctant to join a movement which officially rejected the concept of race, and many more rejected the spiritualist aspects of the Peace Mission, but a sizable contingent of Garveyites saw in Divine's movement the opportunity to continue building a world of their own.

* * *

Two movements based on the promise of repatriation in Africa also attracted substantial numbers of Garveyites in the 1930s: the RastafarI* in Jamaica, and the Peace Movement of Ethiopia and its offshoot, the Ethiopia Pacific Movement, in the United States.

Most early followers of the RastafarI movement, which started in the slums of Kingston in the early 1930s, were from the rank and file of the Jamaican UNIA. At first there were two Rasta groups claiming to have originated the movement, both declaring spiritual guidance from Marcus Garvey and expressing indebtedness to Garvey for the Back-to-Africa idea.* The name RastafarI was taken from the royal line in Ethiopia (articles in Garvey's *Black Man* on the nobleman Ras Nasibu had helped generate interest in Ethiopian royalty). The movement recruited members by offering immediate spiritual transference back to Africa, with the hope of eventual emigration in form as well as in spirit.[29]

Colonial authorities and most Jamaicans considered the RastafarI a cult of religious fanatics; it has, in fact, been primarily a religious and cultural movement. Ferdinand Ricketts, Leopold Howell, and other early leaders made the worship of Ethiopian royalty (as the personification of God) an integral part of the movement on the basis of references to the African features of God in the "seven seals" passage of the book of Revelations. By immersing themselves in deep contemplation, the RastafarI achieved an individual identification with God, in Africa and at home. They conceptualized this transcendental experience with the phrase, "I an I." Followers said they had made a qualitative leap from their surroundings to Africa through psychic experiences achieved by smoking the sacred herb *ganja,* a highly potent variety of marijuana grown in Jamaica.

The desire for repatriation was particularly strong during the Depression years in Jamaica. Chronic unemployment, which had

* The final *I* is capitalized by the RastafarI themselves.

* The leader of one faction, Ferdinand Ricketts, came from a family of active Jamaican Garveyites.

been high since the shift away from sugar before World War I, had grown to alarming proportions by the end of the 1930s. Of 514,000 employable males on the island, 139,000 were unemployed former workers and another 50,000 had never had a steady job.[30] Thus the RastafarI had some reason to declare life in Jamaica untenable. To force the issue of emigration, they refused to accept permanent employment when offered, on the grounds that jobs for a few provided no answer for the thousands who had to continue without a means of livelihood. They also showed disdain for the existing system by wearing ragged clothing with pride and adopting a distinctive hair style: long, braided ringlets which the men grew to shoulder length. These "dreadlocks" make the RastafarI easy to distinguish, and over the past thirty years police have repeatedly harassed and assaulted Rasta men on the streets of Kingston, raided their religious services and closed their communal farms on the pretext of looking for *ganja*. But the movement has continued to grow, most recently with the addition of "dropouts" from the Jamaican upper classes, and there are now probably more than twenty thousand RastafarI on the island. Many more show sympathy with the movement, especially Jamaican youth and those in the new black power movement. The black power newspaper *Abeng* carries weekly comment from RastafarI and news of its activities. The group continues its call for repatriation—although it would now agree to settle in countries other than Ethiopia—and now demands that the government provide temporary employment and permit the use of *ganja*. Said Rasta follower Bongo Jere in an *Abeng* column: "I an I point out that Marcus Garvey's work is still unfinished, relevant and is linked up with the works of Emperor Hyili Silassi I."[31]

In the United States, Garveyites who still sought repatriation found strong support in the Ethiopia Pacific Movement established in Chicago in 1932 by Miss Mittie Gordon, a former lady president of the Chicago division and a leading figure at the 1929 UNIA convention. Miss Gordon and most of her followers were still nominal UNIA members, and the Ethiopia Pacific Movement was a conscious attempt to carry Garveyism forward under a new banner.[32] In the late 1930s, the organization gave enthusiastic support to a bill by Mississippi Senator Theodore Bilbo which would have allocated federal funds to black people who wished to live in Africa. Bilbo was probably the most notorious racist demagogue of his generation, and no friend of the black man, but the many who saw little difference between one white man and another found no reason to reject Bilbo's help if he was willing to aid the Back-to-Africa cause.

Miss Gordon launched a nationwide campaign to obtain signatures from blacks who favored the Bilbo plan. Her contacts among Garveyites helped circulate the petitions, and within eight months some four hundred thousand signatures had been obtained. (There was a claim that additional petitions, never produced, brought the number of signers to two million.) In 1939, some three hundred of Miss Gordon's followers pooled their resources, assembled a fleet of dilapidated trucks, and headed for Washington to lobby for the Bilbo proposal. Most never arrived, as the trucks began breaking down before reaching the Chicago city limits, but their presence would have made no difference in any case. Bilbo's proposal had been a demagogic stunt in the first place, and even his dixiecrat colleagues opposed the expenditures involved.[33]

In August of 1941, Miss Gordon was summoned before federal authorities and charged with influencing blacks to avoid the draft. She denied this, asserting that her organization's principal aim was repatriation for black people. She noted that Abraham Lincoln and Thomas Jefferson had favored similar action: ". . . those men knew the two races couldn't live together. And our race is dying out through amalgamation. There are eight million mulattos in the United States now. Whites should remain white and blacks should remain black. Africa is our country and that's where we want to go—to the soil of Liberia. . . . The government should use the relief money now being spent on blacks here to transport all self-respecting blacks to Liberia." After Pearl Harbor, Miss Gordon again ran afoul of the authorities, this time for advocating the cause of the Japanese and allegedly preaching hatred for the white man.[34]

* * *

There were other aspects of Garveyism which found expression during the decline of the UNIA, for example in the "Don't Buy Where You Can't Work" campaigns led by ad hoc organizations in virtually every major city. Garveyites participated in these campaigns, and some were initiated by local UNIA groups. Their motivation is not difficult to understand. The Depression was doubly oppressive for blacks: New York relief rolls for October 1933 showed 23.9 per cent of the city's blacks on relief, but only 9.2 per cent of the whites; in Philadelphia the ratio was 34.4 per cent to 8.2 per cent, and other cities showed comparable disproportions. Unemployment figures were truly staggering: in 1931, 40.3 per cent of black males in Chicago were unemployed; Pittsburgh had 48 per cent unemployed in 1934.

Blacks were particularly galled when they could not find work in their own neighborhoods. One study of Harlem businesses in May 1931 found fifty-nine per cent owned by whites and employing only whites; another twenty-four per cent were owned by whites who did employ Negroes, but mostly in menial jobs. Black-owned stores accounted for only seventeen per cent of the total.[35] And, as the grip of the Depression tightened, many blacks in the ghetto lost their jobs to hard-pressed relatives of white shop-owners.

In desperation, blacks took to the streets. Starting in Chicago in 1929, the idea of boycotting and picketing discriminatory ghetto stores spread spontaneously across the country: in Washington, D.C., the New Negro Alliance; in Baltimore, the Costanie Movement (which included many Garveyites); the Future Outlook League and the Colored Clerks Circle in St. Louis; the Vanguard League in Columbus, Ohio; the Progressive Negro League (under Garveyite leadership) in Detroit; the Industrial Council (under ex-Garveyites) in Los Angeles—all conducted such campaigns. In New York City, the many movements for jobs included the Harlem Labor Union, Afro-American Federation of Labor, Citizens Committee for Fair Play, and the Greater New York Coordinating Committee, which included the New York UNIA. The rival UNIA Incorporated also conducted boycotts in New York and Philadelphia.[36]

The first of these boycotts was the work of Sufi Abdule Hamid, known for many years in Chicago as Bishop Conshankin, a former religious mystic and an authority on Hindu, Chinese, and other oriental religions. Late in 1929 Hamid started meandering through the black community carrying a stepladder which he would place in front of a discriminatory store. He would mount the ladder and begin to harangue passers-by with slogans like "buy where you can work" and "jobs for Negroes." Members of the Moorish American Science Temple—by then mostly ex-Garveyites—provided much of the legwork, surveying businesses to find out if they would hire blacks. Arna Bontemps claims this display of black power led to the employment of "thousands of Negro men and women in manufacturing plants, stores and offices," and St. Clair Drake Jr. and Horace Cayton credit the Chicago campaign with two thousand jobs.[37] Arguments over tactics and religion lost Hamid most of his campaign workers and he moved to New York late in 1931. His relations with the Garveyites were never good, as he objected to their "pacifist approach," as he termed it.

These movements were often far from peaceful: recurrent outbreaks of violence marked the Chicago campaign; police jailed picketers in Boston, New York, and Philadelphia; and the movement was severely intimidated in the Deep South.[38] At first, the boycotts had a working-class flair, with militant leaders who, like Sufi Hamid, were close to the grass roots and hostile toward whites. Hamid was accused of threatening racist shop owners with physical reprisals, and in New York he was called the "Harlem Hitler" for referring to the "kike," "wop," or "dago" owner of a particular establishment.[39] Bishop Kiowa Costanie in Baltimore and street-corner orator Arthur Reid of the African Patriotic League in New York were both accused of being racist demagogues. "If we can solve our economic problem, then to hell with the white man—and that is exactly what we propose to do," said Lionel Francis, who led the UNIA Incorporated boycott movement in New York.[40] These actions were often almost leaderless and loosely organized—as was one conducted in Brooklyn by a group of housewives and black veterans.[41]

Those who promoted these campaigns had a hard time widening their base of support. Only a handful of black newspapers dared draw the wrath of their advertisers, many of whom owned the very businesses being boycotted. The weekly Atlanta *World* promoted a campaign against A & P stores in 1932, but soon changed its mind after threats from its advertisers. The Chicago *Whip* actively supported Sufi Hamid's campaign and published lists of discriminatory businesses until loss of advertising forced the *Whip* to cease publication in 1932. Its rival, the Chicago *Defender,* didn't even mention the jobs movement, much less endorse it; and the New York *Amsterdam News* excused itself because such support would cause a "fearful loss of advertising." The *Negro World* was one of the few papers to support the campaigns.[42]

By the late 1930s, however, the movement had begun to attract members of the black establishment. In Chicago and in St. Louis, the NAACP and Urban League allowed boycotters to use mimeograph machines and office supplies, though they refrained from endorsing the campaigns.[43] When the picket lines finally appeared in the nation's capital, the middle class quickly stepped in to keep the movement "respectable." This particular campaign started when a hamburger grill in the heart of Washington's ghetto discharged its black employees and replaced them with whites. As Ralph Bunche reported, "Several young Negroes happened to witness the discharge of the Negro employees and the injustice of the situation struck them with full force. They decided to organize a picket line in front of the grill and in a surprisingly short time the discharged Negro workers were back in their jobs." This was the beginning of the New Negro Alliance, which developed a broad program including pressure tactics for jobs, "the creation of bigger and better Negro business through increased earning power of Negroes," support for all businesses which employed Negroes, and Afro-American research into new fields for business and labor. In 1934 the Alliance began to issue its own newspaper, the *New Negro Opinion,* and in 1939 it produced a yearbook detailing its successes in integrating chain stores and other establishments in Washington.[44]

In Harlem the riot of 1935 provided the shock needed to bring a sizable coalition behind the boycott movement. The riot had been engendered almost entirely by rage at job discrimination, and when it was over virtually every white-owned store along the 125th Street shopping center had been smashed and looted.[45] Soon after, fifty prominent Harlemites (including Adam Clayton Powell, the Reverend William Lloyd Imes, Arthur Reid, local Communist leader James W. Ford, and the UNIA's Rudolph Smith and A. L. King) joined together in the Greater New York Coordinating Committee. By 1938, the Committee had won an agreement from Harlem shopowners under which they pledged to fill job vacancies with black people until at least one-third of their employees were black. The militant Harlem Labor Union, originated by Sufi Hamid's followers, rejected the agreement and continued to fight for one hundred per cent black employment.[46]

Garveyites involved in the "Don't Buy Where You Can't Work" movement exemplified those within the UNIA who had asked for greater emphasis on local problems. The New York splinter group,

UNIA Incorporated, joined the jobs movement in Harlem in 1931, and the parent organization followed suit a year later.

During the Depression, the Communist party made a concerted effort to win Garveyite support by developing a program purporting to grant black power and national independence for blacks. In their concern for the plight of the black man, the Communists of the 1930s were far ahead of all other white political groups in America. Communists became active in black communities, where they sought support from laborers, day workers, the unemployed and the young—in effect, the group which had been the foundation of the UNIA. Though they had far smaller numbers than the Garveyites, the Communists proved capable organizers. During the 1930s they arranged parades, demonstrations and rallies which rivaled the best of the UNIA's productions in size. And, like the Garveyites in their heyday, the Communists gave the man on the street a skepticism about both the white power structure and the black bourgeoisie. Unlike the Garveyites, however, Communists found black nationalism an idea that could be dropped easily, and they also proved capable of almost instantaneous changes in their relationship with the power structure, black and white.

The Communists' black nationalist program called for the generation of a separate black republic in the American South after the revolution. The plan attracted no support from prominent Garveyites or ex-Garveyites. The Communists claimed to have won over many of the UNIA rank and file, but only one (Louis Campbell, who became a community organizer in Harlem) was ever elevated to a position of authority in the Party.[47] Nonetheless, the Communists had a deep effect on the strength of the Garvey movement—by emphasizing black nationalism they won away young blacks who were potential recruits for the UNIA. In the late 1930s, the Communist leaders dropped their nationalist program and eased their black converts into a coalition with Franklin D. Roosevelt's liberal New Deal.* Thus the long-range effect of the Communist venture into black nationalism was to help draw a young generation of black militants into the ranks of integrationists. Communist-style black nationalism was worked out in Moscow in 1928 by the former

---

*Some black communists (Campbell, for one) resigned in protest; others, including most of those from the old ABB, dropped out of leading positions when the change occurred.[48]

African Blood Brotherhood leader Harry Haywood and the Russian N. Nasanov. It was an attempt to apply Lenin's program for national minorities in the Soviet Union to the United States—an idea which had inspired Cyril Briggs to found the ABB years earlier. At the Fourth International Communist Conference in 1928, Haywood proposed that black Americans should win a separate republic within the continental United States.[49] (A similar proposal had been discussed some years before at UNIA conventions, but was rejected as impractical.) Haywood argued that blacks, like national minorities in the Soviet Union, dominated a geographical area, had their own culture and social institutions, and were entitled to a federal republic once the revolution had been accomplished. The Black Belt Republic, as it was called, was to include the sixty counties in the South where blacks were a majority—a long, thin line stretching from the Brazos River country of Texas through central Louisiana, Mississippi and Alabama, and on up through Richmond, Virginia. As with federal states in the USSR, foreign affairs and economic policy would be decided upon by the United States in conjunction with the regional states. The new republic was not to be exclusively racial; blacks would be in control only because they were in the majority. Those blacks living outside the republic would be expected to assimilate into the social and economic life of the larger, white community. Communists were to engage in a thorough battle against all forms of racism all over the country to prepare for the Black Belt Republic and to make assimilation in the North possible.[50]

The program did draw support: while the Party had a mere two dozen black members in 1927, by the late 1930s there were between eight and ten thousand black Communists, and many more became members for a short time early in the Depression.[51] Thus the Communist party included blacks in a proportion—ten per cent—comparable to their presence in the society at large. In the North, the Communists gained support in two ways: by disarming nationalists with arguments that the Party had adopted their program and by pointing to Communist-led civil rights struggles as signs of interest in blacks which would be directed toward nationalist ends as soon as Communist activity got a foothold in the South.

The Communists never obtained their foothold in the South, despite an intensive effort. A tenant farmers union in Arkansas and a sizable sharecroppers union in Alabama did thrive for a time, and Communists made important steps toward organizing labor in heavy industry in Birmingham. But the work was arduous, and cost the lives of many a Communist organizer and Southern sympathizer. One woman was shot and killed in Gastonia, North Carolina, while addressing an outdoor meeting of textile workers. In 1931, a black organizer working with Alabama sharecroppers was shot and killed; in 1933, two other sharecropper organizers were lynched following a gun battle with a sheriff's mob. In addition, there were a number of pitched battles between sharecroppers and lynch mobs inflamed with hatred for the "race-mixing" Communists [52] —even in the Black Belt, the Communists insisted upon integrated unions and community action.

Harry Haywood himself was assigned to the South. In 1932, he was organizing in Memphis, where blacks were being murdered at a rate of almost one a day by "Boss " Crump's police. Haywood and a white comrade convinced witnesses to one of these murders that they should testify in an unofficial "trial" in a black church. The police were "convicted" and Haywood asked the local NAACP and black business leaders to join in demanding that the guilty be tried in a regular court of law. The black leaders refused and the NAACP denounced outside intervention by the Communists. Shortly afterward, a key witness disappeared and Haywood received an anonymous phone call warning that he would be next. With Haywood posing as the chauffeur of his white colleague, the two managed to get out of town.[53]

Difficulties with the NAACP, such as the one in Memphis, kindled Haywood's anger at the black establishment and helped make him the Party's chief denouncer of "petit-bourgeois reformists" and "arch race mis-leaders." Garveyites also received a large share of his venom. Haywood and other proponents of the Black Belt Republic were trying in this fashion to reassure the white Party members who doubted that the republic was a legitimate Communist idea. A good many white comrades, themselves racist and leery of black power, had to be shown that the Black Belt Republic would not be racial or connected with "petit-bourgeois nationalism"—allegedly typified by the UNIA. Haywood, with his passionate hatred for the bourgeoisie, was the best man for the job.

Haywood also proved quite adept at arguing the intriguing notion

235

that the black republic would not be racial. "Marxism nowhere places the question of an oppressed people . . . as a race question," he wrote. "Race as a social question exists only for the ideologist of the bourgeoisie and in the minds of those deluded by them."[54] He insisted that blacks were an oppressed national minority, not a racial group, and told the 1934 Communist Party Convention, "The greatest menace to our work among Negroes are . . . the petit-bourgeois nationalists." Such logic led the party to lump "Don't Buy Where You Can't Work" campaigns, the UNIA, and all its nationalist offshoots together with the NAACP and Urban League.[55] This approach, demonstrated at Party conventions and in Party publications, assured troubled white Communists that the program for blacks was consistent with the goal of proletarian unity.

Of course, Communists often had to take a different tack at local levels, or the Party would never have gathered some ten thousand black followers. Communist organizers in the South, for instance, spoke with two voices: among blacks, they talked of a total restructuring of Southern society—political, social, and economic; among whites, they emphasized instead the immediate monetary gains that unions and community programs would bring. For blacks, integrated union meetings, schools and the like were to be the first steps toward eventual power in the Black Belt. Obviously, white comrades would have a place in the new republic, but in the South this point was a bit more acceptable to blacks than to whites. In fact, the monetary rewards of trade unionism were about all white Southern workers could accept—even those willing to join a Communist-sponsored trade union feared giving power to blacks. (Consequently, the Communist party had proportionally more support in the South among blacks than whites.)

In the South especially, Communists found their work jeopardized time after time by white workers' fear of black power. The Communists' response was not only to assure whites that communism did not mean independent black power, but also to refuse power to blacks. In Alabama, for example, after sharecroppers and their organizers had been shot at, beaten and jailed repeatedly, a black caucus within the union asked permission to form separate black and white locals. This group hoped to avoid racist attacks on "miscegenationism," but they were, in effect, also asking for independent power, since most union members were black and an autonomous white local would have little chance of succeeding.[56] The Party hierarchy's response—after two years' delay—was to "liquidate" the sharecroppers' union. Its organizers were asked to work elsewhere as part of the new drive to involve the Party in various New Deal government agencies starting to operate in the South.[57]

This shift reflected a new nationwide policy adopted in 1935: the Party had decided to work within the liberal establishment and try to take it over, rather than building separate revolutionary bases of power. By working to improve the work of New Deal agencies— which were supposed to function without regard to race, creed or color, but often displayed rampant racial discrimination—the Communists could claim to be fighting discrimination against blacks, while avoiding difficult questions of black power. But businessmen and landowners controlled key agencies in the South, and Communist challenges to this control proved unsuccessful, except in the National Youth Administration. In time, the whole scheme turned into a major disaster when a more conservative federal government simply "liquidated" the agencies in the 1940s, leaving the Communists without any base of operations.*

In the North, Communists prided themselves on their activities in black communities and could legitimately point with scorn to the record of other interracial organizations. The Communist weekly *Harlem Liberator* quoted a Socialist Party organizer as having said, "Let us first liberate the white workers, then we'll work for the Negroes,"[58] and Communists noted that the NAACP had no economic program for black people—a weakness which eventually caused Du Bois to quit the Association he had helped create back in 1910. Cyril Briggs (by then editor of the *Liberator*) described the conversion to Communism of Louis Campbell, "the staunch Garveyite of 1929." It was a typical story of the co-opting of a militant. Campbell had participated in a number of CP-sponsored unemployment demonstrations and had been arrested several times for his militancy. "These experiences firmly convinced him that he could only serve the Negro masses by helping to build a fighting alliance of Negro and white workers against their common enemy. Whereupon

---

* In one sense, Communists had manipulated the black struggle, but to a far greater extent the CPUSA had been manipulated by its liberal allies—a fact Communists themselves acknowledged in the forties, when it was too late to do anything about it.

he entered the Workers school to train for leadership in the struggles of the toilers."[59] While other groups deliberated, Communists organized massive parades and rallies to protest inadequate relief payments, poor housing, and Southern lynchings. They ran rent strikes and formed a powerful Domestic Workers Union which effectively eradicated the Bronx "slave mart"—a street near Yankee Stadium where black women lined up daily to be picked by white housewives from the suburbs for a day's labor at ridiculously low wages.

Communists also organized an "anti-eviction militia." When the landlord appeared with a sheriff and an eviction notice, the mother would send one of her children to "get the Reds." Within minutes, a small army of men would have gathered on the sidewalk. As the sheriff's assistants carried the furniture out, the "Reds" would carry it back inside.[60] These actions were not always peaceful: on one occasion, more than five thousand marched from a Communist street rally in Chicago when they heard of an attempt to evict a seventy-two-year-old woman. Police, seeing the crowd, panicked and started shooting into the crowd. Three of the protesters were killed, and in the subsequent scuffle two policemen were badly injured. As a consequence, the Municipal Court temporarily suspended the service of eviction warrants—an expensive victory.[61]

Despite all their feverish activity in the black community, Communists refused to endorse the "Don't Buy Where You Can't Work" movement. The *Party Organizer* described this as a "campaign against the foreign-born workers" raised by "Negro reformists." And Haywood, speaking before the 1934 Communist convention, listed the "Don't Buy Where You Can't Work" movement among the "petit-bourgeois nationalist" activities which were dividing the working class.[62] In the Communist view, power for the black worker could come only through unity with white workers. Rent strikes, anti-eviction militias, demands for equitable relief payments, did not jeopardize that unity; but job campaigns exposed the racism of white workers, and especially of trade unions, and the Party preferred to handle this touchy matter more gently. For example, the *Party Organizer* could report with satisfaction the work of an organizer in South Carolina: white laborers in one textile factory opposed the entry of any blacks into their union. Blacks in the community were asking not only admission to the union, but also guaranteed fair employment. The Communist organizer won a compromise: the handful of blacks already employed in the factory were allowed into the union, but the fair employment policy was omitted, because he felt this was the only way to save the union.[63]

But militants in the North were not about to accept such a compromise. One white Harlem butcher, for example, told a boycott leader his shop was organized by the AFL Butchers Union, and to bring hiring problems to the union. The boycott leader replied, "To hell with the AFL; they are downtown and we are in Harlem. They can't help you if we throw a picket line around this place."[64] The more militant boycott movements in New York—the Afro-American Federation of Labor and the Harlem Labor Union—were attempts to build a black alternative to racist white trade unions, but Communists were reluctant to support genuine black power. In 1934, when Cyril Briggs arranged an "integrated" boycott of the Fifth Avenue Bus Company, which ran through the black community but employed only whites, his *Harlem Liberator* pictured black and white "comrades" picketing bus company offices in an obvious attempt to show a "respectable" boycott and to discredit more nationalistic actions. In the late thirties the Harlem CP cooperated with the respectable Coordinating Committee of Adam Clayton Powell; Communists also managed to integrate a boycott in Boston. Elsewhere in the country, Party members followed official policy and consistently opposed the jobs campaigns.[65]

Communists also opposed the widespread cooperative movement among blacks as "petit-bourgeois." The biggest of the cooperatives, the Colored Merchants Association, was indeed an organization of black businessmen, created by the National Negro Business League, which was dedicated to the conservative principles of its founder, Booker T. Washington. The CMA was nonetheless one expression of black power. It attempted to pool the resources of black retailers across the nation so they could purchase merchandise at a lower price, and virtually every black organization supported it.[66] Blacks initiated smaller independent cooperatives in all parts of the country, especially early in the Depression. One study of seven "Rochdale" consumer-producer cooperatives started by blacks in the 1930s showed that all had predominantly working-class membership, and had been founded by blacks from the lower middle class.[67] Cooperatives were still being formed in the late thirties, but the movement lost strength as more and more blacks began working with trade unions or New Deal agencies.

The New Deal itself was immediately beneficial to blacks: new government agencies provided many jobs and built low-income housing and parks in the ghetto; the president of the United States even established a "Black Cabinet" of Negro advisors.

Yet in the long run, the New Deal proved harmful to blacks. The Agricultural Adjustment Administration's policy of closing farms with marginal productivity made black land ownership drop sharply. The AAA curtailed sharecropping, only to replace it with the widespread use of migrant labor. Although key trade unions were integrated, the percentage of blacks employed in the automobile, steel, and maritime industries remained the same until World War II.[68] New Deal liberals put an end to the practice of mob lynchings—and let the courts do the work: between 1930 and 1960, 396 black people were put to death "legally" in Southern states, compared to only 16 whites. The modern welfare agency created by New Deal liberals has become the plague of the ghetto resident. Finally, the Federal Housing Authority—created to aid the troubled housing industry and a public desperately in need of better housing—worked to keep blacks in the ghetto, while assisting whites to move to the suburbs. The official FHA Underwriting Manual of 1938 warned home buyers, "If a neighborhood is to retain stability, it is necessary that properties shall continue to be occupied by the same social and racial group." The FHA urged mortgage evaluators to ascertain whether "effective restrictive covenants against the entire tract are recorded, since these provide the surest protection against undesirable encroachment [by] inharmonious racial groups." This policy went unchanged for better than two decades.[69]

The facade of progress that was the New Deal pushed black nationalism into the background. By 1940, only a handful of active UNIA divisions (now called Garvey Clubs) survived, along with a smattering of small nationalist groups in some of the largest cities. Garveyites everywhere were working primarily through other organizations. Mrs. Garvey wrote to Sidney Young, editor of the Panama *Tribune,* in 1944: "The Garvey movement having outgrown the capacity for one organization, we operate different societies and auxiliaries. . . . But I am working hard to see that we all aim at the final goal, which is Nationhood—for our people wherever they constitute a majority, in any tropical belt of the globe." [70] During World War II, as independence for colonies began to seem more and more likely, Garveyites turned their efforts in this direction, acting through organizations based in London, Africa and New York.*

Ironically, the years of the New Deal also saw the eclipse of those black Communist leaders who had learned their politics in the 1920s in the shadow of the UNIA. Their mixture of self-determination and assimilation was too nationalistic for the younger breed of Communists caught up in the struggles to integrate the trade unions and the New Deal itself. Cyril Briggs was asked to resign as editor of the *Liberator* early in 1935. He later moved to the West Coast and worked with Charlotta Bass on her *California Eagle* and then with the ardent black nationalist Pat Patterson on her paper the Los Angeles *Herald Dispatch*—one of the first weeklies to carry Elijah Muhammad's editorial column. Harry Haywood, who went off to fight in the Spanish Civil War, returned in 1938 to find that the CP had "liquidated" many of his pet projects in the South. He left the leadership, and quit the Party altogether in the mid-fifties. [72] Grace Campbell, former African Blood Brotherhood member and a Communist leader in Harlem during the early 1930s, quit in 1938, along with ex-Garveyite Louis Campbell. The two (unrelated) Campbells objected to the Party's insistence on having whites in leadership positions of the Harlem Federal Writers Project, and to its opposition to black cooperative movements. [73] Richard B. Moore, another former ABB member, resigned in 1940 because his superiors would not allow him to determine policy for the publishing company he had inaugurated to reprint old works by black writers. [74] George Padmore, who had written one of the early treatises on the Black Belt Republic, quit in 1934 when he learned that the Communists planned to cooperate with the liberals of the New Deal, to change

---

* The Pan-African Congress Movement in London, the West African Student Union, the West African Press Delegation, the African News Service, the *African* magazine (many Garveyites contributed articles to this magazine, the organ of the Pan-African movement), the African Study Circle of the World, the League of Colored People in London, the African National Congress in South Africa, and the Trade Union Congress of Nigeria. These movements had as their elder statesmen the Garveyites William Sherrill, Rudolph Smith, Bishop G. A. McGuire, Eric Walrond, Dr. D. D. Lewis, Samuel Haynes, Vernal Williams, Arden A. Bryan, George Weston, Marie Barrier Houston, Adrian Johnson, Dr. Willis N. Huggins, William Ferris (until his death in 1941), and Amy Jacques Garvey. [71]

their approach in the Black Belt, and to adopt a go-slow policy in colonial Africa. Padmore, head of the international operation for Communist activity in Africa when he resigned, became a bitter foe of the Communists. In the 1950s he was the foremost political theorist in Kwame Nkrumah's Ghana.

Briggs, Haywood, Padmore and the other black Communists were unsuccessful for two reasons. One was the hierarchical structure of the Communist party itself and its leaders' slavish subordination to the Soviet Union. The other involved their approach to the Black Belt Republic. The essential idea has merit, but black Communists insisted upon integrating power bases both North *and* South. Briggs, Haywood, Padmore and others found it logical to seek the aid of white revolutionaries, but in so doing they overlooked the realities of the black situation in the United States. Without careful safeguards, cooperation leads to co-optation for blacks. This had been a major reason for Garveyite refusal to participate in interracial organizations. Garveyites retained their separatist stance in the face of the New Deal not because they opposed social security and government aid to the poor, artists, and the young, but because they realized that without black power no amount of government help could make the blacks' living standard comparable to that of whites, even though both races might gain in absolute terms.

This was not a universal reaction. Garveyites were astute enough to know the value of economic reform. If they stood aloof from certain economic struggles in the United States, it was because they knew racists would twist those struggles to suit their own ends. When there appeared to be safeguards for black control, Garveyites did work within interracial organizations. In 1936 some 580 black and interracial organizations came together to form a National Negro Congress. Representatives of the Chicago and New York UNIA were present at the formative meeting. By 1940 the Congress had come under the control of trade unionists, Communists and others tied to whites, and the Garveyites and other independent-minded groups had withdrawn. In Harlem the local UNIA joined in Adam Clayton Powell's Coordinating Committee, which included many interracial groups, one of which was the Harlem branch of the Communist party. The Coordinating Committee was solidly based in the black community.

In Jamaica, the UNIA had, as early as 1929, demanded virtually every social reform later proposed by the New Deal. In that year the UNIA-initiated Peoples Political Party of Jamaica issued a twenty-six-point manifesto (printed on handbills and in the *Black Man*) demanding concrete action on immediate issues, including: (1) representation to the Imperial Parliament for a larger modicum of self-government; (3) a minimum wage for the laboring and working classes of the island; (4) a law to protect the working and laboring classes of the country by insurance against accident, sickness and death caused during employment; (6) the expansion and improvement of city, town or urban areas without the encumbrance or restraint of private proprietorship; (7) an eight-hour working day throughout Jamaica; (8) a law to encourage the promotion of native industries; (9) land reform; (11) a Jamaican university and polytechnic school; (12) a free government high school and a night school in the capital town of each parish; (13) a public library in the capital town of each parish; (14) a national opera house with an academy of music and art; (16) the compulsory improvement of urban areas from which large profits are made by trusts, corporations, combines and companies; (18) the creation of a legal aid department to render advice and protection to such persons who may not be able to have themselves properly represented and protected in courts of law; (24) a law to establish clinical centers from which trained nurses are to be sent out to visit homes in rural districts and to teach and demonstrate sanitary and better health methods in the care of home and family; (25) a law to empower the parochial boards of each parish to undertake under the direction of the central government the building of sanitary model homes for the peasantry by a system of easy payments to cover a period of from ten to twenty years.[75]

Other points on the platform related to reforms of similar nature. During the 1930s the struggle begun by the UNIA in 1920 became a united front effort including Jamaican leftists and liberals, as well as black nationalists. Conservative elements in the coalition eventually succeeded in driving the UNIA and other militants into the background and two new political parties were formed. By the time of Jamaican independence, the militants were in opposition to both major political parties. Nevertheless, co-optation in Jamaica has not had the same results as in the United States. Point 25 on the Peoples Political Party platform called for low-income housing. When the

Jamaican government sets out to throw a sop to the poor by building a few houses, at least there is the satisfaction of knowing that all
the houses will be for blacks, since virtually everyone on the island
is black; on the other hand, for every black American assisted in
home purchasing by the American government there have been a
hundred whites given such aid. Promoters of liberal reforms claim
that, where the need is great, a little is better than nothing at all.
When Garveyites stood apart from liberal and left reform movements in the United States, it was because they thought the little
was too small to bother with.

* * *

In Jamaica Marcus Garvey is today a national hero, acknowledged
as such even by Jamaicans who fought him during his lifetime.
There are a Garvey Drive and a Garvey Street in Kingston. Garvey's
picture is on a ten cent Jamaican postage stamp. Even Jamaican
tourist pamphlets include a biography of Marcus Garvey. At the
Marcus Garvey national shrine, above the casket containing his
body, is a large bust of the UNIA founder, and behind it an impos-
ing free-form sculpture. Periodically visitors to Jamaica pay their
respects to Garvey by placing a wreath at the base of the shrine.
Garvey died in London in 1940, but his remains were taken to his
homeland in 1956. Impressive re-interment services were held;
attending were a number of representatives of the Jamaican legislature, the leader of the independence movement and head of the
Jamaican labor movement Sir Alexander Bustamante, the heads of
the Anglican and Catholic churches, a delegation of American
Garveyites led by William Sherrill, leaders of today's Jamaican black
power movement Ken Hill and Bernard Lewis, and numerous other
civil rights leaders.[76] The eulogy was delivered by William Sherrill,
who said of his fallen leader: "His greatness is proven by the standard which measures greatness. Greatness is determined by the
impact a man's work and teaching has on his times. When viewing
the individual and his work, we ask ourselves—was the world different because he lived? The answer to this question as it relates to
Marcus Garvey places him in the company of the Great. . . . So great
were the goals he set for his race that small minds criticized, and
little men laughed. Laughed as they always have at every new idea
or venture. Some called him a fool. Others branded him a charlatan
and buffoon; while the more charitable called him a dreamer. Too

blind and shortsighted to realize the possibility of black men building for themselves, they sought to belittle his work by terming it a dream. Little did they realize that in calling Garvey a dreamer, they instantly placed him in the ranks of the Great." [77]

The work and philosophy of Marcus Garvey have left their mark on the black world in many ways. An ever-growing awareness of the Garveyite tradition is reflected in the numerous approaches to black nationalism and black power. Garvey did more than anyone else in this century to stimulate race pride and confidence among the black masses. The black writer Roi Ottley noted during the 1940s that in stimulating race consciousness the Garveyites were developing the "ethical standard by which most things are measured and interpreted." [78] This was the standard of race first and other considerations later. Although his critics denied it, Garvey proved that for blacks "chauvinistic nationalism" was not racism; and that a fierce pride and spirit of defiance need not destroy the beauty and compassion in "The Souls of Black Folk."

The black historian John Hope Franklin has called the Garvey movement "the first and only real mass movement among Negroes in the history of the United States. . ." [79] Yet Franklin and other historians have ignored the significance of this fact. They write of the black renaissance of the 1920s and 1930s and how it developed pride in African and Afro-American culture, but they fail to note that the UNIA brought this pride from the lofty plane of literary and artistic achievement to the level of the average man. Scholars also note that the militance of the World War I period permanently put an end to the myth of the docile Negro, but they neglect to acknowledge that it was the UNIA which broadened and institutionalized this militancy in black society. Franklin and most other historians have failed to even consider the possibility that Garveyism might be *the* political ideology for the black man.

Scholars have been more willing to acknowledge Garvey's role in guiding the liberation struggle in Africa, perhaps because so many African independence leaders have publicly acknowledged his inspiration and guidance. Jomo Kenyatta of Kenya heard Garvey lecture several times in London and considered himself a member of the UNIA. One of Kenyatta's political rivals, the late labor leader Tom Mboya, also acknowledged "having followed very closely the writings and speeches of Marcus Garvey." Kwame Nkrumah of

Ghana has said, "I think that of all the literature I studied, the book that did more than any other to fire my enthusiasm was the philosophy of Marcus Garvey published by his wife." [80] Godfrey Binaisa, Uganda's first attorney general, credits copies of the *Black Man,* illegally smuggled into his country, for showing him the black man could stand up and demand his rights. Joseph Mobutu, president of the Congo (Leopoldville), is a staunch admirer of Marcus Garvey. Dr. Nnamdi Azikiwe, the first president of Nigeria, and Kenneth Kaunda, president of Zambia, have acknowledged their indebtedness to Garvey, as has Felix Eboué of the Central African Republic. [81]

Black leaders have most often acknowledged Garvey's ability "to give millions of Negroes a sense of dignity and destiny and make the Negro feel he was somebody," as Martin Luther King said in a speech at the Garvey shrine in Kingston in 1965. [82] George Padmore evaluated Garvey's impact on Africa in similar terms. In *Black Metropolis,* St. Clair Drake and Horace Cayton wrote, "Garvey didn't get many Negroes back to Africa, but he helped to destroy their inferiority complex, and made them conscious of their power." Noting the religious side of Garveyism, Thomas Hodgkin wrote in *Nationalism and Colonial Africa* that the Garvey movement was "probably the most important single stimulus" in "spreading the idea of independent African Churches as an instrument of African liberation." [83] And in 1960, C. Eric Lincoln commented, "Garveyism lives on not really as a movement but as a symbol—a symbol of the militant Negro nationalism which so many black Americans see as their only alternative to eternal frustration and despair." [84]

Garveyites in London and in the Americas helped organize the Pan-African Congress of 1945. Held in London, with many future heads of African states as delegates, the Congress was a spring-board for the post–World War II independence movement. Dr. DuBois, once the UNIA's arch-enemy, wrote to Garvey's widow asking assistance in attracting delegates, and she replied with a lengthy letter containing the names and addresses of her many contacts in and out of the UNIA. [85] The UNIA itself was represented at the Congress by J. A. Linton. The historian George Shepperson described the program of the 1945 Congress as "the merging of the two schools of Pan-Africanism," those of Garvey and of DuBois. [86]

Nation-building in black Africa continues. The difficulties of the task have been evident in the tragedy of the Congo in the early 1960s, in the Nigeria-Biafra conflict, and in nearly a score of military coups in the newly independent African states. It is a battle against European and American interests which have conspired to keep tribal prejudices alive, create class divisions, and destroy national unity. Garveyism is as relevant in this struggle against neocolonialism as it was in the fight for independence. This is clearly recognized in Jamaica and in Barbados, where black power movements today explicitly trace their heritage to Marcus Garvey.[87] In the United States, the relevance of Garveyism to contemporary struggles is beginning to be recognized. Photographs of Garvey now adorn the office walls of black power organizations as much as photos of Che, Mao, and Lenin fill the offices of the New Left. On the East Coast, red, black, and green buttons are pinned to the lapels of young militants as a black power symbol. Scholarly approaches to Garveyism are being fostered by the spread of black studies departments in colleges across America. Growing ties between the black power movement in America and in the West Indies have added to this awakening interest. While some of today's black power programs and principles are explicitly borrowed from Garvey, most are simply the logical consequences of the historical processes Garvey helped to mold.

* * *

In Jamaica, Marcus Garvey Jr. (Mwalimu Marcus Garvey) has recently issued a program for a new political party in his country. It calls for "promotion of cultural ties with Africa and the study of African languages in all schools. Promotion of commercial links with Africa. Membership of the organization of African unity, and withdrawal from the organization of American states. Nationalization of large scale expatriate holdings in accordance with the principles of African socialism. Repatriation of all Africans in Jamaica wishing to return to the motherland of Africa to be arranged with African governments. An agrarian reform plan to place land in the hands of the landless. . . . [Formation of] people's cooperatives to enable the Africans to gain control of the trade and commerce of the nation."[88] These demands are eminently reasonable, and, in the best tradition of constructive, progressive change. They are also a logical updating of the philosophy of Garveyism.

During his lifetime, Marcus Garvey senior was called a charlatan, a chauvinist and a reactionary. The modern student of black power knows otherwise. Today, the greatest drawback to an appreciation of Garvey and Garveyism is the racial prejudice against black political theorists held by almost all whites, and not a few blacks. In addition there is the prejudice of the Left against theorists who do not appear to develop their ideas out of a socialist ideology—which is almost always a hazily defined concept. However, as these prejudices are broken down, the ideology and tactics of Marcus Garvey will doubtless aid the struggles against colonialism and neo-colonialism in the Third World, and may prove useful in places like Quebec and Northern Ireland. Garvey's synthesis of cultural, economic and political struggle might also prove of value to the alienated white youth of America.

Not so many years ago, one often heard the argument that blacks should follow the example of Irish-Americans, German-Americans and other hyphenated minorities who had found "equality" through assimilation into middle-America. However, racial prejudice has blocked assimilation for the black American. In addition, the hyphenated American whites are now discovering that they gave up their identity for the equality of wage slaves, powerless under the might of a master class. Today the old argument is being reversed. The youth of white America are attempting to follow the example of blacks in building alternative identities to the melting pot. Organization around life-styles is replacing the old alignments of laborers vs. employers. Even in the ranks of labor, it is blacks, chicanos, long-haired whites, and other alternative life-style enthusiasts who are leading the movement to reform the trade unions. While in England recently I ran across a group of London anarchist hippies who were attempting to gain support among the poor white cockney laborers in the slums of Stepney. "We have set up offices in this neighborhood," one of the anarchists told me, "because it is here that you find Englishmen who are treated like Negroes are treated in your country." My anarchist friend is on the right track, and would benefit from a study of the Garvey movement. He would be hard pressed to find a better example of organization based on cultural identity, providing international consciousness, aimed at assuming power for the powerless, and looking forward to a world of peace and brotherhood for all humanity.

A NOTE ON
RESEARCHING
BLACK RADICALISM

A word to the researcher wishing to delve into the history of twentieth-century black nationalism: in an age in which there is readily available source material for most historical studies, there is a paucity of material on a wide area of black studies. It has always been difficult to get independent black opinion into print, especially black nationalist opinion. White publishers have been reluctant to accept written works directed exclusively toward a black readership, arguing that there would not be enough black readers to make the venture profitable, and lack of funds has made it difficult for blacks to enter the publishing field. In the case of the Garvey movement, writings by Garveyites have been printed with UNIA funds, most of them in limited editions. Today there are re-issues available of *Philosophy and Opinions* and of *Garvey and Garveyism.* Other works that should be re-issued are Garvey's *Tragedy of White Injustice* and *Selections from the Poetic Meditations of Marcus Garvey;* Rabbi J. Arnold Ford's *Universal Ethiopian Hymnal,* printed by his black Jewish congregation; and Zebedee Green's *Why I Am Dissatisfied,* published in Pittsburgh in 1922 by a short-lived UNIA printing company set up by George Weston. A re-issue of Len Nembhard's *Trials and Triumphs of Marcus Garvey* would be a valuable aid to the study of Garveyism in the West Indies.

There remains today a crying need for scholarly works based upon primary source materials dealing with black nationalism and other forms of black radicalism. Most of the standard Negro history texts available today were written by men who developed their views during the New Deal, and their writings reflect the biases of that period.

The researcher must be prepared to face considerable difficulty in gathering materials—which has led me to conclude that there has been an attempt to suppress data concerning black nationalism. I have been unable to locate a single issue of the Garvey daily *Negro Times* in any library in the United States, England, or Jamaica. There is a collection of the *Negro World,* comprising about one-third of the issues from 1926 to 1933, in the Schomburg Collection in New York, and there are microfilm reels of this collection in some major college libraries. However, I have been able to locate fewer than twenty complete issues of the *Negro World* for the years 1918 to 1926. The Schomburg Collection has clippings from early issues, but not one complete newspaper. The Collection did have a file of early *Negro World*s, but this file was destroyed! (Jean Hutson, the Schomburg librarian, told me that the issues had been prepared for microfilming and sent down to the main library. In transit they fell off the back of the truck and and were scattered about: someone decided they were ruined, and so this precious collection was burned.)

While I was in Jamaica, Mrs. Amy Jacques Garvey showed me some letters from a friend in London, Richard Hart. Hart had been researching into UNIA activities in West Africa and had found a listing in the British Colonial Office index to a file dealing with Garveyite activities in Senegal and Sierra Leone. "Opposite the entry are stamped the words 'Destroyed Under Statute.' This means that the Colonial Office destroyed their file, or at least their copy of the petition. But the Superintendent of the Reading Room tells me that material of this importance is seldom destroyed unless it has been printed and may be found elsewhere." [1] Six months later, Hart was still looking.*

Proceedings of the UNIA conventions were regularly printed up in sizable blue folders and distributed to UNIA officials. None of the leading Garveyites to whom I have been able to talk has retained any of these. The files of these convention proceedings were part of the cache of UNIA records seized for the mail fraud trial, and were destroyed by the United States government. [3]

Recently, a very large cache of New York UNIA records was uncovered in an abandoned building in Harlem. Extensive financial records, membership lists, and correspondence from the late 1920s

---

*The historian Robert G. Weisbord was also unable to locate this file. [2]

and early 1930s were found crammed in a number of old file cabinets. From all reports this collection should be a great boon to researchers at some time in the future when it is made available. At present, the question of who owns the collection is being taken to court.

The New York cache was originally discovered by members of the Community Thing, an organization dealing with the youth drug problem. The Community Thing still holds the major part of the find, but a substantial amount of material was carted off to the Schomburg Collection and additional files were stolen at gunpoint by persons apparently bent on ransoming the data to the highest bidder. Bernice Sims of the Community Thing has contacted numerous former members of the New York UNIA and has received their endorsement for her claim. Contesting the ownership of the find are a host of government agencies, and the Schomburg Collection. The issue has become embroiled in politics. Bernice Sims argues that the citizens of Harlem—and especially the Garveyites—should have control over the material. City officials have tried to legitimize their claim by enlisting the support of Dr. Kenneth Clark, a man at odds with numerous black nationalists in New York. In charge of that part of the collection now in the Schomburg library is librarian Ernest Kaiser, an editor of *Freedomways* magazine, which has generally opposed black nationalism. Asked about the availability of the Schomburg segment of the find, Kaiser responded, "The collection is very controversial." When he was asked to elaborate, he said, "These records are in a similar category to our collection of Paul Robeson papers, which were given to us on the stipulation that they be withheld from the public until his death." [4]

The home of Amy Jacques Garvey is piled high with UNIA records, including a collection of *Negro World*s placed, for lack of space, in a baby crib. Garvey's widow also has a sizable collection of correspondence, some of it dating from the earliest years of the UNIA, and a large file on the *Black Man.* Although Garvey is a national hero in his homeland, the Jamaican Institute has been reluctant to aid Mrs. Garvey in cataloging her files, copying them, or placing them for preservation in humidity-proof rooms.

The researcher into black militancy must be alert for mislabeled data. The pictorial history *Harlem on My Mind* provides an example. This book includes a section devoted to protest and social movements of the 1920s, in which there are a number of photographs of Garveyites. There are pictures of the Black Cross Nurses, African Legionnaires, Marcus Garvey, and the Black Star Line ship, the *Yarmouth*. From this collection it is obvious that Garveyites were an important part of the Harlem scene. On the other hand, the collection contributes to the general misunderstanding of the UNIA. In between the properly identified photographs of the Garveyites there is a dramatic picture titled, "A Protest Parade—1924." [5] The caption fails to say that this is a UNIA parade! With this omission the viewer of this collection receives the impression that the Garveyites were interested in steamships and the wearing of colorful attire, while others were engaged in protest. Another photograph in this section is captioned, "A Group of Harlem Black Jews." [6] The caption does not note that the man in the picture holding the bass fiddle is Rabbi J. Arnold Ford, UNIA musical director, and that the group is standing in front of Ford's storefront synagogue for his Garveyite Beth B'nai Abraham congregation.* The omissions from these two captions detract immeasurably from the impact of the Garvey section. Properly identified, these and other photographs would have shown the UNIA to be the most impressive phenomenon ever to come to Harlem.

Garveyism is not the only black radical viewpoint to be ignored or suppressed. Of the numerous post–World War I radical magazines there are few copies anywhere today, with the exception of Randolph's *Messenger*. There are two anthologies of black radical publications of the World War I period; ironically, they were both compiled by right-wing government agents. Attorney General Mitchell Palmer's "Radicalism and Sedition among the Negroes as Reflected in Their Publications" was published in 1919; and "Revolutionary Radicalism: A Report of the Joint Legislative Committee of New York Investigating Seditious Activities" appeared in 1920. The Schomburg Collection and leading college libraries have collections of pamphlets, broadsides, flyers and the like put out by the NAACP, other civil rights organizations, and black Communists and Socialists. But the libraries have very little of this type of material dealing with the UNIA, the Muslims, the Abyssinians, Noble Drew

---

*The caption gives the date as 1929, which is apparently incorrect since Rabbi Ford was in Ethiopia throughout 1929.

Ali's Moors, the ABB, or other nationalist movements. All organizations put out material of this kind, and Mrs. Garvey has a collection of ephemerae pertaining to the UNIA.

Here and there, in bits and snatches, the story of black radicalism can be gleaned from the pages of the black establishment's weekly newspapers. But the losses of the *Negro World* and *Negro Times* files are tragic because the UNIA press was virtually the only free press available to black people in the 1920s and 1930s. Other black publishing concerns were usually tied to white money. Even the *Negro World* had its Bayer Aspirin advertising account, but most of its ads were from blacks, and its financial solvency was backed up by the Association. The NAACP journal *Crisis* was self-supporting, but when its editor, Dr. DuBois, started sounding like a nationalist during the early 1930s, he was pressured into resigning by the NAACP leadership.

In 1926, a group of Harlem Renaissance writers pooled their meager resources to bring out an independent magazine of literary opinion. It was called *Fire,* "the idea being," as one of the group— Langston Hughes—said, "it would burn up a lot of the old, dead, conventional Negro-white ideas of the past, [and help] younger Negro writers and artists, and provide us with an outlet for publication not available in the limited pages of the small Negro magazines then existing, the *Crisis, Opportunity,* and the *Messenger.*" *Fire* had only one issue, and its attempt at new literary forms was roasted by critics for *Crisis* and the Baltimore *Afro-American,* while white literary journals took no notice of it at all.[7] Another journal of independent black literary opinion, the *New Challenge,* lasted for only a few issues in 1936.

In 1940, the former African Blood Brotherhood leader Richard B. Moore, then a follower of Communism, attempted to launch his own publishing company to bring back in print old works by Negroes. He brought out the first twentieth-century publication of *The Life and Times of Frederick Douglass.* But his plans for other works were questioned by his Communist comrades who wanted to control which books would be published. Moore dissolved his company in anger and quit the Communist Party.[8]

In the mid-1930s Dr. W. E. B. DuBois was commissioned to write a book on the Negro and the New Deal for the Bronze Booklet Series of Howard University, which had published small volumes on the Negro in the arts, business, etc. DuBois sent in his manuscript and was paid for his efforts, but the book was never published. The publishers found the book too critical of the New Deal.[9] This was a nationalistic period for DuBois, and he did publish one treatise with this view—*Dusk of Dawn*, published in 1940. The 1960s saw the re-issuing of most of DuBois's works, and *Dusk of Dawn* was one of the last to be so honored, in 1968.

The present-day black power spokesman John O. Killens suffered censorship similar to that which plagued many earlier writers, who found themselves unable to publish their true feelings and were forced to write pap which would satisfy white publishers. Killens came out of World War II eager to write a novel about a race riot involving black and white American troops stationed in Australia during the war. Such a riot had indeed occurred. It was one of many military engagements between blacks and whites during the war, and for the most part it was played down or not reported at all. Killens's wife got a job as a secretary in the office of a left-wing trade union to earn money to put him through writing school. His left-wing friends promised to help him find a publisher and to promote his book when published, but they were not enthusiastic about his plan to write about the race riot; the subject seemed to smack of black nationalism. Killens conceded and turned out a polite novel about the civil rights struggle in the South. Only years later did he write *And Then We Heard the Thunder,* a significant novel in that it describes a race war from the black point of view without resorting to reverse racism.[10]

The researcher into black nationalist history has one sizable and almost untapped source—which will soon be gone. A number of aged Garveyites are still alive, along with early Black Muslims, Moors, members of the African Blood Brotherhood, and other radicals. Their stories should be recorded, not only because they can help us understand the problems and tasks of blackness, but also because these people deserve to be remembered as individuals. To hold black nationalism or black power views in their day was to run against the conventional wisdom. Today's bandwagon attracts the shallow-minded as well as the politically astute.

APPENDIX 1

THE DECLARATION
OF RIGHTS OF THE
NEGRO PEOPLES OF THE WORLD

The following declaration was drafted and adopted at the 1920 UNIA convention in New York. The declaration was signed by 122 convention delegates. Some fifty signers went on to take leading roles in the affairs of the Association; their names are noted by an asterisk in the list of prominent Garveyites in Appendix 2.

Among the other signers were Garvey's secretaries, Janie Jenkins and Mary E. Johnson; J. J. Cranston, head of the Baltimore division; Reynold F. Austin, head of the Brooklyn division; the Jamaican delegates Frederick Samuel Ricketts, Carrie M. Ashford and James Young; heads of Canadian divisions, Richard Edward Riley, T. H. Golden and I. Braithwaite; Edward Alfred Taylor of Pittsburgh; Frank O. Raines of New York; Shedrick Williams of Cleveland; Emily Christmas Kinch of Liberia; Prince Alfred McConney; and UNIA field representative Sara Branch.

PREAMBLE

Be it Resolved, That the Negro people of the world, through their chosen representatives in convention assembled in Liberty Hall, in the City of New York and United States of America, from August 1 to August 31, in the year of our Lord, one thousand nine hundred and twenty, protest against the wrongs and injustices they are suffering at the hands of their white brethren, and state what they deem their fair and just rights, as well as the treatment they propose to demand of all men in the future.

We complain:

I. That nowhere in the world, with few exceptions, are black men accorded equal treatment with white men, although in the same situation and circumstances, but on the contrary, are discriminated against and denied the common rights due to human beings for no other reason than their race and color.

We are not willingly accepted as guests in the public hotels and inns of the world for no other reason than our race and color.

II. In certain parts of the United States of America our race is denied the right of public trial accorded to other races when accused of crime, but are lynched and burned by mobs, and such brutal and inhuman treatment is even practised upon our women.

III. That European nations have parcelled out among them and taken possession of nearly all of the continent of Africa, and the natives are compelled to surrender their lands to aliens and are treated in most instances like slaves.

IV. In the southern portion of the United States of America, although citizens under the Federal Constitution, and in some states almost equal to the whites in population and are qualified land owners and taxpayers, we are, nevertheless, denied all voice in the making and administration of the laws and are taxed without representation by the state governments, and at the same time compelled to do military service in defense of the country.

V. On the public conveyances and common carriers in the Southern portion of the United States we are jim-crowed and compelled to accept separate and inferior accommodations, and made to pay the same fare charged for first-class accommodations, and our families are often humiliated and insulted by drunken white men who habitually pass through the jim-crow cars going to the smoking car.

VI. The physicians of our race are denied the right to attend their patients while in the public hospitals of the cities and states where they reside in certain parts of the United States.

Our children are forced to attend inferior separate schools for shorter terms than white children and the public school funds are unequally divided between the white and colored schools.

VII. We are discriminated against and denied an equal chance to earn wages for the support of our families, and in many instances are refused admission into labor unions, and nearly everywhere are paid smaller wages than white men.

VIII. In Civil Service and departmental offices we are everywhere discriminated against and made to feel that to be a Black man in Europe, America and the West Indies is equivalent to being an outcast and a leper among the races of men, no matter what the character and attainments of the Black man may be.

IX. In the British and other West Indian Islands and colonies, Negroes are secretly and cunningly discriminated against, and denied those fuller rights of government to which white citizens are appointed, nominated and elected.

X. That our people in those parts are forced to work for lower wages than the average standard of white men and are kept in conditions repugnant to good civilized tastes and customs.

XI. That the many acts of injustice against members of our race before the courts of law in the respective islands and colonies are of such nature as to create disgust and disrespect for the white man's sense of justice.

XII. Against all such inhuman, unchristian and uncivilized treatment we here and now emphatically protest, and invoke the condemnation of all mankind.

In order to encourage our race all over the world and to stimulate it to a higher and grander destiny, we demand and insist on the following Declaration of Rights:

1. Be it known to all men that whereas, all men are created equal and entitled to the rights of life, liberty and the pursuit of happiness, and because of this we, the duly elected representatives of the Negro peoples of the world, invoking the aid of the just and Almighty God do declare all men women and children of our blood throughout the world free citizens, and do claim them as free citizens of Africa, the Motherland of all Negroes.

2. That we believe in the supreme authority of our race in all things racial; that all things are created and given to man as a common possession; that there should be an equitable distribution and apportionment of all such things, and in consideration of the fact that as a race we are now deprived of those things that are morally and legally ours, we believe it right that all such things should be acquired and held by whatsoever means possible.

3. That we believe the Negro, like any other race, should be governed by the ethics of civilization, and, therefore, should not be deprived of any of those rights or privileges common to other human beings.

4. We declare that Negroes, wheresoever they form a community among themselves, should be given the right to elect their own representatives to represent them in legislatures, courts of law, or such institutions as may exercise control over that particular community.

5. We assert that the Negro is entitled to even-handed justice before all courts of law and equity in whatever country he may be found, and when this is denied him on account of his race or color such denial is an insult to the race as a whole and should be resented by the entire body of Negroes.

6. We declare it unfair and prejudicial to the rights of Negroes in communities where they exist in considerable numbers to be tried by a judge and jury composed entirely of an alien race, but in all such cases members of our race are entitled to representation on the jury.

7. We believe that any law or practice that tends to deprive any African of his land or the privileges of free citizenship within his country is unjust and immoral, and no native should respect any such law or practice.

8. We declare taxation without representation unjust and tyrannous, and there should be no obligation on the part of the Negro to obey the levy of a tax by any law-making body from which he is excluded and denied representation on account of his race and color.

9. We believe that any law especially directed against the Negro to his detriment and singling him out because of his race or color is unfair and immoral, and should not be respected.

10. We believe all men entitled to common human respect, and that our race should in no way tolerate any insults that may be interpreted to mean disrespect to our color.

11. We deprecate the use of the term "nigger" as applied to Negroes, and demand that the word "Negro" be written with a capital "N."

12. We believe that the Negro should adopt every means to protect himself against barbarous practices inflicted upon him because of color.

13. We believe in the freedom of Africa for the Negro people of the world, and by the principle of Europe for the Europeans and Asia for the Asiatics, we also demand Africa for the Africans at

home and abroad.

14. We believe in the inherent right of the Negro to possess himself of Africa, and that his possession of same shall not be regarded as an infringement on any claim or purchase made by any race or nation.

15. We strongly condemn the cupidity of those nations of the world who, by open aggression or secret schemes, have seized the territories and inexhaustible natural wealth of Africa, and we place on record our most solemn determination to reclaim the treasures and possession of the vast continent of our forefathers.

16. We believe all men should live in peace one with the other, but when races and nations provoke the ire of other races and nations by attempting to infringe upon their rights, war becomes inevitable, and the attempt in any way to free one's self or protect one's rights or heritage becomes justifiable.

17. Whereas, the lynching, by burning, hanging or any other means, of human beings is a barbarous practice, and a shame and disgrace to civilization, and we therefore declare any country guilty of such atrocities outside the pale of civilization.

18. We protest against the atrocious crime of whipping, flogging and overworking the native tribes of Africa and Negroes everywhere. These are methods that should be abolished, and all means should be taken to prevent a continuance of such brutal practices.

19. We protest against the atrocious practice of shaving the heads of Africans, especially of African women or individuals of Negro blood, when placed in prison as a punishment for crime by an alien race.

20. We protest against segregated districts, separate public conveyances, industrial discrimination, lynchings and limitations of political privileges of any Negro citizen in any part of the world on account of race, color or creed, and will exert our full influence and power against all such.

21. We protest against any punishment, inflicted upon a Negro with severity, as against lighter punishment inflicted upon another of an alien race for like offense, as an act of prejudice and injustice, and should be resented by the entire race.

22. We protest against the system of education in any country where Negroes are denied the same privileges and advantages as other races.

23. We declare it inhuman and unfair to boycott Negroes from industries and labor in any part of the world.

24. We believe in the doctrine of the freedom of the press, and we therefore emphatically protest against the suppression of Negro newspapers and periodicals in various parts of the world, and call upon Negroes everywhere to employ all available means to prevent such suppression.

25. We further demand free speech universally for all men.

26. We hereby protest against the publication of scandalous and inflammatory articles by an alien press tending to create racial strife and the exhibition of picture films showing the Negro as a cannibal.

27. We believe in the self-determination of all peoples.

28. We declare for the freedom of religious worship.

29. With the help of Almighty God, we declare ourselves the sworn protectors of the honor and virtue of our women and children, and pledge our lives for their protection and defense everywhere, and under all circumstances from wrongs and outrages.

30. We demand the right of unlimited and unprejudiced education for ourselves and our posterity forever.

31. We declare that the teaching in any school by alien teachers to our boys and girls, that the alien race is superior to the Negro race, is an insult to the Negro people of the world.

32. Where Negroes form a part of the citizenry of any country, and pass the civil service examination of such country, we declare them entitled to the same consideration as other citizens as to appointments in such civil service.

33. We vigorously protest against the increasingly unfair and unjust treatment accorded Negro travellers on land and sea by the agents and employees of railroad and steamship companies and insist that for equal fare we receive equal privileges with travellers of other races.

34. We declare it unjust for any country, State or nation to enact laws tending to hinder and obstruct the free immigration of Negroes on account of their race and color.

35. That the right of the Negro to travel unmolested throughout the world be not abridged by any person or persons, and all Negroes are called upon to give aid to a fellow Negro when thus molested.

36. We declare that all Negroes are entitled to the same right to travel over the world as other men.

37. We hereby demand that the governments of the world recognize our leader and his representatives chosen by the race to look after the welfare of our people under such governments.

38. We demand complete control of our social institutions without interference by any alien race or races.

39. That the colors, Red Black and Green, be the colors of the Negro race.

40. Resolved, that the anthem "Ethiopia, Thou Land of Our Fathers," etc., shall be the anthem of the Negro race.

THE UNIVERSAL ETHIOPIAN ANTHEM
(poem by Burrell and Ford)

Ethiopia, thou land of our fathers,
Thou land where the gods loved to be,
As storm cloud at night suddenly gathers
Our armies come rushing to thee.
We must in the fight be victorious
When swords are thrust outward to gleam;
For us will the vict'ry be glorious
When led by the red, black and green.

Chorus:
Advance, advance to victory,
Let Africa be free;
Advance to meet the foe
With the might
Of the red, the black and the green.

II

Ethiopia, the tyrant's falling,
Who smote thee upon thy knees,
And thy children are lustily calling
From over the distant seas.
Jehovah, the Great One has heard us,
Has noted our sighs and our tears,
With His spirit of Love he has stirred us
To be One through the coming years.

Chorus: Advance, advance, etc.

III

O Jehovah, thou God of the ages
Grant unto our sons that lead
The wisdom Thou gave to Thy sages
When Israel was sore in need.
Thy voice thro' the dim past has spoken,
Ethiopia shall stretch forth her hand,
By Thee shall all fetters be broken,
And Heav'n bless our dear fatherland.

Chorus: Advance, advance, etc.

41. We believe that any limited liberty which deprives one of the complete rights and prerogatives of full citizenship is but a modified form of slavery.

42. We declare it an injustice to our people and a serious impediment to the health of the race to deny to competent licensed Negro physicians the right to practice in the public hospitals of the communities in which they reside, for no other reason than their race and color.

43. We call upon the various governments of the world to accept and acknowledge Negro representatives who shall be sent to the said governments to represent the general welfare of the Negro peoples of the world.

44. We deplore and protest against the practice of confining juvenile prisoners in prisons with adults, and we recommend that such youthful prisoners be taught gainful trades under humane supervision.

45. Be it further resolved, that we as a race of people declare the League of Nations null and void as far as the Negro is concerned, in that it seeks to deprive Negroes of their liberty.

46. We demand of all men to do unto us as we would do unto them, in the name of justice; and we cheerfully accord to all men all the rights we claim herein for ourselves.

47. We declare that no Negro shall engage himself in battle for an alien race without first obtaining the consent of the leader of the

Negro people of the world, except in a matter of national self-defense.

48. We protest against the practice of drafting Negroes and sending them to war with alien forces without proper training, and demand in all cases that Negro soldiers be given the same training as the aliens.

49. We demand that instructions given Negro children in schools include the subject of "Negro History," to their benefit.

50. We demand a free and unfettered commercial intercourse with all the Negro people of the world.

51. We declare for the absolute freedom of the seas for all peoples.

52. We demand that our duly accredited representatives be given proper recognition in all leagues, conferences, conventions or courts of international arbitration wherever human rights are discussed.

53. We proclaim the 31st day of August of each year to be an international holiday to be observed by all Negroes.

54. We want all men to know we shall maintain and contend for the freedom and equality of every man, woman and child of our race, with our lives, our fortunes and our sacred honor.

These rights we believe to be justly ours and proper for the protection of the Negro race at large, and because of this belief, we, on behalf of the four hundred million Negroes of the world, do pledge herein the sacred blood of the race in defense, and we hereby subscribe our names as a guarantee of the truthfulness and faithfulness hereof in the presence of Almighty God, on the 13th day of August, in the year of our Lord one thousand nine hundred and twenty.

APPENDIX 2
PROMINENT GARVEYITES

The following is an alphabetical list of prominent Garveyites, with their UNIA positions. Each of the men and women listed played an important role in one or more of the UNIA conventions, or was otherwise noteworthy in the international affairs of the movement. Where known, each individual's occupation and place of national origin are given. Asterisks denote signers of the 1920 Declaration of Rights of the Negro Peoples of the World.

J. J. Adams, head of the San Francisco division and UNIA Ambassador to France; educator; Haiti.

Thomas W. Anderson, assistant president general, minister of industries, and head of the Negro Factories Corporation; USA.

Charlotta Bass, lady president of the Los Angeles division; journalist; USA.

Clifford Bourne,* high chancellor and treasurer and head of the Guatemalan UNIA; civil service clerk; Barbados.

John "Grit" Bruce, *Negro World* columnist; journalist; USA.

Arden A. Bryan,* Black Star Line official and head of membership recruiting; Jamaica.

LeRoy Bundy, head of the Cleveland division and assistant president general; physician; USA.

Percival Burrows, assistant president general; *Negro World* columnist.

G. Emonie Carter, secretary general; accountant; USA.

J. A. Craigen, head of the Detroit division; USA.

George Creese,* head of the Nova Scotia division; West Indies.

Cyril Crichlow,* head of the UNIA delegation to Liberia; Jamaica.

Arnold S. Cunning,* head of the Cuban UNIA; laborer; Jamaica.

Adrian Daily, official in the Jamaican UNIA and one of the founders of the UNIA; Jamaica.

Gertrude Davis,* lady president of the Cleveland division; USA

Henrietta Vinton Davis,* international organizer; actress; USA.

S. Sydney DeBourg,* leader of the West Indies UNIA; laborer; Trinidad.

Madame M. L. T. DeMena, international organizer and head of the Nicaraguan UNIA; Nicaragua.

J. R. L. Diggs, chaplain general; educator and minister; USA.

Warner A. Domingo, *Negro World* editor; journalist and businessman; Jamaica.

Evelyn R. Donawa,* head of the Dominica UNIA: domestic worker; Dominica.

J. C. St. Clair Drake, international organizer; educator; Barbados.

Marie Duchaterlier,* official in the New York UNIA; domestic worker; Haiti.

James W. H. Eason,* leader of American Negroes; minister; USA.

Frances W. Ellegor,* high commissioner; minister; Guiana.

William Ferris, assistant president general and *Negro World* editor; educator and minister; USA.

J. Arnold Ford,* UNIA musical director; musician and rabbi; Barbados.

T. Thomas Fortune, *Negro World* editor; journalist; USA.

John W. Fowler, minister of industries and head of the Oakland, California, division; businessman; USA.

Lionel Francis,* head of the Philadelphia division and the New York division; physician; West Indies.

Napoleon Francis,* head of the Haiti UNIA; Haiti.

E. L. Gaines, minister of legions; professional soldier; USA.

Eli Garcia, auditor general and Black Star Line official; clerk; Haiti.

Amy Jacques Garvey; journalist and writer; Jamaica.

Marcus Garvey,* president general and provisional president of Africa; race leader; Jamaica.

Joseph Gibson,* surgeon general; physician.

J. D. Gordon,* assistant president general; minister; West Indies.

Arthur S. Gray, head of the California UNIA and *Negro World* columnist; businessman; USA.

Walter Smith Green,* Black Star Line official; Jamaica.

Lionel Greenidge,* member of New York Division of the UNIA; electrician; Barbados.

James A. Hassell, head of Seattle UNIA; USA.

Samuel A. Haynes, registrar, *Negro World* columnist and head of the Pittsburgh division; British Honduras.

Cyril Henry, international organizer; agricultural specialist; Jamaica.

R. Henry Hodge,* head of the Syracuse, New York division and field organizer; West Indies.

Marie Barrier Houston,* UNIA choir; musician; USA.

Florida Jenkins,* lady president of the Kansas City division.

Adrian Johnson,* chairman of the convention; physician; Jamaica.

Gabriel Johnson,* potentate; government official; Liberia.

S. M. Jones, head of the Jamaican UNIA; minister; Jamaica.

Howard Kirby,* head of the Washington, D.C., division and an official in the Chicago division.

D. D. Lewis,* head of the Montreal division; physician; Nigeria.

Levi F. Lord, auditor general and assistant president general; West Indies.

George Alexander McGuire,* chaplain general; minister; Antigua.

Ernest E. Mair, *Negro World* columnist; Jamaica.

George O. Marke,* deputy potentate; civil servant and journalist; Sierra Leone.

William C. Matthews,* counsel general; attorney and civil rights leader; USA.

Sir Isaiah Morter; businessman; British Honduras.

H. G. Mugdal, head of the Trinidad division and *Negro World* editor; journalist and educator; India.

J. Austin Norris, head of the Philadelphia division; attorney; USA.

James O'Meally, high commissioner; educator; Jamaica.

J. J. Peters, head of the Boston division, the Chicago division, and the New Orleans division, and assistant president general; minister; USA.

Charles A. Petioni,* official in the New York UNIA; physician; Trinidad.

H. Vinton Plummer,* publicity director; realtor; USA.

Arthur M. Poston, minister of labor; realtor; USA.

Robert L. Poston, assistant president general; journalist; USA.

Ulysses S. Poston, minister of industries and *Negro World* and *Negro Times* editor; journalist; USA.

R. Van Richards, Liberian UNIA assistant chaplain general; minister; Liberia.

William Sherrill, assistant president general; businessman, USA.

Rudolph Smith,* leader of the West Indies UNIA; journalist and minister; Guyana.

Soloman Smith, official in the Cuban and Jamaican UNIA; laborer; Jamaica.

Wilford E. Smith,* assistant counsel general; attorney; USA.

Gabriel Stewart,* high chancellor; educator; Jamaica.

Prince Kojo Tavalou, potentate; political leader; Dahomey.

A. B. Thomas,* head of the Panama UNIA; attorney; Panama.

Norton G. Thomas, assistant president general and *Negro World* editor; accountant; USA.

Noah Thompson, head of the Los Angeles division and *Negro World* columnist; journalist and realtor; USA.

Orlando Thompson, Black Star Line official; clerk.

George Tobias, Black Star Line official; laborer.

Richard Tobitt,* leader of the West Indies UNIA; carpenter; Bermuda.

Fred Toote,* Black Star Line official, head of the Philadelphia division, and assistant president general; minister; Bahamas.

William A. Wallace, head of the Chicago division and assistant president general; minister; USA.

Eric Walrond, *Negro World, Negro Times,* and *Black Man* editor; journalist and writer; Guyana.

William Ware,* head of the Cincinnati division; laborer; USA.

George Weston, head of the Pittsburgh division and the New York division; laborer; Antigua.

Vernal Williams,* assistant counsel general; attorney; Jamaica.

Andrew N. Willis,* head of the Bocas Del Toro, Panama, division; Panama.

James B. Yearwood,* assistant president general and secretary general; school teacher and laborer; Barbados.

APPENDIX 3
SOURCES

The following newspapers and magazines carried information on the UNIA and related organizations. They are arranged roughly in order of their value as source materials. The magazines with continual coverage of black militancy are listed by name only. Those with isolated contributions are listed with the dates of pertinent issues. An asterisk indicates that few copies are available.

NEWSPAPERS

Negro World; New York *Age;* Baltimore *Afro-American;* New York *World* (the most informative of white newspapers); Chicago *Defender;* Pittsburgh *Courier; Voice of Freedom;** Kingston, Jamaica, *Daily Gleaner;* New York *Daily Worker* (exceptional coverage of the 1924 UNIA Convention); Los Angeles *California Eagle;* New York *Inter-state Tattler;* Washington *Bee;* New York *Amsterdam News;** *New York Times; Afro-American* (Washington edition); Philadelphia *Tribune;* Philadelphia *American;* Cleveland *Gazette;* New York *Emancipator;** Los Angeles *Citizen Advocate;* Oakland *California Voice; Harlem Liberator,* also titled *Negro Liberator* and *Liberator* (circa 1930); Kingston *Record* (circa 1920); Kingston *Abeng* (late 1960s); New York *People's Voice* (circa 1940); Atlanta *Independent;* Columbia, South Carolina, *Indicator* (circa 1920); Savannah *Tribune;* Portland, Oregon, *Advocate.*

MAGAZINES

Black Man (circa 1930); *Negro Churchman;** *Crusader;** *African Times and Orient Review,* also titled *African and Orient Review;*

Messenger (bound volumes of reprints now available); NAACP *Crisis;* Urban League *Opportunity; Negro Voice;* Challenge;* Colored American Review;* New Challenge; New Masses; African* (circa 1940); *Liberator* (circa 1920); *Communist Party Organizer.*

Current History (March 1921, June 1923, June 1935); *Century* (February 1923); *Nation* (28 Dec. 1921, 18 Aug. 1926, 15 May 1935); *Literary Digest* (19 Aug. 1922, 19 March 1921); *World's Work* (Dec. 1920, March 1921, Jan. 1921); *Independent* (26 Feb. 1921, 3 Jan. 1925); *London Communist Review* (April 1922); *Christian Century* (8 June 1955); *Outlook* (18 Aug. 1923); *New Republic* (11 July 1923, 31 Aug. 1927); *Overseas* (April 1921); *Worker's Monthly* (April 1926, Oct. 1924); *World Tomorrow* (Sept. 1920, June 1921); *Ebony* (March 1960); *Forum* (Aug. 1923); *New Statesman* (4 April 1961); *Survey* (March 1925); *Public Opinion* (3 November 1956); *L'Illustré* (14 Oct. 1922); *Revue Indigène* (Nov.-Dec. 1922); *Les Oeuvres libres* (Jan. 19); *Science and Society* (Summer 1968).

* * *

Much of the material in this book is based on the following collections of correspondence or ephemerae:

The UNIA Papers in the Schomburg Collection of the New York Public Library; 130 West 135th St., New York, New York.

The John Bruce Papers, also in the Schomburg Collection.

The Amy Jacques Garvey collection (referred to in the notes as the Garvey Papers); 12 Mona Rd., Kingston, Jamaica.

The UNIA collection in the Jamaican Institute, Kingston, Jamaica.

William Taylor's collection of Cyril Briggs's papers (referred to in the notes as the Briggs Papers); 5737 South St. Andrew's Place, Los Angeles, California.

NOTES

AN INTRODUCTION TO GARVEYISM

1 W. E. B. DuBois, *Souls of Black Folk* (Blue Heron Press edition; New York, 1953), p. 13.

2 Roi Ottley, *New World A-Coming* (World; Cleveland & New York, 1943), p. 81.

3 *Philosophy and Opinions of Marcus Garvey* was originally published in two volumes, edited by Amy Jacques Garvey. Volume 1 was published in 1923 by the Universal Publishing House of the UNIA in New York, under the title *Philosophy and Opinions of Marcus Garvey;* volume 2 was published in 1926, under the title *Philosophy and Opinions of Marcus Garvey, or Africa for the Africans.* The first of the reissues appearing in the past few years is the 1967 compilation of volumes 1 and 2 by Frank Cass & Company of London with a new introduction by E. U. Essien-Udom of the University of Ibadan, Nigeria. All page references in this book are to the Cass & Company edition. This reissue is the first book of the Africana Modern Library series, which is under the direction of Professor Essien-Udom. Other recent editions include the two-volume compilations by Arno Press in New York and the Atheneum Press in New York. The Richardson press in San Francisco has produced a new issue of volume 1.

4 Amy Jacques Garvey, *Garvey and Garveyism* (published by the author; Kingston, Jamaica, 1963), has been issued in 1970 by The Macmillan Company and in paperback by P. F. Collier, Inc., both of New York.

5 Len S. Nembhard, *Trials and Triumphs of Marcus Garvey* (Gleaner Publishing Company; Kingston, Jamaica, 1940).

6 Edmund David Cronon, *Black Moses: The Story of Marcus Garvey and the Universal Negro Improvement Association* (University of Wisconsin Press; Madison, 1955).

7 Ibid., p. 221.

8 Ibid., p. 199.

9 Ibid., p. 222.

10 Albert B. Cleage Jr., *The Black Messiah* (Sheed and Ward; New York, 1968), pp. 11–12.

11 *Philosophy and Opinions*, vol. 1, p. 19.

12 The Declaration is included in *Philosophy and Opinions*, vol. 2, pp. 135–43. Also see Appendix 2 of this volume.

13 Quoted in the Baltimore *Afro-American*, 19 Nov. 1920.
14 *Negro World*, 16 Oct. 1918; quoted in W. F. Elkins, "Suppression of the *Negro World* in the British West Indies" (MS prepared for *Science and Society*).
15 *Philosophy and Opinions*, vol. 2, p. 81.
16 Pittsburgh *Courier*, 26 April 1924.
17 *Negro World*, 6 Feb. 1932.
18 *Negro World* 18 Dec. 1920; quoted in Robert G. Weisbord, "Marcus Garvey, Pan-Negroist: the View from Whitehall," *Race* (London), April 1970.
19 *Philosophy and Opinions*, vol. 1, p. 31.
20 Eldridge Cleaver, "Minister of Information Black Paper" (pamphlet published by the Black Panther Party for Self-Defense; Oakland, Calif., 1968).
21 *Philosophy and Opinions*, vol. 2, p. 140.
22 *Negro World*, 16 Aug. 1924.
23 Speech by Stokely Carmichael at the Black Panther Party rally in celebration of Huey P. Newton's birthday, Oakland, California, 17 Feb. 1968.
24 *Philosophy and Opinions*, vol. 2, p. 72.
25 Ibid., vol. 1, p. 41.
26 Baltimore *Afro-American*, 12 Aug. 1921.
27 *Daily Worker*, 12 Aug. 1924.
28 *Philosophy and Opinions*, vol. 2, p. 72.
29 Marcus Garvey, *The Tragedy of White Injustice* and *Selections from the Poetic Meditations of Marcus Garvey* (published by Amy Jacques Garvey; New York, 1927).
30 *Black Man*, July–Aug. 1936. This monthly magazine was published irregularly during the 1930s by Marcus Garvey; the first six issues were published under the name *Blackman*.
31 *Philosophy and Opinions*, vol. 2, p. 69.
32 *Negro World*, 25 June 1927.
33 *Blackman*, Dec. 1969. This monthly magazine has been published in Kingston, Jamaica, since 1969 by the African Nationalist Union; Marcus Garvey Jr., editor.

THE NEW NEGRO: GARVEYITES AND OTHERS

1 Baltimore *Afro-American*, 11 Aug 1917; 13 Oct. 1917.
2 Interview with St. Clair Drake Jr., Oct. 1970.
3 *Crisis*, May 1919.
4 Cronon, *Black Moses*, p. 31.
5 In Philadelphia, a three-day riot in the summer of 1918 left two blacks and one white dead: see the Baltimore *Afro-American*, 2 Aug. 1918. On a significant Harlem battle in the summer of 1917, see the Chicago *Defender*, 2 June, 1917.
6 Chicago *Defender*, 2 Aug. 1919; Washington *Bee*, 2 Aug. 1919. Note also the map of casualties in the Chicago Commission on Race Relations, *The Negro in Chicago* (University of Chicago Press; Chicago, 1922).
7 Washington *Bee*, 21 June 1921.

8 Thomas Hodgkin, *Nationalism in Colonial Africa* (Frederick Muller; London, 1956), pp. 124-25. For background information see W. F. Elkins, "The Influence of Marcus Garvey on Africa: a British Report of 1922," *Science and Society,* Summer 1968; W. F. Elkins, "Black Power in the West Indies: the Trinidad Longshoremen's Strike of 1919," *Science and Society,* Winter 1969; W. F. Elkins, "A Source of Black Nationalism in the Caribbean," *Science and Society,* Spring 1970; W. F. Elkins, "The Suppression of the *Negro World* in the British West Indies," MS prepared for *Science and Society.* See also Robert G. Weisbord, "Marcus Garvey, Pan-Negroist, the View from Whitehall," *Race* (London), April 1970.

9 W. F. Elkins, "A Source of Black Nationalism in the Caribbean."

10 Ibid.

11 The picture is reprinted on the first page of "Revolutionary Radicalism, a Report of the Joint Committee of New York Investigating Seditious Activities" (J. B. Lyon; Albany, New York, 1920), vol. 2.

12 Claude McKay, *Harlem Shadows* (Harcourt, Brace; New York, 1922), p. 53. This poem was first published in the *Liberator,* later in the *Messenger* and other magazines.

13 The manifesto is quoted in full in Cronon, *Black Moses,* p. 17.

14 Cronon, *Black Moses,* p. 41; Cyril V. Briggs, "Notes for an Autobiography," Cyril Briggs Papers.

15 Baltimore *Afro-American,* 30 June 1917.

16 Harold Cruse, *The Crisis of the Negro Intellectual* (Morrow; New York, 1967), p. 119.

17 *Negro World,* 11 Oct. 1919.

18 Chicago *Defender,* 2 Aug. 1919; Washington *Bee,* 2 Aug. 1919; Pittsburgh *Courier* quoted in John Hope Franklin, *From Slavery to Freedom* (Knopf; New York, 1956), p. 477.

19 *New York Times,* 28 July 1919.

20 The origins of Randolph's title are discussed in Arna Bontemps, "The Most Dangerous Negro in America," in *Negro Digest,* Sept. 1961.

21 See Mitchell A. Palmer, "Radicalism and Sedition among the Negroes as Reflected in their Publications," report of the United States Department of Justice, vol. 12 of Senate Documents, no. 153, 66th Congress, 1st Session, 1919, pp. 161-187. Also the Lusk Committee Report, "Revolutionary Radicalism, A Report of the Joint Legislative Committee of New York Investigating Seditious Activities," vol. 2.

22 *Messenger,* Aug. 1922.

23 *Messenger,* Dec. 1919.

24 Republished from *Crusader* in *Negro Yearbook, 1918-1919* (Negro Yearbook Publishing Company; Tuskegee, Alabama, 1919); there is a mention of a catechism in Briggs, "Notes for an Autobiography."

ALTERNATIVES TO GARVEYISM

1 For biographical information on Abbott, see Richard Bardolph, *Negro Vanguard* (Vintage; New York, 1961), pp. 192-94; also see Metz T. P. Lochard, "Phylon Profile XII: Robert S. Abbott, 'Race Leader,' " *Phylon,* second quarter 1947, pp. 124-28.

2 Chicago *Defender,* 9 Oct. 1920; 16 Oct. 1920.
3 *Negro Yearbook,* 1931; James S. Allen, "The American Negro" (pamphlet; International Publishers; New York, 1932), pp. 14-15.
4 Allen, "The American Negro," pp. 14-15.
5 See the Washington *Bee,* 4 June 1921.
6 *Crusader,* Nov. 1921; *Philosophy and Opinions,* vol. 2, p. 300.
7 Lerone Bennett, *Before the Mayflower* (Johnson; Chicago, 1964), p. 276.
8 *Who's Who of the Colored Race,* 1915.
9 *Crisis,* Feb. 1918.
10 *Crisis,* Jan. 1930; Nov. 1931; April 1933; June 1933.
11 DuBois, *Dusk of Dawn* (Harcourt, Brace; New York, 1940), pp. 274–75.
12 George Padmore, *Pan-Africanism or Communism?* (Dennis Dobson; London, 1956), p. 123.
13 DuBois, *Dusk of Dawn,* p. 275.
14 DuBois himself asked for Garveyite support; see W. E. B. DuBois to Amy Jacques Garvey, 8 April 1944, in the Garvey Papers, Kingston, Jamaica.
15 New York *Age,* 11 July 1919; 21 Aug. 1920.
16 *Negro World,* 16 July 1929.
17 *Garvey and Garveyism,* pp. 66–67.
18 George Shepperson, "Pan-Africanism, Some Historical Notes," *Phylon,* Winter 1962, p. 354.
19 *Crisis,* Jan. 1921.
20 *Crisis,* May 1924.
21 *Crisis,* Oct. 1912.
22 Speech by Herbert Aptheker at the University of California, Berkeley, 11 Feb. 1965.
23 *Crisis,* Sept. 1931; July 1932, May 1933; James W. Ford, "World Problems of the Negro People" (pamphlet; Harlem Branch of the Communist Party, circa 1932).
24 New York *Inter-state Tattler,* 7 April 1932 (part of a series of articles published posthumously in the *Tattler* through the efforts of Robert's brother, Ulysses Poston); interview with Ted Poston, 1966.
25 Alain Locke, ed., *The New Negro* (Boni; New York, 1925), pp. 403-408.
26 W. E. B. DuBois, *Darkwater* (Harcourt, Brace; New York, 1920), pp. 90–104.
27 In Herbert Aptheker, *Documentary History of the Negro People* (Citadel Press edition; New York, 1964), vol. 2, p. 753.
28 Also see DuBois, *Darkwater,* p. 49; *Crisis,* May 1933.
29 National Educational Television documentary film, "A. Philip Randolph," 1966.
30 Biographical data in *Who's Who in Colored America,* 1927 (Who's Who Publishing Company, New York); Arna Bontemps, biographical sketch of Randolph, *Negro Digest,* Sept. 1961; John Henrik Clark, biographical sketch of Randolph, *Negro Digest,* March 1967.
31 Charles Lionel Franklin, *Negro Labor Unionist of New York* (Columbia University Press; New York, 1936), p. 94; Sterling D. Spero & Abram Harris, *Black Worker* (Atheneum; New York, 1963), p. 394.
32 Spero & Harris, *Black Worker,* p. 390. (During the early 1920s Abram Harris was a contributing editor to the *Messenger.*)
33 *Messenger,* July 1919.

34 Ibid.
35 Washington *Bee,* 21 Jan. 1920.
36 *Messenger,* Jan. 1918; May–June 1919.
37 Spero & Harris, *Black Worker,* p. 395.
38 *Messenger,* Aug. 1923.
39 *Messenger,* Jan. 1923.
40 Chicago *Defender,* 12 Aug. 1922.
41 Chicago *Defender,* 26 Aug. 1922.
42 *L. I. D. Monthly,* March 1930.
43 Wilson Record, *The Negro and the Communist Party* (University of North Carolina Press; Chapel Hill, 1951), p. 18.
44 Baltimore *Afro-American,* 6 Jan. 1922.
45 Domingo's report was reprinted in "Revolutionary Radicalism: A Report of the Joint Legislative Committee of New York Investigating Seditious Activities," vol. 2 (J. B. Lyon; Albany, New York, 1920); also in New York *Age,* 5 July 1919.
46 Brailsford R. Brazeal, *The Brotherhood of Sleeping Car Porters* (Harpers; New York, 1946), pp. 19–20.
47 Ibid., pp. 16–20.
48 Ibid., pp. 50–56.
49 *Opportunity,* Feb. 1926.
50 Johnson, *Negro Americans, What Now?* (Viking; New York, 1934), pp. 3–18.
51 On the peculiar evolution of George Schuyler see E. Franklin Frazier, *The Negro Family in the United States* (University of Chicago Press; Chicago, 1939), p. 17; Georgiana Schuyler in *Negro Digest,* Sept. 1944; Pittsburgh *Courier,* 18 Jan. 1967. On Schuyler and the Socialist Party in Syracuse see *Negro Digest,* Nov. 1948.
52 Interview with Harry Haywood, June 1966.
53 Pickens, *The Heir of Slaves* (Pilgrim Press; Boston, New York and Chicago, 1911); interview with Amy Jacques Garvey, July 1969; interview with Rudolph Smith, July 1969.
54 William Pickens to Marcus Garvey, reprinted in the Chicago *Defender,* 29 July 1922.
55 Chicago *Defender,* 12 Aug. 1922.
56 See the *Crusader,* Feb. 1921.
57 *Crusader,* Nov. 1921.
58 Washington *Bee,* 11 June 1921.
59 Chicago *Defender,* 11 June 1921.
60 Interview with Harry Haywood, June 1966; Cyril Briggs to Theodore Draper, 17 March 1958, Briggs Papers.
61 Program published in *Communist Review* (London), April 1922.
62 Baltimore *Afro-American,* 1923 *passim.*
63 *Who's Who of the Colored Race,* 1915; interview with Harry Haywood, June 1966.
64 *Colored American Review,* 15 Sept. 1915; 15 Oct. 1915. Copies in the Briggs Papers.
65 Briggs, "Notes for an Autobiography," in the Briggs Papers.
66 *Crusader,* Sept. 1919.
67 Interview with Harry Haywood, June 1966.

68 *Colored American Review,* 15 Oct. 1915; interview with Harry Haywood, June 1966; interview with Richard B. Moore, May 1968; *Crusader,* Nov. 1921.
69 *Crusader,* reprinted in the 1918-1919 *Negro Yearbook.*
70 *Crusader,* Nov. 1919.
71 Cyril Briggs to Sheridan W. Johns III, 7 June 1961, Briggs Papers.
72 Cyril Briggs to Theodore Draper, 17 March 1958, Briggs Papers.
73 *Crusader,* Oct. 1919.
74 *Crusader,* Feb. 1921.
75 *Colored American Review,* 15 Oct. 1915.
76 *Crusader,* Nov. 1919.
77 *Crusader,* Nov. 1921; Washington *Bee,* 29 Oct. 1921.
78 Burgit Aron, "The Garvey Movement" (master's thesis, Columbia University, 1947), p. 18.
79 *Crusader,* Nov. 1921; interview with Harry Haywood, June 1966; *Garvey and Garveyism,* pp. 64–65; New York *World, 20 Aug. 1921.*
80 *Crusader,* Nov. 1921.
81 Ibid.
82 Interview with Harry Haywood, June 1966; interview with Richard B. Moore, May 1968; interview with William Taylor, curator of the Briggs Papers, Aug. 1969; Cyril Briggs to Theodore Draper, 17 March 1958, Briggs Papers.
83 Cyril Briggs to Sheridan W. Johns III, 10 April 1961.
84 Cyril Briggs to Theodore Draper, 17 March 1958; interview with William Taylor, Aug. 1969.
85 *Crusader,* Nov. 1921.
86 *Crusader,* Jan. 1921.
87 *Communist Review* (London), April 1922.
88 *Philosophy and Opinions,* vol. 2, pp. 333–34.
89 Cyril Briggs to Theodore Draper, 17 March 1958; interview with Harry Haywood, June 1966; interview with Richard B. Moore, May 1968.
90 Interview with Harry Haywood, June 1966; Briggs, "Notes for an Autobiography."
91 Interview with Harry Haywood, June 1966.
92 Chicago *Defender,* 22 Jan. 1921; Chicago Commission on Race Relations, *The Negro in Chicago,* pp. 59–64.
93 Chicago *Defender,* 20 June 1920; 3 July 1920.
94 Chicago *Defender,* 15 Jan. 1921.
95 Chicago Commission on Race Relations, *The Negro in Chicago,* pp. 59–64.
96 MS for *Negro World* articles in the John Bruce Papers, Schomburg Collection.
97 Chicago *Defender,* 22 Jan. 1921.
98 *Negro World* quoted in *The Negro in Chicago,* p. 64; William H. Briggs was also a contributor to the *Colored American Review,* 15 Oct. 1915.
99 Chicago *Defender,* 22 Jan. 1921.
100 Chicago *Defender,* 2 July 1921.

THE ORIGINS OF THE UNIA

1. Biographical information on Garvey is taken from *Philosophy and Opinions; Garvey and Garveyism;* Cronon, *Black Moses;* and from interviews with Amy Jacques Garvey, James B. Yearwood, Len Nembhard, and Rudolph B. Smith.

2 *Negro Yearbook,* 1926–1927 (Negro Yearbook Publishing Co., Tuskegee, Alabama).

3 Cronon, *Black Moses,* p. 14.

4 *African Times and Orient Review,* July 1921.

5 Duse Mohammed, *In the Land of the Pharaohs* (Stanley Paul; London, 1911) pp. 1–3.

6 Ibid., pp. 3–5.

7 Ibid., pp. 105–10, 66, 121–22.

8 Ibid., pp. 121–22.

9 *African Times and Orient Review,* Sept. 1913.

10 Ibid., Oct. 1913.

11 *African and Orient Review,* May 1920—the *African Times and Orient Review* was renamed in 1920.

12 Duse Mohammed, *In the Land of the Pharaohs,* p. 5.

13 *African Times and Orient Review,* Oct. 1913.

14 *African and Orient Review,* June 1920.

15 Interview with Rudolph Smith, July 1969.

16 Interview with James B. Yearwood, Aug. 1969; *Negro World,* 12 June 1920.

17 Interview with Rudolph Smith, July 1969.

18 See the John Bruce Papers, in the Schomburg Collection, New York.

19 Interviews with Rudolph Smith, July 1969; James B. Yearwood, Aug. 1969; and Richard B. Moore, Sept. 1968; *African Times and Orient Review,* Sept. 1913; Sept. 1917; Oct. 1917; Oct. 1913; *African and Orient Review,* June 1920; Dec. 1920; *Negro World,* 15 April 1933.

20 *Philosophy and Opinions,* vol. 2, p. 126.

21 J. G. Monaghan to Marcus Garvey, Kingston, 14 May 1915; J. H. Levy to Marcus Garvey, 5 July 1916; Garvey Papers. Also see George Shepperson, "Pan Africanism, Some Historical Notes."

22 "A Talk With Afro-West Indians by Marcus Garvey" (pamphlet of the UNIA and African Communities League, circa 1915), in the Jamaican Institute, Kingston.

23 London *Times,* 27 Oct. 1914.

24 "A Talk With Afro-West Indians by Marcus Garvey."

25 MS notes in the John Bruce Papers, Schomburg Collection.

26 *Philosophy and Opinions,* vol. 2, p. 128; also see the reprint of an advertisement for a 1917 address by Garvey in Amy Jacques Garvey, "Black Power in America" (pamphlet printed by Amy Jacques Garvey; Kingston, 1968).

27 *Philosophy and Opinions,* vol. 2, p. 129; Cronon, *Black Moses,* p. 43.

28 Samuel Duncan to His Excellency the Governor of St. Lucia quoted in *Philosophy and Opinions,* vol. 2, p. 359.

29 *Garvey and Garveyism,* p. 91.

30 Cronon, *Black Moses,* p. 50.

31 *Philosophy and Opinions,* vol. 2, p. 97.

32 *Negro World,* 1 Jan. 1921; reprinted in the Baltimore *Afro-American* Jan. 7, 1921.
33 Washington *Bee,* 2 Aug. 1919.

THE GARVEY MOVEMENT IN ITS PRIME

1 George Padmore, *Pan Africanism or Communism?* (Dennis Dobson; London, 1956), p. 96; interview with Amy Jacques Garvey, July 1969; W. F. Elkins, "Suppression of the *Negro World* in the British West Indies."
2 Kingston *Gleaner,* 13 Dec. 1919; 15 Dec. 1919.
3 Marie Duchaterlier to John Bruce, from Panama City, 12 Jan. 1920, in the John Bruce Papers, Schomburg Collection.
4 New York *Evening Journal,* 18 Aug. 1920.
5 Interview with James B. Yearwood, Aug. 1969.
6 Savannah *Tribune,* 4 Aug. 1921.
7 Interview with Amy Jacques Garvey, July 1969.
8 The attendance of ABB members at early UNIA conventions has been acknowledged in interviews with Richard B. Moore, Sept. 1968, and with Harry Haywood, June 1966, and in the *Crusader,* Nov. 1921; however, the prominent ABB members were present only as observers, rather than as official delegates.
9 *New York Times,* 18 Aug. 1920; for the initial proposal of the Black House see the *New York Times,* 18 Aug. 1919.
10 Biographical sketch of Bishop McGuire in the New York *World,* 3 Aug. 1924.
11 New York *World,* 4 Aug. 1920; 7 Aug. 1920.
12 New York *Age,* 28 Aug. 1920.
13 *California Eagle,* 24 Dec. 1921; *Messenger,* March 1923.
14 *Garvey and Garveyism,* p. 46; also see Cronon, *Black Moses,* pp. 63–64.
15 *New York Times,* 4 Aug. 1920; New York *World,* 5 Aug. 1920.
16 New York *World,* 5 Aug. 1920.
17 New York *World,* 4 Aug. 1920; 5 Aug. 1920.
18 New York *Age,* 21 Aug. 1920.
19 Pittsburgh *Courier,* 22 March 1930; *Philosophy and Opinions,* vol. 2 pp. 135–43.
20 *Negro World,* 11 Sept. 1920; reprinted in *Independent,* 26 Feb. 1921. The Baltimore *Afro-American,* 20 Aug. 1920, also emphasized the refusal-to-fight clause in its analysis of the UNIA declaration.
21 A list of UNIA officers was carried in the New York *Age,* 4 Sept. 1920.
22 Interview with James B. Yearwood, Aug. 1969.
23 Baltimore *Afro-American,* 27 Aug. 1920.
24 New York *World,* 27 Aug. 1920.
25 *Philosophy and Opinions,* vol. 2, pp. 278–79; New York *Age,* 19 Aug. 1922.
26 Cronon, *Black Moses,* p. 59.
27 Ibid., p. 59
28 Baltimore *Afro-American,* 15 Sept. 1922.
29 "Menu: First Annual Court Reception, Sat. August 27, 1921," in the Garvey Papers; interview with Amy Jacques Garvey, July 1969.
30 New York *World,* 22 Aug. 1922.
31 Interview with Amy Jacques Garvey, July 1969.

32 New York *World,* 13 Aug. 1922.
33 M. K. Gandhi to Amy Jacques Garvey, 5 May 1926, Garvey Papers.
34 Baltimore *Afro-American,* 16 Sept. 1921.
35 *Negro World,* 16 Aug. 1924.
36 George Padmore, *Pan-Africanism or Communism,* p. 96.
37 *Negro World,* 26 Oct. 1918. Quoted in W. F. Elkins, "Suppression of the *Negro World* in the British West Indies."
38 W. F. Elkins, "Suppression of the *Negro World* in the British West Indies."
39 *Negro World,* 21 Oct. 1921.
40 Interview with Ted Poston, July 1967.
41 *Messenger,* Dec. 1922.
42 *Negro World,* 13 Aug. 1927.
43 *Negro World,* 15 April 1933; interview with Amy Jacques Garvey, July 1969.
44 Personal information about the Garvey family from interviews with Amy Jacques Garvey, July 1969; Len Nembhard, July 1969; and Herbert Hill, Aug. 1969.
45 Interview with Herbert Hill, Aug. 1969.
46 Interview with James B. Yearwood, Aug. 1969.
47 *Negro World,* 3 July 1926.
48 Interview with Ruth Beckford, April 1970.
49 *Negro World,* 7 June 1919.
50 *Daily Worker,* 12 Aug. 1924.
51 New York *World,* 15 Aug. 1922; 26 Aug. 1922.
52 *Negro World,* 22 Nov. 1930.
53 New York *World,* 7 Aug. 1920.
54 New York *World,* 3 Aug. 1924.
55 Ibid.; interview with James B. Yearwood, Aug. 1969.
56 New York *World,* 3 Aug. 1924.
57 Quoted in Cronon, *Black Moses,* p. 180.
58 Ibid.
59 New York *World,* 3 Aug. 1924. The 1968 *World Almanac* listed the African Orthodox Church as having 24 congregations and 6,000 members.
60 New York *World,* 26 Aug. 1922.

PERSONALITIES AND MOTIVATIONS

1 On Cyril Henry see the Kingston *Gleaner,* 13 Dec. 1919. On Gabriel Stewart see the *Gleaner,* 13 Dec. 1919; 15 Dec. 1919. There is an autobiographical sketch of Samuel Haynes in the *Negro World,* 13 Aug. 1927.
2 *Garvey and Garveyism,* p. 75.
3 *Christian Century,* 8 June 1955, quoted in *Garvey and Garveyism,* p. 251..
4 Marie Duchaterlier to John Bruce, 12 Jan. 1920, John Bruce Papers.
5 "Maloney" to John Bruce, 3 Jan. 1923, John Bruce Papers.
6 Interview with Lionel W. Greenidge, July 1969; interview with Muriel Petioni, daughter of Charles A. Petioni, Aug. 1969.
7 Interview with Alfred A. Smith, June 1969.
8 On Louis Campbell see *Harlem Liberator,* 1 July 1933; 2 Sept. 1933; and Claude McKay, *Harlem: Negro Metropolis,* (Dutton; New York, 1940), pp. 237–39. New York Age, 14 Aug. 1920.

9 New York *Age*, 14 Aug. 1920.
10 W. E. B. DuBois, *Darkwater*, pp. 81–104.
11 Elliott M. Rudwick, *Race Riot at East St. Louis July 2, 1917* (World; Cleveland, 1966), pp. 119–32, 261.
12 *Who's Who of the Colored Race*, 1915; interview with James B. Yearwood, Aug. 1969.
13 *Who's Who of the Colored Race*, 1915; interview with Ted Poston, July 1967; New York *Age*, 26 May 1923; *Who's Who in Colored America*, 1927
14 *Who's Who of the Colored Race*, 1915; interview with Ted Poston, July 1967.
15 Interview with Ted Poston, July 1967.
16 *Messenger*, Dec. 1922; Feb. 1923; *Negro World*, 7 Aug. 1926.
17 See Christian A. Lokko, Parkra via Accra, Gold Coast, to Marcus Garvey, 12 Aug. 122, John Bruce Papers, Schomburg Collection.
18 Interview with Amy Jacques Garvey, March 1970.
19 Claude McKay, *Harlem: Negro Metropolis*, pp. 168–69; Roi Ottley, *New World A-Coming* (World, Cleveland, 1943), p. 71; *Negro World*, 4 June 1927.
20 John Bruce to Florence Bruce, 2 Jan. 1924; Casely Hayford, Seccondee, Gold Coast, to John Bruce, 24 Nov. 1923, John Bruce Papers.
21 Interview with Amy Jacques Garvey, July 1969.
22 New York *Age*, 19 Aug. 1922.
23 Chicago *Defender*, 6 Jan. 1923.
24 "Maloney" to John Bruce, 3 Jan. 1923, John Bruce Papers, Schomburg Collection.
25 *Daily Worker*, 9 Aug. 1924; 11 Aug. 1924; 12 Aug. 1924; interview with Charlotta Bass, Nov. 1961; Charlotta Bass, *Forty Years, Memoirs from the Pages of a Newspaper* (Charlotta Bass; Los Angeles, 1960), p. 198; interview with Len Nembhard, July 1969; Kingston *Gleaner*, 15 Dec. 1919; 26 March 1921; 14 June 1921; *Crusader*, Feb. 1921; Nov. 1921; *Negro World*, 25 July 1931; 1 Aug. 1931.
26 *Garvey and Garveyism*, p. 164; *Negro World*, 24 July 1926; 25 June 1927; 10 Aug. 1927.
27 Interview with St. Clair Drake, Aug. 1970.
28 Ibid.; Shepperson and Price, *Independent African* (Edinburgh University Press; Edinburgh, 1963), pp. 225, 250–58.
29 Interview with St. Clair Drake, Aug. 1970.

A WORLDWIDE MOVEMENT

1 Estimates of the sizes of the divisions were obtained from statements about the number of members and from references to the size of weekly meetings in the *Negro World* and other newspapers and periodicals.
2 *Negro World*, 5 June 1920; 12 June 1920; 22 Oct. 1921; 17 Dec. 1921; 24 April 1924.
3 *Negro World*, 22 Oct. 1921.
4 Passport regulations are set out in the *UNIA Constitution and Book of Laws*, copy in the Garvey Papers.
5 Savannah *Tribune*, 14 Sept. 1922.
6 Baltimore *Afro-American*, 23 March 1923.

7 Interview with Amy Jacques Garvey, July 1969.
8 See, for example, issues of the Los Angeles *Citizen Advocate,* and the Oakland *California Voice.*
9 *California Eagle,* 2 July 1921; Los Angeles *Citizen Advocate,* 12 March 1921.
10 Discussions with Charlotta Bass, Nov. 1961; Charlotta Bass, *Forty Years.*
11 *California Eagle,* 28 May 1921; 8 Oct. 1921.
12 *California Eagle,* 8 Jan. 1921.
13 *Negro World,* 25 July 1931; 1 Aug. 1931; Communist reply in *Negro Worker,* Aug. 1931.
14 *Negro World,* 11 Sept. 1926; 2 July 1927.
15 *Crusader,* Nov. 1921; W. F. Elkins, "Suppression of the *Negro World* in the British West Indies"; for background information see W. F. Elkins, "Influence of Marcus Garvey in Africa"; "Black Power in the British West Indies"; "A Source of Black Nationalism in the Caribbean."
16 *Crusader,* Nov. 1921.
17 Kingston *Gleaner,* 13 Dec. 1919; 15 Dec. 1919.
18 Kingston *Gleaner,* 15 Aug. 1921.
19 Kingston *Gleaner,* 13 Dec. 1919; 15 Dec. 1919; 26 March 1921; 11 May 1921.
20 Kingston *Gleaner,* 26 March 1921.
21 Kingston *Gleaner,* 2 June 1921; Amy Jacques Garvey, "Black Power in America," p. 18.
22 Amy Jacques Garvey, "Black Power in America," p. 18.
23 W. F. Elkins, "Influence of Marcus Garvey on Africa"; interview with Muriel Petioni, Aug. 1969.
24 *Negro World,* 12 June 1920.
25 Kingston *Gleaner,* 8 June 1921; 10 May 1921. The *Gleaner* covered Garveyite activity throughout the Caribbean.
26 *Crusader,* Jan. 1921, Nov. 1921.
27 Kingston *Gleaner,* 4 April 1921.
28 See the *Negro World,* 1926–28 passim.
29 *Handbook of British Honduras, 1925* (The West Indian Committee, London).
30 George Padmore, *Pan-Africanism or Communism?,* p. 96; W. F. Elkins, "Influence of Marcus Garvey in Africa"; Robert Weisbord, "Marcus Garvey, Pan-Negroist"; Richard Hart to Amy Jacques Garvey, 6 March 1969, Garvey Papers.
31 Interview with Amy Jacques Garvey, July 1969; Amy Jacques Garvey to W. E. B. DuBois, 24 April 1944; Sidney Young to Amy Jacques Garvey, 12 April 1944, both in the Garvey Papers.
32 Roi Ottley, *New World A-Coming,* (World; Cleveland, New York, 1963), p. 76; Baltimore *Afro-American,* 16 Sept. 1921.
33 Interview with Amy Jacques Garvey, July 1969. John Bruce's evaluation of Hayford's work is in an undated MS in the John Bruce Papers, Schomburg Collection.
34 Marcus Garvey's membership card in the CDRN is in the Garvey Papers.
35 *Negro World,* 17 July 1926, 1927–28 passim; Ronald Segal, *African Profiles* (Penguin; London, 1962), p. 197.
36 *Negro World,* 24 July 1926; 28 Aug. 1926; 11 Sept. 1926; 30 April 1927.

37 On Dr. Burnham and the UNIA see *Negro World,* 25 June 1924; 14 Aug. 1926; on Johnson and the UNIA see *Negro World,* 30 April 1927.

38 For Garvey and the African labor movement see Thomas Hodgkin, *Nationalism in Colonial Africa* (Muller; London, 1956), pp. 101–2; A. A. Adio-Moses to Amy Jacques Garvey, 9 Jan. 1946, Garvey Papers; for the AOC in Uganda see Robert Rotberg, *A Political History of Tropical Africa* (Harcourt Brace & World; New York, 1965), pp. 340–41.

39 Interview with Rudolph Smith, July 1969.

40 See former UNIA member Stanley A. Davis's *This is Liberia* (William Frederick; New York, 1953), p. 117; Charles Henry Huberich, *Political and Legislative History* (Central Book; New York, 1947), vol. 2, pp. 819, 871, 1207–10.

41 *Philosophy and Opinions,* vol. 2, pp. 399–405.

42 Edwin Barclay to UNIA, 14 June 1920, reprinted in *Philosophy and Opinions,* vol. 2, p. 365.

43 Ibid., p. 366.

44 Quoted in Cronon, *Black Moses,* pp. 125–26; for examples of the manner in which the British authorities kept watch on the Liberian UNIA, see Robert G. Weisbord, "Marcus Garvey, Pan-Negroist."

45 Cronon, *Black Moses,* p. 126.

46 *Garvey and Garveyism,* p. 147; Huberich, *Political and Legislative History,* vol. 2, pp. 869, 871–72, 986, 1207–10; Nathaniel Richardson, *Liberia Past and Present* (Diplomatic Press; London, 1959), pp. 283, 287. On the political career of Gabriel Johnson see C. L. Simpson, *The Symbol of Liberia* (Diplomatic Press; London, n.d.) pp. 155–56.

47 Pittsburgh *Courier,* 8 Aug. 1924; *Philosophy and Opinions,* vol. 2, pp. 371, 375.

48 New York *Age,* 22 March 1924; Pittsburgh *Courier,* 22 March 1924; 3 May 1924.

49 As reported in *Philosophy and Opinions,* vol. 2, p. 379.

50 Pittsburgh *Courier,* 3 May 1924.

51 New York *Age,* 23 Aug. 1924; also see Baltimore *Afro-American,* 11 May 1923.

52 *Garvey and Garveyism,* p. 144.

53 Pittsburgh *Courier,* 5 Sept. 1924.

54 New York *Evening Bulletin,* 24 Aug. 1924, quoted in *Garvey and Garveyism,* pp. 146–47.

55 Interview with Amy Jacques Garvey, July 1969; *Garvey and Garveyism,* p. 78; Baltimore *Afro-American,* 11 Aug. 1922.

56 New York *World,* 31 Aug. 1922; Baltimore *Afro-American,* 11 Aug. 1922; Cronon, *Black Moses,* p. 148. For a historical account of the delegation see *Negro World,* 11 June 1932.

57 Cronon, *Black Moses,* p. 148; *Negro World,* 16 Aug. 1924; Washington *Bee,* 1 Dec. 1921; Baltimore *Afro-American,* 25 Nov. 1921; Pittsburgh *Courier,* 23 Nov. 1923.

DISSENSIONS AND THE DECLINE OF GARVEYISM

1 Interview with Amy Jacques Garvey, July 1969.

2 See Walter White, *Fire in the Flint* (Knopf; New York, 1924); *Rope and Faggott* (Knopf; New York, 1929); and *A Man Called White* (Viking; New York, 1948).

3 Interview with Amy Jacques Garvey, July 1969; New York *Age*, 22 July 1922.
4 New York *Age*, 22 July 1922.
5 William Pickens to Marcus Garvey, 24 July 1922, printed in the Chicago *Defender*, 29 July 1922.
6 For Briggs and Manoedi see Chicago *Defender*, 12 Aug. 1922; Mokete Manoedi, "Garvey and Africa, by a Native African" (pamphlet published by the New York *Age* Press; New York, 1922).
7 Chicago *Defender*, 12 Aug. 1922.
8 Ibid.
9 Mokete Manoedi, "Garvey and Africa."
10 New York *Age*, 23 Sept. 1922.
11 New York *Age*, 30 June 1923.
12 For the retraction see the Washington *Bee*, 21 Jan. 1922; Briggs's lawsuit is covered in the *Bee*, 29 Oct. 1921.
13 *Philosophy and Opinions*, vol. 2, p. 240.
14 Baltimore *Afro-American*, 18 Aug. 1922.
15 Quoted in the Chicago *Defender*, 26 Aug. 1922; for the UNIA leadership struggle see the *Defender*, 29 July 1922; 5 Aug. 1922.
16 New York *World*, 23 Aug. 1922; the second quote is from the Chicago *Defender*, 26 Aug. 1922.
17 New York *World*, 17 Aug. 1922; Chicago *Defender*, 26 Aug. 1922. The account in the *World* is more complete.
18 New York *Age*, 2 Sept. 1922; New York *World*, 27 Aug. 1922.
19 *Negro World* article by Poston quoted in the New York *Age*, 23 Sept. 1922.
20 New York *World*, 13 Aug. 1922.
21 New York *World*, 24 Aug. 1922.
22 *California Eagle*, 5 Nov. 1921; 12 Nov. 1921; 26 Nov. 1921.
23 *California Eagle*, 3 Dec. 1921.
24 *California Eagle*, 6 May 1922; 3 June 1922.
25 New York *World*, 24 Aug. 1922; 26 Aug. 1922; *California Eagle*, 11 Nov. 1922; New York *Age*, 23 Sept. 1922; *Philosophy and Opinions*, vol. 2, p. 296.
26 *New York Times*, 11 Sept. 1922.
27 Baltimore *Afro-American*, 18 Aug. 1922.
28 New York *Age*, 14 Oct. 1922.
29 The charge is made in a letter from leading anti-Garvey blacks to the U.S. attorney general, dated 15 Jan. 1923. The letter is reprinted in *Philosophy and Opinions*, vol. 2, pp. 296–97.
30. Ibid., pp. 296–98. Eason's assassination was covered by the *New York Times*, 13 Jan. 1923; New York *Age*, 13 Jan. 1923; New Orleans *Times-Picayune*, 2 Jan. 1923. There is an obituary sketch of Eason in the New York *Age*, 13 Jan. 1923.
31 *Philosophy and Opinions*, vol. 2, pp. 299–300; Cronon, *Black Moses*, p. 111.
32 *Philosophy and Opinions*, vol. 2, pp. 301–8.
33 Fourth Federal Reporter, Second Series; Circuit Court of Appeals, Second Circuit, pp. 974–75.
34 Interview with Amy Jacques Garvey, July 1969; New Orleans *Times-Picayune*, 18 Jan. 1923.

35 *Negro World,* 24 Feb. 1923; Baltimore *Afro-American,* 23 Feb. 1923.
36 *New York Times,* 30 May 1923.
37 Interview with Amy Jacques Garvey, July 1969; interview with Rudolph Smith, July 1969; interview with Alfred A. Smith, Aug. 1969; *Philosophy and Opinions,* vol. 2, pp. 145–46; Amy Jacques Garvey, "United States of America v. Marcus Garvey, Was Justice Defeated?" (pamphlet published by A. J. Garvey; New York, 1925), Schomburg Collection.
38 *Garvey and Garveyism,* p. 108; New York *Age,* 26 May 1923.
39 Quoted in Cronon, *Black Moses,* pp. 100–101; also see pp. 112–18. There are excerpts from the trial transcript and an analysis of the trial in *Philosophy and Opinions,* vol. 2, pp. 145–216.
40 Cronon, *Black Moses,* p. 115.
41 New York *World,* 13 June 1923.
42 *Philosophy and Opinions,* vol. 2, pp. 169–73.
43 Ibid., pp. 146–48.
44 Baltimore *Afro-American,* 21 Sept. 1923.
45 New York *Age,* 23 Sept. 1922; *Philosophy and Opinions,* vol. 2, p. 296; interview with James B. Yearwood, Aug. 1969.
46 *Negro World,* 12 April 1924; 26 April 1924.
47 *Negro World,* 16 Aug. 1924.
48 *Daily Worker,* 14 Aug. 1924.
49 The Klan resolution is discussed in the *Daily Worker,* 14 Aug. 1924.
50 *Philosophy and Opinions,* vol. 2, p. 148.
51 Interview with Alfred A. Smith, Aug. 1969. Smith was a seaman on the *General Goethals* during its voyage for the UNIA.
52 *Negro World,* 16 Aug. 1924; *Daily Worker,* 9 Aug. 1924; 12 Aug. 1924.
53 *Daily Worker,* 18 Aug. 1924.
54 Pittsburgh *Courier,* 5 Sept. 1924.
55 *Daily Worker,* 9 Aug. 1924.
56 Ibid.
57 *Daily Worker,* 9 Aug. 1924; 11 Aug, 1924.
58 *Daily Worker,* 9 Aug. 1924; 11 Aug. 1924; 14 Aug. 1924; 18 Aug. 1924.
59 *Daily Worker,* 9 Aug. 1924.
60 Interview with Amy Jacques Garvey, July 1969; interview with James B. Yearwood, Aug. 1969.
61 The visitor, Lionel Francis, reported the conversation in the New York *Age,* 30 Aug. 1924.
62 New York *Age,* 6 Aug. 1924.
63 *Daily Worker,* 18 Aug. 1924.
64 Ibid.
65 *Negro World,* 28 July 1928; 11 Aug. 1928; 29 Sept. 1928.

TWILIGHT ACHIEVEMENTS

1 Interview with Amy Jacques Garvey, July 1969.
2 Chicago *Defender,* 4 Sept. 1926; New York *Age,* 21 Aug. 1926.
3 Pittsburgh *Courier,* 7 Aug. 1926; New York *Age,* 21 Aug. 1926; Chicago *Defender,* 7 Aug. 1926.
4 *Negro World,* 10 Dec. 1927; Kingston *Gleaner,* 15 Dec. 1927.
5 *Garvey and Garveyism,* p. 176; Cronon, *Black Moses,* p. 142.
6 Pittsburgh *Courier,* 13 Aug. 1932.

7 The estimate is based on letters to the editor and fund-raising contribution lists in *Negro World*, 1930–1933; and *Black Man* 1930–1938.

8 The figures are based on statements of support in issues of *Black Man* for the late 1930s; the UNIA *Voice of Freedom*, 15 May 1945; issues of *The African* magazine for the late 1930s and early 1940s; interviews in the summer of 1969 with Amy Jacques Garvey, Rudolph Smith, James B. Yearwood, Reynold R. Felix, Lionel Winston Greenidge, Alfred A. Smith, Len Nembhard, relatives of Garveyites Charles A. Petioni, Sybil Donawa, Marie Duchaterlier; interview with Ted Poston, July 1967.

9 New York *People's Voice*, 25 March 1944.

10 Interview with Len Nembhard, Aug. 1969.

11 Ibid.; interview with Amy Jacques Garvey, July 1969.

12 Ulysses Poston arranged to have a history of the UNIA in the United States written by Marcus Garvey published serially in the Pittsburgh *Courier* of 1930–interview with Ted Poston, Sept. 1967.

13 UNIA flyers of 1932 and 1937, Garvey Papers; the *Negro World*, 3 July 1926; 7 May 1927; *Voice of Freedom*, 15 May 1945. The latter was a short-lived Garveyite newspaper based in New York.

14 *Negro World*, 15 April 1933; a similar analysis by Haynes from the *Negro World*, 6 May 1933, is reprinted in *Garvey and Garveyism*, p. 213.

15 *World Almanac*, 1968.

16 Pittsburgh *Courier*, 7 Aug. 1926; interview with Amy Jacques Garvey, July 1969.

17 Interview with Amy Jacques Garvey, July 1969; also see Amy Jacques Garvey, "Black Power in America."

18 Arna Bontemps and Jack Conroy, *They Seek a City* (Doubleday, Doran & Company; Garden City, New Jersey, 1965), pp. 176–77.

19 Quoted in E. U. Essien-Udom, *Black Nationalism* (University of Chicago Press; Chicago, 1962), p. 63.

20 Bontemps and Conroy, *They Seek a City*, pp. 177–83; Essien-Udom, *Black Nationalism*, pp. 33–35.

21 Essien-Udom, *Black Nationalism*, pp. 4, 67–69. For the Muslims and the government see Bontemps and Conroy, p. 183.

22 Essien-Udom, *Black Nationalism*, pp. 122–42; Elijah Muhammad, *Message to the Blackman* (Muhammad Mosque no. 2; Chicago, 1965), pp. 1–29.

23 Elijah Muhammad, *Message to the Blackman*, pp. 173–75.

24 Essien-Udom, *Black Nationalism*, pp. 166–67.

25 Interview with Amy Jacques Garvey, July 1969.

26 Quoted in Claude McKay, *Harlem: Negro Metropolis*, p. 37.

27 See Robert A. Parker, *The Incredible Messiah* (Little, Brown & Company; Boston, 1937); John Hoshor, *God in a Rolls Royce* (Hillman-Curl; New York, 1936).

28 Claude McKay, *Harlem: Negro Metropolis*, p. 51.

29 See study report, *Rastafari* (University of the West Indies; Kingston, 1962); *Black Man*, Jan. 1937; current issues of *Abeng*, a black power weekly in Jamaica; *Bongo-Man*, a current Jamaican youth magazine; and current issues of *Blackman*.

30 *Abeng*, 8 Feb. 1969.

31 *Abeng*, 27 June 1969.

32 Len Nembhard, *Trials and Triumphs of Marcus Garvey*, pp. 138–41.

33 Bontemps and Conroy, *They Seek a City*, pp. 184–85; Gunnar Myrdal, *American Dilemma* (Harpers; New York, 1944), pp. 813–14.

34 Bontemps and Conroy, *They Seek a City*, pp. 184–85; Chicago *Defender*, 15 June 1940.

35 Herbert Garfinkel, *When Negroes March* (Free Press; Glencoe, Illinois, 1959), pp. 18–19; James S. Allen, "The American Negro" (pamphlet, International Publishers; New York, n.d.) pp. 14–15; E. Franklin Frazier in *Science and Society*, Fall 1938.

36 General coverage of the jobs movement in Charles Radford Lawrence, "Negro Organizations in Crisis" (Ph.D. thesis, Columbia University, n.d.); Ralph Bunche, "Programs, Ideologies, Tactics and Achievements of Negro Betterment and Interracial Organizations" (MS prepared for the Myrdal study *American Dilemma*, in the Schomburg Collection). On UNIA involvement in the jobs movement see *Negro World*, 1 Aug. 1931; 26 Dec. 1931; 2 Jan. 1932; 2 April 1932; Pittsburgh *Courier*, 21 Jan. 1933. Information on the UNIA Incorporated from interview with Muriel Petioni, Aug. 1969.

37 Bontemps and Conroy, *They Seek a City*, p. 157; St. Clair Drake and Horace Cayton, *Black Metropolis* (Harcourt Brace; New York, 1945), pp. 83–85, 295–96, 412, 743.

38 *Harlem Liberator*, 10 March 1934; 17 March 1934; Charles Radford Lawrence, "Negro Organizations in Crisis," pp. 286–92.

39 New York Federal Writers Project, "Biographical Sketches—Sufi Hamid," MS in the Schomburg Collection; Claude McKay, *Harlem: Negro Metropolis*, pp. 198–200.

40 Quoted in Gunnar Myrdal, *American Dilemma*, p. 813.

41 New York *Age*, 17 June 1933; 24 June 1933.

42 *Amsterdam News*, quoted in Charles Radford Lawrence, "Negro Organizations in Crisis," pp. 289–90; *Negro World*, 1 Aug. 1931; 26 Dec. 1931; 2 Jan. 1932; 2 April 1932.

43 Charles Radford Lawrence, "Negro Organizations in Crisis," pp. 186–92.

44 Ralph Bunche, "Programs, Ideologies, Tactics," pp. 388–90.

45 See James W. Ford, "Hunger and Terror in Harlem" (pamphlet, Harlem Communist Party, circa 1935), Schomburg Collection.

46 Emmett Coleman, *Adam Clayton Powell* (Bee Line; New York, 1967), pp. 35–38; New York *Age*, 13 Aug. 1938.

47 *Harlem Liberator*, 1 July 1933; 2 Sept. 1933.

48 Claude McKay, *Harlem: Negro Metropolis*, pp. 237–40; interviews with Harry Haywood, June 1966; Richard B. Moore, May 1968.

49 Interview with Harry Haywood, June 1966; Theodore Draper to Cyril Briggs, 20 March 1958; Cyril Briggs to Theodore Draper, 24 March 1958, both in the Briggs Papers.

50 See Harry Haywood, *Negro Liberation* (International Publishers, New York, 1947).

51 Interview with William Taylor, Oct. 1969; Wilson Record, *The Negro and the Communist Party* (University of North Carolina Press; Chapel Hill, 1951), pp. 299–300.

52 Interview with Harry Haywood, July 1966; *Harlem Liberator*, 22 July 1933; 29 July 1933; 16 Sept. 1933; *Daily Worker*, 25 Feb. 1933; Wilson Record, *The Negro and the Communist Party*, pp. 71–75.

53 Interview with Harry Haywood, July 1966.

54 *Communist,* Aug. 1930.

55 Harry Haywood, "The Road to Negro Liberation," Report to the 1934 CPUSA Convention (International Publishers; New York, 1934).

56 *Daily Worker,* 2 March 1933.

57 Interview with Harry Haywood, June 1966.

58 *Harlem Liberator,* 4 Nov. 1933.

59 *Harlem Liberator,* 1 July 1933.

60 Drake and Cayton, *Black Metropolis,* pp. 85–87.

61 *Negro World,* 31 Aug. 1931; Chicago *Defender,* 11 Aug. 1931; New York *Inter-state Tattler,* 6 Aug. 1931.

62 *Party Organizer,* April 1931; Harry Haywood, "Road to Negro Liberation."

63 *Party Organizer,* May 1931.

64 Quoted in Lawrence, "Negro Organizations in Crisis," pp. 288–89.

65 *Harlem Liberator,* 3 March 1934; 10 March 1934; 17 March 1934; Emmett Coleman, *Adam Clayton Powell,* p. 35.

66 *Negro World,* 29 Aug. 1931; 2 Jan. 1932; Pittsburgh *Courier,* 19 April 1930; 7 Oct. 1933; *California Eagle,* 14 March 1930; *Crisis,* April 1933; Jan. 1932.

67 John Hope II, "Rochdale Cooperatives among Negroes," *Phylon,* first quarter 1940.

68 See Gunnar Myrdal, *America Dilemma,* for an extensive analysis of the Negro and the New Deal.

69 Quoted in Nathan Wright Jr., *Ready to Riot* (Holt, Reinhart & Winston; New York, 1968), p. 51.

70 Amy Jacques Garvey to Sidney Young, 12 April 1944, Garvey Papers.

71 Interview with Amy Jacques Garvey, July 1969; interview with Rudolph Smith, July 1969; A. A. Adio-Moses to Amy Jacques Garvey, 9 Jan. 1946; "Memorandum to Representatives of the United States" by Amy Jacques Garvey, 1945; W. E. B. DuBois to Amy Jacques Garvey, 8 April 1944; Amy Jacques Garvey to W. E. B. DuBois, 24 April 1944; *Voice of Freedom,* 15 May 1945.

72 Interview with Harry Haywood, June 1966.

73 Claude McKay, *Harlem: Negro Metropolis,* pp. 223–24, p. 238.

74 Interview with Richard B. Moore, Sept. 1968.

75 In Amy Jacques Garvey, "Black Power in America," pp. 20–21.

76 *Garvey and Garveyism,* p. 275.

77 Ibid., pp. 281–82.

78 Roi Ottley, *New World A-Coming,* p. 81.

79 John Hope Franklin, *From Slavery to Freedom* (Alfred A. Knopf; New York, 1956), p. 483.

80 Amy Jacques Garvey, "Black Power in America," pp. 32–34; Kwame Nkrumah, quoted by Essien-Udom in the introduction to the Cass edition of *Philosophy and Opinions,* p. xxv, from *Ghana: Autobiography of Kwame Nkrumah* (Thomas Nelson & Sons; New York, 1957), p. 45.

81 Amy Jacques Garvey, "Black Power in America," p. 34; Ronald Segal, *African Profiles* (Penguin; Baltimore, 1962), pp. 196–98; Amy Jacques Garvey to W. E. B. DuBois, 24 April 1944; Amy Jacques Garvey to Max Yergan, 22 May 1944, both in the Garvey Papers.

82 Amy Jacques Garvey, "Black Power in America," pp. 7–8.

83 George Padmore, *Pan-Africanism or Communism?*, p. 304; Drake and Cayton, *Black Metropolis*, p. 752; Thomas Hodgkin, *Nationalism in Colonial Africa* (Muller; London, 1956), pp. 101–2. The role of the African Orthodox Church in Uganda is discussed in Robert Rotberg, *A Political History of Tropical Africa* (Harcourt Brace & World; New York, 1965), pp. 340–41.

84 C. Eric Lincoln, *The Black Muslims in America*, p. 66.

85 W. E. B. DuBois to Amy Jacques Garvey, 8 April 1944; Amy Jacques Garvey to W. E. B. DuBois, 24 April 1944, both in the Garvey Papers.

86 George Padmore, *Pan-Africanism or Communism?*, p. 169; George Shepperson, "Pan-Africanism; Some Historical Notes," *Phylon*, Winter 1962.

87 For Jamaica see issues of *Abeng*, 1969–1970.

88 Flyer for the African Nationalist Union, enclosed in a letter from Amy Jacques Garvey to the author, 28 Oct. 1970.

RESEARCHING BLACK RADICALISM

1 Richard Hart to Amy Jacques Garvey, 6 March 1969, in the Garvey Papers.

2 In Robert G. Weisbord, "Marcus Garvey, Pan-Negroist; the View from Whitehall," *Race* (London), April 1970.

3 Interview with Amy Jacques Garvey, July 1969; interview with Alfred A. Smith, Aug. 1969.

4 Interview with Ernest Kaiser, May 1970; telephone interview with Bernice Sims, May 1970.

5 Allon Schoener, editor, *Harlem on My Mind, 1900–1968* (Random House; New York, 1968), p. 105; Amy Jacques Garvey to the author, 29 July 1970.

6 *Harlem on My Mind*, p. 91.

7 Langston Hughes, *The Big Sea* (Hill and Wang; New York, 1963), pp. 235–37.

8 Interview with Richard B. Moore, May 1968.

9 Address by Herbert Aptheker at the University of California, Berkeley, 11 Feb. 1965.

10 Personal recollections of the author, whose family was close to the Killens family during the early 1950s.

INDEX

Ricketts, Ferdinand, 227
Riley, Richard Edward, 111
Robeson, Paul, 72
Robinson, James H., 153
"Rochdale" cooperatives, 239
Rogers, Joel A., 73, 160
Roosevelt, Franklin D., 233
Roosevelt, Theodore, 156
Royal African Motor Corps, 102

Savage, Augusta, 130, 159
Savannah *Tribune*, 168
Schomburg, Arthur, 97
Schuyler, George, 58, 72
Seattle General Strike, 64
Separatism, 14, 16-17, 20-21, 70,
    93-95, 190, 219, 222
Sherrill, William, 153, 184, 195, 197,
    210, 213-14, 217, 241, 244-45
Shepperson, George, 246
Shuffle Inn Music Hall, 67
Sims, R. T., 62
Smith, Alfred A., 155
Smith, Alfred E., 214, 219
Smith, Harry, 54
Smith, Rudolph, 39, 97, 221, 232,
    241
Smith, Wilford, 155
Socialism, 14, 41, 43, 45, 63-64, 95,
    166, 248
Socialist party (USA), 45, 59, 63-68,
    71-72, 79, 237
Spaulding, C. C., 66
Star Order of Ethiopia and Ethiopian
    Missionaries to Abyssinia. *See*
    Abyssinians.
Sterling, Spero D., 64
Steady, I. G., 160
Stephens, Theodore, 97, 175
Stewart, Gabriel, 39, 152
Stokes, J. C. Phelps, 82
Stokes, Rose Pastor, 81-82

Taranto rebellion, 35-36
Tavalou, Prince Kojo, 153, 158, 176,
    177, 206
Third International, 14
Third World, 28-29, 33, 42-43, 57
Thomas, Norman, 68
Thompson, Noah, 169-70, 198

Thompson, Orlando, 200, 202-3
Toote, Fred, 218
Trade Union Committee for Organiz-
    ing Negro Workers, 68
Trade Union Congress of Nigeria, 241
Trade union movement, 28, 55, 58-
    59, 63-70, 110, 125, 173, 226,
    248
Tragedy of White Injustice, The, and
    *Selections from the Poetic Medita-
    tions of Marcus Garvey,* 15, 251
*Trials and Triumphs of Marcus
    Garvey,* 15, 251
Tropic Death, 160
Trotter, William Monroe, 44, 56, 59,
    71, 112, 156, 161
Tulsa, Oklahoma, riot of 1921, 74-75
Tuskegee Institute, 55

United Fruit Company, 93, 110, 171
United Mine Workers Union, 155
Universal Ethiopian Hymnal, 251
Universal Loyal Negro Association,
    110
Universal Negro Improvement Associ-
    ation and African Communities
    League: and Africa, 18, 20, 57-58,
    97, 109-11, 151-52, 158, 176-85,
    199, 205-8, 252; and African
    Blood Brotherhood, 45, 78, 81-
    83, 191, 193-94, 209; branch divi-
    sions of, 109, 165-85; in Canada,
    110-11, 151, 165; in Central
    America, 97, 110-11, 128, 165,
    171, 174-75, 208; Civil Service of,
    167; and Communism, 79, 82-84,
    170, 232-33, 234, 236-37, 242;
    Constitution of, 112, 114-15,
    122, 126-27, 193, 212; Conven-
    tions of, 14, 105, 109, 112-27,
    134, 191, 196-99, 204-6, 209-11,
    213-14, 217-18, 252; Declaration
    of Rights of, 19, 20-21, 23, 112,
    114-19; and "Don't Buy Where
    You Can't Work" movement,
    229-33, 242; economics of, 18,
    25, 47, 61, 101-4, 126, 166-67,
    172-73, 195, 203-4; and electoral
    politics, 18-20, 112, 120, 210,
    214, 218-19, 243-44; and Ethi-